YEN
FOR
DEVELOPMENT

Japanese Foreign Aid & the Politics of Burden-Sharing

EDITED BY
SHAFIQUL ISLAM

COUNCIL ON FOREIGN RELATIONS PRESS
NEW YORK

COUNCIL ON FOREIGN RELATIONS BOOKS

The Council on Foreign Relations, Inc., is a nonprofit and nonpartisan organization devoted to promoting improved understanding of international affairs through the free exchange of ideas. The Council does not take any position on questions of foreign policy and has no affiliation with, and receives no funding from, the United States government.

From time to time, books and monographs written by members of the Council's research staff or visiting fellows, or commissioned by the Council, or written by an independent author with critical review contributed by a Council study or working group are published with the designation "Council on Foreign Relations Book." Any book or monograph bearing that designation is, in the judgment of the Committee on Studies of the Council's Board of Directors, a responsible treatment of a significant international topic worthy of presentation to the public. All statements of fact and expressions of opinion contained in Council books are, however, the sole responsibility of the author.

For more information about Council publications, please write the Council on Foreign Relations, 58 East 68th Street, New York, NY 10021, or call the Publications Office at (212) 734-0400.

Library of Congress Cataloguing-in-Publication Data

Yen for development: Japanese foreign aid and the politics of burden-sharing/edited by Shafiqul Islam.
    p. cm.
    Includes bibliographical references and index.
    ISBN 0-87609-096-X : $18.95
    1. Economic assistance, Japanese—Developing countries.
  I. Islam, Shafiqul.
  HC60.Y46   1991
  338.9' 15201724–dc20   90-25335
                                              CIP

91   92   93   94   95   96   PB   10   9   8   7   6   5   4   3   2   1

Cover Design: Whit Vye

CONTENTS

PART IV: THE HUMAN DIMENSION

PART V: YEN DIPLOMACY & U.S. FOREIGN POLICY

LIST OF TABLES

FOREWORD

James D. Robinson III

Japan—no longer recovering from World War II—has become the second-largest market economy in the world, with enormous trade and capital surpluses. Japan's newfound economic prowess has led to expectations and pressures for Japan to take on more responsibilities in global affairs. Policymakers and private-sector leaders from the United States to countries in the developing world are calling on Japan to play a greater role in addressing the world's economic, social, and political problems.

In 1986, I had the opportunity to put forth a proposal—that Japan, in the spirit of the Marshall Plan, take the lead in a global security initiative to promote economic growth in the developing world.

My proposal rested on four assumptions:

- First, global peace and security depend on economic growth and prosperity, not just military preparedness.

- Second, over one hundred countries with a large proportion of the world's population were stalled in the early stages of development. Scarce capital limited their ability to translate human and natural resources into strong economic growth.

- Third, the United States, the world's postwar leader in mobilizing capital through foreign aid and multilateral lending to help less-developed countries (LDCs) grow, was stymied by its enormous budget and trade deficits, and by the costs of its extensive military and defense responsibilities.

- Fourth, thanks to booming exports, high domestic savings, and a low defense burden, Japan had generated the world's largest capital surplus. More than ever, Japan's future depended on a peaceful, growing world economy, including the developing world. Why not have Japan use its capital surplus to promote economic growth and political stability in the developing world, to complement the military security provided by the United States?

Since 1986, Japan has in fact significantly expanded its official development assistance, or ODA (it now surpasses the United States in dollar value); its backing for the World Bank, the International Monetary Fund, and other multilateral institutions; its financial support for special initiatives such as the Brady Plan for LDC debt; and its private sector's investment overseas.

But, as Japan's role in assisting economic development has grown, many practical questions—political, diplomatic, economic, fiscal, operational, and organizational—have also surfaced. What are or should be Japan's goals in economic assistance? What ideas and theories of economic development should guide Japan's aid? Whose interests are being served and should be served by this aid? Should Japanese aid be coordinated with the United States, and if so, how? Is Japan contributing enough money, or is money the wrong answer? How should Japanese capital, which is primarily in the private sector, be marshalled to achieve public-sector goals? What responsibilities and powers should Japan assume if it is providing more money, and how much responsibility and power will the United States share with Japan? Does Japan have the technical and intellectual infrastructure to mount and sustain an expansion in its development aid?

To address these questions, the Council on Foreign Relations in 1988 launched a study group on Japan's role in development finance, which I had the honor of chairing. The study group was an effort to define, refine, and answer the key practical questions surrounding Japan's expanded role in international economic development. It was a unique opportunity for experts from Japan, the United States, and the multilateral institutions to share views on Japan's role and dilemmas. (A list of the study group members can be found in the Appendix.)

For myself, and I think for all the participants in the discussions, the study group was very much a learning process. Assumptions were challenged; knowledge was shared; new ideas and awareness were created. While full agreement on the *answers* was neither achieved nor expected, a general consensus on the key *questions* was reached. Both the consensus on the key questions about Japan's new international role and the wide range of views on the answers are fully reflected in the product: *Yen for Development,* edited by a well-known authority on the subject, Shafiqul Islam.

The bottom-line is this—Japan *is* and *will be* playing a larger role in international economic development, and the relationship between the United States and Japan will have to evolve in response. The issue is whether the expansion of Japan's role, and the resulting evolution of what Ambassador Mike Mansfield has correctly called, "the most important bilateral relationship in the world," occurs in ways that strengthen U.S.–Japan relations and benefit the world, or strain that relationship and damage the world economy. How that issue is resolved depends in turn on answers to questions posed in this book.

James D. Robinson III is the chairman and chief executive officer of American Express Company.

PREFACE

This volume grew out of a study group convened in 1988 at the Council on Foreign Relations. It was formally known as the C. Peter McColough Study Group on Japan's Role in Development Finance. James D. Robinson III chaired the group, I directed it, and the members were mostly Americans and Japanese from various communities: academia, government, business, media, and international agencies (see the Appendix for a complete list).

At each of the study group's four sessions (which took place between May and November 1988), a large subset of the 40-odd distinguished individuals discussed and debated one or another key aspect of Japan's role in a changing world and, in particular, Japan's growing involvement in development cooperation. Typically, a Japanese expert presented the lead paper, Americans and officials from multilateral development and financial institutions offered formal comments, and intense discussion and dialogue ensued. The intention was to create a forum for experts, opinion leaders, and decision makers—from the United States, Japan, and the developing countries—to conduct a frank exchange of views, to present facts and raise questions, and even search for some answers. We were largely successful in this endeavor, thanks to the superb chairmanship of Jim Robinson.

Yen for Development emerged from that process but, with time, took on a life of its own. Thus it contains chapters that were presented in 1988 but were more or less rewritten in 1990. Other chapters and all the comments were written for the first time in 1990. And some pieces that were presented to the study group simply failed to find their place in the volume. So, yes, the volume owes its origin to the study group, but it has matured into a collection that takes the reader out of the transforming 1980s into the unknown 1990s.

From the planning of the study group to the publication of the product, I have incurred such massive debts to so many people in such myriad ways that what follows represents neither a comprehensive nor a coherent account of my gratitude. In addition to the study group participants, I wish to offer special thanks to those who attended the authors' review group: Shinji Asanuma, Andrew Bartels, Lori Foreman, Javed Hamid, Masamichi Hanabusa, Bruce MacLaury, Frank McNeil, Kazuharu Nogami, and Stephen Quick. They read the entire manuscript with unusual care, and offered many critical comments and constructive suggestions, most of which contributed to major revisions of the structure and content of the book. I am particularly indebted to Bruce MacLaury who graciously agreed to chair the review group in the middle of a very busy week. He did a masterful job of guiding the discussion and summing up the central points, and left me with ideas and insights that proved invaluable during revisions.

At the Council, Peter Tarnoff, John Temple Swing, David Kellogg, C. Michael Aho, and Alan D. Romberg provided unwavering support—and the much-needed nudge—throughout the process. William H. Gleysteen, Jr., former vice president of Studies, remained a guide and mentor even after he left the Council. He served as a discussant at the opening session of the study group and contributed a very thoughtful comment on the lead chapter of the volume. Nicholas X. Rizopoulos picked up right where Bill Gleysteen left off, always ready to lend a helping hand at every stage, including with the choice of the title for this volume.

Outside the Council, many people—Americans, Japanese, and others—offered their help at various stages of the enterprise. Among the Japanese, Tadashi Yamamoto of the Japan Center of International Exchange always found time to invite me to breakfast or for a drink at the Hotel Okura, to answer my naive questions, and to arrange for me to meet key Tokyoites. His associate in New York, Hiroshi Peter Kamura, has been a constant source of help and advice. I also deeply appreciate the hospitality and assistance of several officials at the Economic Cooperation Bureau of the Japanese Ministry of Foreign Affairs (MOFA), most notably Koiichira Matsuura and Kenzo Oshima.

And I would like to thank Yoshiji Nogami of the Japan Institute of International Affairs; while in the Embassy in Washington, he was a fountain of ideas, advice, and assistance. Several officials of the Japan Export-Import Bank, most notably Reiichi Shimamoto (former deputy president), Toshihiko Kinoshita, and Kazuharu Nogami, taught me a great deal about the Recycling Plan and met my frequent demands for the most recent data. Koji Yamazaki, the Japanese executive director at the International Monetary Fund, was an active participant in the study group and responded immediately whenever I needed new information. And Shinji Asanuma of the World Bank and Yukio Iura, then at the Institute of International Finance, always made me think by challenging the conventional wisdom.

I also wish to acknowledge my special debt to Ambassador Masamichi Hanabusa. We met when he was director-general of MOFA's Economic Cooperation Bureau in Tokyo. I invited him to participate in the second session of the study group and he accepted. His involvement with the book began when he came to New York as the Japanese consul-general. I first persuaded him to write a comment on Japanese foreign aid, and then to participate in the authors' review group. The reviewers liked his piece so much that we concluded he should transform it into a chapter. Under group pressure Ambassador Hanabusa obliged, and even with his hectic schedule delivered the product on time. Let me also take this opportunity to acknowledge the help and cooperation of a number of his current and former colleagues at the Consulate General, most notably Kojiro Shiojiri and Hideo Sato.

Among the Americans, I am indebted to the late David McEachron and John Wheeler of the Japan Society for their invaluable assistance in the organization of the study group and in establishing my contacts in Japan. I also wish to thank Ellen Frost of Westinghouse for many helpful tips at the initial stage of this project, and Richard E. Bissel, formerly of the U.S. Agency for International Development (AID), for stimulating conversations and insightful comments on parts of the manuscript. Besides Jim Robinson, there are two other individuals from American Express to whom I am especially grateful: Joan Spero and Andrew Bartels. Both helped me immensely in planning each session of the study group and shaping its agenda. On behalf of the Council, I thank them for arranging—and Jim Robinson for hosting—luncheons for our Japanese guests. As editor, I would also like to thank Andrew Bartels for helping to resolve some controversial issues about the purpose and the audience of the volume.

Needless to say, this volume would not have been published without the patient cooperation of the authors and their willingness to put up with the editor's repeated demands that they revise, clarify, tighten, and elaborate parts of their pieces—and do so on short notice. What needs to be said, however, is that there are quite a few individuals whose names do not appear in the volume without whose help and involvement *Yen for Development* would never have seen the light of day. To begin with, Peter Oppenheimer and Alyson Piro helped organize the study group sessions and take care of all the indispensable logistics. Anita Hawner assisted in communicating—often overseas—with the authors, editing and re-editing the fourteen-odd pieces, as well as diligently handling all the administrative issues, including typing the revisions and some of the drafts into the Council's wordprocessing system. Dore Hollander did a superb job of copyediting the final version of the manuscript. At this stage, Barbara Brodeur and Elizabeth Halliday helped to do all that is necessary to transform the manuscript into the galleys.

The person who played the most pivotal role in creating a coherent volume out of a series of drafts is Suzanne Hooper, the Council's associate director of publications. She took charge when the manuscript was ready for production, and it was her disciplined devotion, insistence for consistency, attention to detail, and dedication to deadlines that minimized the adverse impact of some of my bad habits on the quality of the volume and on the time it took to send it to the printers.

Shafiqul Islam
New York

January 1991

INTRODUCTION

Shafiqul Islam

Foreign aid and foreign policy experts around the world agree that Japan should give money—lots of it—to the Third World. They disagree, however, on why Japan should do such a thing. Some say Japan, now a global power, must assume global responsibility, and giving foreign aid is the way. They argue that the Third World is in grave economic crisis, and no other country is better placed than Japan to respond effectively to this crisis by launching a major global initiative of economic assistance.

For many Americans the key rationale is *burden-sharing*: Japan has taken a "free ride" to economic preeminence as the United States has fallen behind, burdened with defending the "free world"; massive aid to the Third World is one way Japan can correct its "unfair burden deficit." Yet others invoke political macroeconomics to seek Japanese money: the usual macroeconomic policy tools cannot correct Japan's huge current account surplus; recycling this surplus to the Third World is therefore the most effective way of meeting the resource needs of the poor South while at the same time easing trade tensions in the rich North. Finally, to the aid experts of the South itself, the logic is simple: they need the money, America does not have it, and Japan does.

While experts fiddle, Tokyo gives. In 1989, with net official development assistance (ODA) disbursements totalling $9 billion, Japan replaced the United States as the world's top donor nation for the first time in the history of development aid. Throughout the year, as Washington celebrated the collapse of communism in Europe, Tokyo raced to become the unchallenged Santa Claus for the world's poor and needy. In the spring, when U.S. Treasury Secretary Nicholas Brady launched a reconstructed Japanese plan for reduction of bank debts of the troubled Third World debtors, Japan promised $4.5 billion of

1

official money—raised later to $10 billion—to help implement the plan; the United States and other major industrialized nations refused to put up a penny. In the summer, at a July 3–5 meeting of nineteen donor nations and seven international financial institutions, Tokyo pledged almost $1 billion to another plan that originated in Washington, the so-called mini–Marshall Plan for the Philippines; the Bush administration committed $200 million, which it ultimately failed to deliver, as the U.S. Congress—the original brain behind the plan—refused to appropriate more than $160 million.

A week later, as President François Mitterrand celebrated the bicentennial of the French Revolution at the Paris Economic Summit, Prime Minister Sosuke Uno unveiled a plan for adding $35 billion to the almost-fully-committed "Nakasone Recycling Plan" of $30 billion for the developing world. Prime Minister Uno also committed $2 billion of environmental aid to the Third World and added $100 million to Tokyo's $500 million untied nonproject grant aid package for least-developed countries.

As the new decade dawned, Tokyo's aid initiative began in Eastern Europe. On January 9, 1990, speaking only blocks from the Berlin Wall, Prime Minister Toshiki Kaifu unveiled an aid package of $2 billion for Poland and Hungary. Six months earlier, President George Bush had stopped in Poland on his way to the Paris Summit; he had cheered the Polish people for their bold march toward democracy and capitalism, and promised to help them with an aid package of $200 million (an embarrassed Congress raised it to $840 million a few months later).

Tokyo's development assistance efforts are becoming increasingly global. Japan is already the top donor in 30 countries; it allocates 70 percent of its aid to low-income countries (whereas Uncle Sam allocates less than 50 percent to those countries); it gives more aid, mostly untied, to Sub-Saharan Africa than the United States does; and it gives more money to environment-related projects than any other donor. For a country that was repaying its World Bank loans until July 1990, all this adds up to a stunning feat unparalleled in history.

And yet no one is happy. New criticisms, frustrations, and tensions are emerging around the globe as the old ones refuse to disappear. One reason is the needs of the developing countries are vast; and Japan's rising financial contributions, while substantial, still fall far short of making up for the dramatic decline of net resource flows from other donors, especially the United States. At a time when the 1980s have been characterized as the lost decade of development, the feeling in much of the Third World and among concerned observers of the First World therefore is: yes, Japan is doing more, but it is not doing enough. This frustrated expectation is compounded by the fact that while Japan is rich in financial capital, it is poor in human capital: shortage of aid staff and lack of diplomatic skills prevent Japan from taking the policy and political lead in development cooperation. Bluntly put, Tokyo gives the money, but it fails to use its mouth to speak its mind.

Another reason for unhappiness involves the bilateral politics of the U.S.–Japan relationship. On this side of the ocean, criticisms and indictments result from the vicious cycle driven by America's loss of confidence in its ability to compete and its image of Japan as a selfish superpower free riding to unfair economic supremacy. On the other side, frustrations and resentment accumulate as too few people push too much money with too little sense of why, and feel harassed by the seemingly unending stream of criticisms of "unfair aid practices" and demands for bearing a "fair share of the burden." As a newcomer in the Old Boys' Club, Japan is treated as a selfish upstart trying to buy respect with money and is kept busy either defending itself against foreign attacks or devising schemes to address them. While Japan's old preoccupation with narrowly defined national interest is no longer acceptable to the international community, its new attempts to act like a global power also meet resistance.

The purpose of this volume is to help ease this adjustment process and improve the quality of the policy debate by addressing the myths, misperceptions, and miscommunications that characterize the philosophy, economics, and politics of Japan's emerging role in Third World development. The volume attempts to accomplish this goal in three ways. First, it examines the various rationales for Japan's assuming a leading role in development cooperation and seeks to determine whether a common ground exists between the development implications of Japanese foreign aid and the political imperatives of U.S. foreign policy. Second, it presents an informed debate on what the real issues are, guided by facts that define the situation of the early 1990s, and discourages unnecessary controversies based on the relics of the 1960s and 1970s. Finally, it draws implications of the end of the Cold War for the bilateral politics of foreign aid, as well as for U.S. and Japanese foreign policy, and offers suggestions as to where and how the world's top two donors can fruitfully cooperate to promote Third World development.

Yen for Development does not attempt to accomplish these goals with a single voice, but by offering an informed and frank dialogue and discussion among academics, aid experts, and officials from Japan, the United States, and multilateral development institutions. There are thus disagreements; however, they do not arise from ignorance or misunderstanding of facts, as is usually the case with politicians, power brokers, and the press. Instead, they reflect informed differences regarding the philosophy of aid or its impact on economic development—matters on which reasonable people can agree to disagree.

The core of this volume consists of an extensive analysis of Japan's evolving role in financing and promoting economic development of the Third World. One may view the issues involved as the legs of a tripod. The first leg is ODA, or what is popularly known as foreign aid. The second leg is the role the Japanese private sector plays in developing countries. The third leg is the human dimension—Japan's leadership, managerial, and intellectual role—in the multilateral development and financial institutions.

The volume consists of five parts. Part 1 analyzes the global context in which Japan's role in Third World development has become a Japanese as well as a U.S. foreign policy goal of critical importance. Here, Takashi Inoguchi, an eminent political scientist from Tokyo University, compares the feasibility and desirability of four scenarios of the future world order. The most likely, he thinks, is a regime where the United States retains its leadership but needs a little help from allies and friends to exercise it. In this world order, Japan, committed to maintaining its postwar pacifism, takes a lead in development cooperation while continuing to defer security matters to the United States. Commenting on Inoguchi's scenarios, William H. Gleysteen, Jr., president of the Japan Society and a former top Asia hand at the State Department, puts Japan's role in Third World development in the context of the economic and psychological problems that plague the politics of Washington-Tokyo relations, and suggests policy steps to reduce "the risk of drifting mindlessly into failure."

Parts 2–4 represent the three legs of the development cooperation tripod. Part 2, focusing on ODA, contains four chapters and two comments. An overview by Toru Yanagihara & Anne Emig, two aid experts from academia, sets the stage for a more detailed examination of Japanese ODA. Their summary covers issues ranging from an analysis of the evolution of Japanese ODA, recent trends, quantity, quality, and administration to "strategic aid" and the complexities of the so-called Japanese Recycling Plan. Julia Chang Bloch, a former top official of the U.S. Agency for International Development (AID), examines the limits and possibilities of U.S.–Japan cooperation in development assistance and offers several concrete suggestions. Next, Masamichi Hanabusa, a former top aid official of the Japanese Ministry of Foreign Affairs, gives his candid personal views on the philosophy, administration, quality, and effectiveness of Japanese development assistance.

In their comments, Shinji Asanuma, one of the few Japanese senior World Bank officials, and Ernest H. Preeg, another former high-ranking U.S. AID official, extend the discussion in a number of directions. Asanuma explains the observed characteristics of Japan's foreign aid in terms of a historical process involving "a series of concentric waves of trading, investment, and aid activities spreading through the Third World as Japan's economic power . . . has grown," and questions the traditional premises of U.S.–Japan aid cooperation. Preeg focuses on five key aspects of the U.S.–Japan aid relationship, including such controversial issues as tied aid and burden-sharing; he advocates, among other things, a "common approach based on the momentum of private-sector, export-driven economic growth in many parts of the developing world."

Part 2 also contains a comparative analysis of Japanese and American aid in the Philippines—the only chapter in the volume where two experts from a developing country offer a recipient-country perspective on the strengths and the weaknesses of Japanese ODA. A discussion of Japanese ODA limited to views from the United States, Japan, and multilateral institutions risks becoming a self-serving and unbalanced "dialogue of the donor"; the chapter by Filologo Pante, Jr., & Romeo A. Reyes provides the missing balance. For several reasons, the Philippines is a suitable choice for the purpose at hand: it is a recipient country where Japan (the donor under scrutiny) and the United States (the donor most critical of Japan) have long histories of substantial and comparable involvement and continuing security interests; it also represents a rare case where both donors have successfully *cooperated* in putting together an aid package.

Part 3, with two chapters and one commentary, examines the opportunities and challenges Japan's private capital faces as it courts the Third World in the pursuit of profits. Hiroya Ichikawa, a development expert at Keidanren (a leading association of the Japanese business community), argues that Japanese foreign direct investment can play a critical role in Third World development, but urges the public sector (the Japanese and other creditor governments, as well as multilateral institutions) to share the risk in areas where economic crisis and political instability make it difficult for private investors to go alone. On the prospect of Japanese bank lending to debtor developing countries, Shoji Ochi, deputy president of the Japan Center for International Finance, a highly influential Japanese association of private banks and financial institutions, offers a pessimistic assessment; he sees wholesale withdrawal of long-term bank lending from the debt-distressed countries as the Japanese banks feel discriminated against by what they view as irresponsible and incompetent implementation of the Brady debt plan.

Commenting on the Ichikawa and Ochi chapters, Barbara Stallings, a leading expert on Japan's evolving relationship with Latin America, argues that the debt crisis has driven a wedge between development finance and profit motive, and offers suggestions as to how the public sector can loosen and ultimately remove this wedge.

The final leg of the development cooperation tripod is the subject of Part 4. Ryokichi Hirono, a former high-ranking official of the United Nations Development Programme (UNDP), offers his views on why Japan's leadership role in development cooperation, and its management and intellectual contributions in international financial and development institutions, lag behind its financial contributions. Ernest Stern, a senior vice president of the World Bank, comments on this subject with the insight of a longtime insider of the World Bank.

Hirono points out that the imbalance between money and management does not characterize Japan's participation at regional organizations within the Asia and Pacific region. To reduce that imbalance at the global level, he calls on the Japanese authorities to reform employment practices, such as by sending government officials to the multilateral institutions for longer periods of time and guaranteeing job security and seniority for those returning home. At the same time, those institutions should invite Japanese officials and experts to participate in conferences, symposia, and seminars held abroad, as well as hold such meetings in Japan and involve Japanese from all walks of life. Stern stresses that in a career-oriented organization such as the World Bank, the critical window of influence is not the size of Japan's share of capital (voting rights) but its participation at the staff level; a limited role here deprives the Bretton Woods institutions and their member-countries of valuable and unique lessons that they could learn from the way Japan manages and develops its economy.

Part 5 contains only one chapter, which I have written with the benefit of having read and edited the others. The purpose of this concluding chapter is neither to summarize the key points of the volume nor to identify the areas of agreements and disagreements. Rather, here I close the circle: the volume starts with the premise that development cooperation is the most effective avenue for a gun-shy Japan to assume global responsibilities; it ends with my thoughts on what that role of Japan implies for U.S. and Japanese foreign aid, their foreign policies, and the politics of burden-sharing, as the two nations try to adjust their imbalances between commitments and capacity.

Future historians may mark 1989 as the year when the West won the Cold War. The Third World, however, may remember 1989 differently: it was the year when America relinquished its *financial* lead in development aid to Japan. Paradoxically, while Japan assumes more of the "nonmilitary burden" of promoting global peace and prosperity, tension and resentment on both sides of the Pacific are likely to rise as an insecure America, long used to the status of a supreme superpower, finds itself increasingly constrained by a *nouveau riche* Japan stumbling along toward becoming a global leader. The efforts that have gone into producing this volume will have been worth it if *Yen for Development* can make a small contribution to easing the pain of realigning the postwar balance of power as the bipolarity that long held the world together crumbles.

I

Global Context

JAPAN'S GLOBAL ROLE IN A MULTIPOLAR WORLD

Takashi Inoguchi

With the 20th century coming to a close, a vague angst is haunting Japan. The current mood can be compared with that prevailing during the early 1800s, when the Tokugawa policy of seclusion started to manifest its contradictions, or that of the early 1900s, when the Meiji state, with its victory over Russia, finally consolidated its national security and recovered from the long-felt humiliation dealt by Western powers. Bereft of a sense of direction and uncertain about the future, Japan is responding with ambivalence to the demands, requests, and suggestions from abroad that it—now a global economic power—assume global responsibility.[1]

One outcome of this loss of direction is a revived emphasis on traditional values, such as perseverance, frugality, diligence, family, community, sacrifice, humility, the spirit of harmony, and deference for the elderly. But these traditional values cannot be the basis for guiding Japan's foreign policy. The question that Japan must confront now is, How does it see its future global position and its global role? Put differently, What scenarios of the world order can one envisage in which Japan may occupy a more prominent position than it has held to date? This chapter addresses these and related questions, especially in relation to burden-sharing and power-sharing with the United States in managing the world economy and international relations.

First, I present results of several opinion polls. These are a useful prelude to analyzing the scenarios of the future conjured up largely by educated elites because opinion polls represent prevailing moods and sentiments of the masses. Second, I outline four scenarios, highlighting their differences in terms of economic, political, and security arrangements. In each case, I indicate Japan's role and degree of burden- and power-sharing with the United States. Third, I discuss the feasibility and desirability of each scenario in terms of three conditions. Finally, I take up the issue of foreign aid and development finance, and assess the desirability of Japan's current burden- and power-sharing arrangements with the United States in light of their implications for the four scenarios.

JAPAN'S GLOBAL ROLE: PUBLIC OPINION POLLS

In its 1987 annual opinion poll on Japanese diplomacy,[2] the Public Relations Department of the Office of the Prime Minister asked the following question: "What kind of roles do you think Japan should play in the community of nations?" The respondents overwhelmingly preferred roles outside security and political matters, such as in economic development and scientific, technological, and cultural exchanges.

Results of a 1986 poll, conducted by an academic team, permit us to compare the priorities Japanese men and women attach to domestic and international roles the government should play.[3] Instead of asking which task respondents wanted to see the government treat as its first priority, the poll asked the following question about eight policy areas: "There are many kinds of government policies nowadays. What do you think about the emphasis the government puts on each of them?" The following proportions of respondents indicated a desire for much *more* emphasis:

- Domestic economic management—56 percent

- Internal security and order—56 percent

- Social welfare—45 percent

- Living standard—45 percent

- Economic power—30 percent

- National solidarity—19 percent

- National security—11 percent

If global economic welfare and economic power correspond roughly to Japan's contribution in the economic field and national security corresponds roughly to Japan's contribution in the security field, then two points are immediately clear: the overwhelming priority of domestic issues; and the overwhelming significance of economic contributions, rather than security contributions, to the desired role of Japan in the world.

Further evidence of the Japanese reluctance to make a commitment to military matters is apparent from a comparison of two opinion polls, conducted in 1956 and in 1980, on the idea of Japan's responding to a hypothetical United Nations (UN) request to send personnel to conflict areas.[4] Interestingly, while support for sending medical teams to UN peacekeeping forces shows an increase (from 24 percent to 37 percent) over the period, that for contributing armed soldiers registers a decline (from 24 percent to 13 percent).

It is critical to keep such evidence on Japanese public opinion in mind as we assess the four schools of thought on the future shape of the world order and Japan's role in it.

SCENARIOS FOR THE FUTURE

The following four scenarios have overlapping elements, but they represent differing expectations—among both Japanese and non-Japanese—for global development, and for the balance of economic and military power in the next 25–50 years.[5]

Pax Americana Phase II

In this scenario, first articulated by the Americans, the United States retains its leading position in the world, deftly prodding and cajoling its allies into an enlightened joint action. The outline of this scenario began to take shape during the latter half of the 1970s, when the post-Vietnam trauma was still strong and Soviet influence appeared somewhat exaggerated. In the parlance of American political science, the key word was "regimes," whereby the United States would retain its enlightened hegemony and control the direction of world development. Such phrases as "after hegemony" and "cooperation under anarchy"—both book titles—epitomize the primary thrust of policy and academic interest in this image of the future.[6]

Different versions of this image have emerged intermittently. Confident of the retention of America's cultural hegemony in the Gramscian sense, Bruce Russett, a Yale political scientist, has likened the declaration of America's decline and imminent demise to the premature report of the death of Mark Twain. More directly and bluntly, Susan Strange, of the London School of Economics, has asserted that U.S. hegemony is not yet gone; lamenting a lost hegemony is the favorite habit of American self-indulgence, she says. Paul Kennedy, of Yale, has presented an image of the revival of American composure and confidence, combined with the somber recognition that national decline is inevitable in the longer term.[7]

In Japan, this image of America's future has been a consistent favorite. Naohiro Amaya, former vice minister of international trade and industry, was fond of talking about "Go-Bei" (later United States), implying that prior to Vietnam, the United States was called "Zen-Bei" (earlier United States).[8] Amaya was thus alluding to the Han dynasty of ancient China: after disappearing for seventeen years, the dynasty was restored, and this so-called later Han dynasty survived another two centuries. Similarly, Yasusuke Murakami, a well-known economist, has argued that the hegemonic cycle observed for the last few centuries has ceased to repeat itself largely because of the world economy's transformation from a fragmented composite of national economies to a tightly integrated global economy. His scenario depicts an America that is an enlightened and experienced primus inter pares in an increasingly multipolar world.[9]

The appeal of this image is due in no small part to its retention of Japan's traditional concentration on an economic role without any drastic increase in its security role; global security, in this scenario, is largely the responsibility of the United

States. Even if Japan increases its security-related assistance to Third World countries—like Pakistan, Turkey, Papua New Guinea, and Honduras—the security leadership of the United States will remain strong. And even if Japan enhances its global security cooperation by sending warships to the Persian Gulf to help shoulder the costs of oil imports, it will be supporting the U.S.-dominated world, rather than becoming a main security provider in the region.

"Bigemony"

This second scenario is the favorite of economists and business-men fascinated by the rapid development and integration of what Robert Gilpin, a Princeton University political scientist, calls the nichibei (Japan–U.S.) economy.[10] That is to say, it portrays the economies of Japan and the United States as becoming one integrated economy of a sort. C. Fred Bergsten, the director of the Institute for International Economics, coined the word "bigemony," denoting the primordial importance of America and Japan in managing the world economy. Zbigniew Brzezinski, former national security adviser to President Carter, coined the term "Amerippon" to describe the close integration of the American and Japanese manufacturing, financial, and commercial sectors and the two economies as something of a whole. This image gains support from the steady rise in the yen's value against the U.S. dollar and the concomitant rise of the Japanese gross national product (GNP), which now accounts for 20 percent of the world GNP.

One of the foremost Japanese advocates of this scenario was Prime Minister Yasuhiro Nakasone. In a meeting with President Reagan, he said that Japan and the United States should forge a single community of the same destiny, although he focused on security rather than economic aspects of the bilateral relationship.[11]

Economic power almost inevitably becomes military power, and Japan does not constitute a historic exception to this rule.[12] But the way Japan's economic power is likely to be translated into military power needs close attention. Under bigemony, the technological, economic, and strategic cooperation or integration of the United States and Japan may become formidable and of the largest scale in history. It is not difficult to foresee, for instance, that advanced fighter aircraft could be jointly developed and manufactured primarily for Japanese use, with primarily Japanese finance and American know-how, but secondarily sold to third countries as well, under the label "Made in the United States."

Japan's regional role in bigemony is an acceleration of the features presented in Pax Americana Phase II. A gigantic Pacific economic community is forged, with Japan's role reminiscent of the role played by the corridor stretching from northern Italy through northeastern France, the Rhineland, and the Low Countries to southern Britain in modern European economic development. Furthermore, the strategic integration of many countries in the region may make it hard to accommodate the Soviet Union within an invigorated bigemonic structure, thus relegating it to a far less important status than it now has, in the absence of other countervailing moves.

Pax Consortis

In the third scenario, the major actors in a world of many consortia are busily forging coalitions among themselves; no single actor can dominate the rest. This image, in its barest outline, resembles Pax Americana Phase II. By contrast, however, while the thrust of this scenario rests on the pluralistic nature of policy adjustments, the first scenario builds on the desirability, or necessity, or even hoped-for inevitability of the administrative guidance or moral leadership by the United States. Many Japanese favor Pax Consortis, not least because Japan is averse to shouldering large security burdens. They also favor it because Japan is not completely happy about America's bossing everyone around, especially when it only grudgingly admits its relative decline.

Kuniko Inoguchi, a Sophia University political scientist, articulates this scenario most eloquently and forcefully in the context of the American debate on posthegemonic stability of the international system.[13] Shinji Fukukawa, former vice minister of international trade and industry, has also advanced this image. Pax Consortis, which accords on the whole with the pacifist sentiment of most Japanese, sees two global roles for Japan.[14] With the strategic nuclear arsenals increasingly neutralized either by de facto U.S.–Soviet détente or by technological breakthroughs, the first role is that of quiet economic diplomacy in forging coalitions and shaping policy adjustments among peers. The other role is that of helping to create a world bereft of military solutions, including, if possible, the diffusion of antinuclear defensive systems to all countries and the extension of massive economic aid tied to cease-fire or peace agreements between belligerents.

Japan's primary regional role in this scenario is to coordinate or promote the interests of the Asian and Pacific countries that have lacked full representation either in the United Nations system or in the economic institutions of the industrialized nations, such as the Organization for Economic Cooperation and Development (OECD). Its secondary regional role is to moderate, especially in security areas.[15] For example, Japan might attempt to serve as an intermediary in the negotiations between North and South Korea, or in the facilitation of neutral peacekeeping forces in Cambodia and Afghanistan.

Pax Nipponica

Ezra Vogel, a Harvard University sociologist, was the first to articulate the Pax Nipponica vision of the future.[16] In this world, Japanese economic power reigns supreme. This scenario is attractive to Americans who are concerned about the visible contrast between America's relative loss of technological and manufacturing competitiveness and Japan's concomitant gain. It has been gaining popularity in Japan as well, reflecting both the dramatic rise in the value of the yen and Japan's number-one position as a creditor country. Japan's internationalization is also contributing to the appeal of this scenario as the intrusion of external economic and social forces into Japanese society invites nationalistic reactions.

Under Pax Nipponica, Japan is best compared with Britain during the nineteenth century, when it functioned as balancer among the continental powers. Britain's global commercial interests presumably helped it play this role. In this scenario, Japan's preeminent global position will enable it to play the leading role in the Asian and Pacific region, as well.

FEASIBILITY OF THE SCENARIOS

To what extent are these scenarios feasible? Under what conditions could they materialize? Before attempting to answer these questions, it is necessary to examine three factors that will critically influence the relative probabilities of the scenarios: the effective neutralization of strategic nuclear arsenals, scientific-technological dynamism, and the burden of history.

Neutralizing the Nuclear Arsenals

Strategic nuclear forces have allowed the United States and the Soviet Union to retain their superpower status and global influence. Whether these weapons will become obsolete remains to be seen. Whether the United States or the Soviet Union or any other country will be able to arm itself with a defensive weapons system that makes it immune to nuclear attacks is another open question. The American Strategic Defense Initiative and its Soviet counterpart are related to this issue, as is the Conventional Defense Initiative; the last, which the United States started in 1987 and subsequently proposed as a partially joint project with Japan, significantly enhances the capabilities of U.S. conventional forces, including those of "smart" weapons and high-power microwaves.

However, with the disarmament process between the United States and the Soviet Union slowly making progress, strategic nuclear forces may not make much difference in determining global development. Some observers maintain that nuclear weapons and even military power in general have already ceased to be a major factor in international politics, and that economic interdependence has deepened sufficiently to make war an obsolete instrument for resolving conflicts of interests, at least among OECD countries and in direct East-West relations.

Scientific and Technological Dynamism

The innovative and inventive capacity of nations—how vigorous they are in making scientific and technological progress and translating it into economic development—will also influence the scenarios' feasibility. Needless to say, forecasting technological development is not easy. Yet, a cursory examination of the social propensity to innovate suggests that the Americans are the more innovative, and the Japanese follow steadily behind. Open competition, abundant opportunities, a strong spirit of individualism and freedom, and high social mobility—conditions that encourage innovation—are more prevalent in the United States than in Japan.

Other evidence, however, appears to indicate that Japan is either about to surpass or has already surpassed America. For example, the number of patents—to exclusively utilize technological innovation for manufacturing—obtained by Japanese companies and individuals in the United States has grown very close to that obtained by Americans; in 1987, the top three companies, in terms of the number of licenses obtained, were Japanese firms—Canon, Hitachi, and Toshiba.[17] Furthermore, Japanese scientists are gaining exposure in the professional literature; they have, for instance, made up the largest group of authors, except U.S.–based authors, published in *Chemical Abstracts* since 1985.[18] Finally, the United States produced as few as five Nobel Prize–winners in the first 30 years of this century, about on par with Japan's seven winners since 1945.[19] The speculation is that Japan might shortly start producing as many Nobel Prize–winners as the United States has been since World War II, when it started to act as the world leader.

The Burden of History

The third determining factor involves the memory among the vanquished nations in World War II of their treatment, primarily at the hands of the Germans and the Japanese. As Hu

Yaobang, former secretary-general of the Chinese Communist Party, has told novelist Toyoko Yamazaki, the memory of people who suffered from war disappears only 80 years after the event.[20] Citing the Boxer intervention in China in 1900, which is now virtually forgotten, he argues that the Second Sino-Japanese War (1937–1945) will not disappear from the memory of the Chinese for another 40 years. For now, according to this view, neither Japan nor West Germany can play a leading global role without facing many emotional barriers.

Pax Americana Phase II

Whether Pax Americana Phase II is realized or not depends greatly on scientific and technological dynamism. The argument for this scenario is based on the free spirit, open competition, and dynamic character of the American society that presumably stimulate the innovative and inventive capacity of the United States.

This scenario has a fairly high feasibility if the United States adopts two essential policies: a close macroeconomic policy cooperation with Japan, and a full-scale interlinking of its economy with the Asian and Pacific economies under U.S. leadership. Whether the United States can execute these policies without igniting Asian nationalism against it remains to be seen.

Bigemony

The feasibility of bigemony depends critically on the legacy of history. Whether Japan's neighbors can be at ease with its leadership in regional and global security matters, even in cooperation with the Americans, is not clear. Furthermore, bigemony requires a very close friendship between the United States and Japan, and the ambiguity of their relationship—the steady progress toward economic integration and defense cooperation, on the one hand, and the recurrent and at times almost explosive friction, on the other—augurs ill for this scenario. Bigemony would best progress only slowly and steadily, because technological progress and economic dynamism are bound to push Japan and the United States much closer.

Pax Consortis

Nuclear neutralization is the key determinant of the feasibility of Pax Consortis. Realization of this scenario is conceivable only in the distant future—say, 50 years from now. The United States and the Soviet Union will need time to give up their superpower status and revert to less important roles, even assuming that their relative decline has already progressed. One can recall Edward Gibbon (an eighteenth century English historian who authored *The Decline and Fall of the Roman Empire*) saying that it took 300 years for the Roman Empire to disappear after its inevitable decline and demise were common knowledge.

How an unknown, perfect antinuclear defensive weapons system might be developed and deployed is beyond speculation. Yet the possibly embryonic form of Pax Consortis can be discerned. As supporting evidence, one may cite several examples: the inability of the superpowers to decisively influence the course of events in Nicaragua and Afghanistan, the increasing importance of monetary and economic policy coordination and consultation among the major powers, the increasing collaboration in research and development, mostly among OECD countries yet increasingly throughout the world, including the United States and the Soviet Union, as well, and the frequent formation of consortia in manufacturing and financial activities throughout the world.

Pax Nipponica

Pax Nipponica's feasibility hinges on neutralization of nuclear weapons and scientific and technological dynamism. If both conditions are satisfied together, the historical factor may become less significant. Japan's innovative and inventive capacity for the next decade or two should not be taken lightly. Beyond that period, however, the expected fall in demographic dynamism (i.e., the increasingly high percentage of those older than 55) and associated social problems that are bound to arise—such as overburdening of the increasingly small productive working population (i.e., those whose age ranges from 25 to 55) to facili-

tate extensive social welfare expenditure and increased contributions to international public goods—throw the feasibility of this
scenario into question.

SPECIFIC JAPAN–U.S. UNDERTAKINGS

Although the four scenarios contain many elements of the evolving global arrangements, the above review did not attempt to
relate them with various cooperative schemes that have been
steadily forged between the United States and Japan, in both
security and economic terms. Here I make a limited effort by
focusing on the economic area—in particular, on U.S.–Japan
cooperation in foreign aid and development finance. In this
context, I also address the issue of burden- and power-sharing. It
is useful to divide the discussion into two parts: development
assistance and security assistance.

Development Assistance

Under the imperative of burden-sharing, Japan's aid has been
complementing U.S. aid, especially outside the Asian and Pacific
region. U.S.–Japan bilateral consultation and implementation
that started in 1985 is one form of burden- and power-sharing.[21]
Furthermore, Senator Albert Gore has proposed the U.S.–
Japan Strategic Environment Initiative to meet head-on the
increasingly menacing global environmental deterioration.
These schemes are consistent with Pax Americana Phase II, and
both the United States and Japan should encourage and enhance them.

Japan has also engaged in bilateral aid cooperations with the
United Kingdom on Africa, and with Australia on the South
Pacific. This kind of scheme is naturally welcome to Japan, which
"is long on yen, short on experts."[22]

Foreign aid should enhance multilateralism more than it
does. Japan's contributions to multilateral institutions—the
World Bank, the Asian Development Bank, and others—have
been very large. But the United States and other major countries
do not seem happy about increasing Japanese influence in these

institutions. For example, given increasing lending to private firms rather than governments, the Asian Development Bank needs to set up a new subsidiary, but the United States and Western Europe resisted the Japanese initiative to establish the Asian Financial Investment Corporation. What America and other major powers seem to have difficulty accepting is that power-sharing must to a certain extent go hand in hand with burden-sharing. This difficulty can throw roadblocks on the path toward Pax Americana Phase II.

Security Assistance

The logic behind Japan's provisions of security assistance is the same: When the United States has difficulties sustaining its world leadership role with its resources alone, its wealthy allies should share the burden of enhancing the ability of Third World countries that are strategically important to the Western alliance. Economic assistance can strengthen their ability to cope with economic difficulties and with security threats. While the United States suffers from both government and trade deficits, Japan is under increasing pressure to provide security assistance.

Cooperation in security assistance, however, entails two problems. First, postwar pacifism limits not only Japan's defense efforts, but also its security assistance. The guiding principle of the Japanese government is the pursuit of nonmilitary solutions to conflicts among states. Granting the need in this area for Japanese involvement, I prefer efforts that are in basic accord with this principle—for example, offering current belligerents postwar assistance in economic reconstruction and in force-level reductions. Japan is moving in that direction: it has taken the initiative to establish the Trust Fund for Peace in the United Nations for the purpose of sustaining the peacekeeping operations, such as those in Afghanistan, Iran, Iraq, Namibia, Cambodia, and Nicaragua.

Second, if pushed too far, Japanese security assistance could easily undermine the hegemonic position of the United States in certain key Third World countries. Japan has already demonstrated steadfastness in keeping its promise to shore up its foreign aid. For example, prior to the Soviet invasion of Afghanistan in 1979, Japanese aid to South Asian countries was not large, but in responding to requests for greater aid, Japan became the largest donor for most of the region, including India.

Masashi Nishihara, of the Japanese Defense College, has proposed a common fund for security assistance.[23] Under his scheme, Japan probably would contribute more than the United States, but the fund's management would be under joint control, thus mitigating both problems associated with cooperation in security assistance. If this initiative can be implemented along the Pax Americana Phase II line, it is worthy of support. The Multilateral Aid Initiative on the Philippines is perhaps another good example of cooperation in security assistance. Although Japan underwrites the bulk of financial bases, the leadership remains with the United States; contributions from seven international organizations and nineteen countries "multilateralize" the program.

CONCLUSION

In this chapter, I have outlined four possible scenarios for the world order and assessed some specific cooperative arrangements between the United States and Japan. Pax Americana Phase II and bigemony are the most feasible scenarios for the next 25 years; of these, Pax Americana Phase II is preferable because it entails less risk to the United States as well as to the rest of the world. Over the longer haul, a mixture of Pax Americana Phase II and Pax Consortis seems more feasible because sustaining Pax Americana Phase II for such a long period of time does not seem a realistic proposition, especially in light of the current difficulties that strain its evolution. To bolster Pax Americana Phase II, Japan must enhance its aid and development finance efforts. Japan's role in this area should focus on economic and technological matters rather than on security matters, even though nonmilitary channels exist for providing security assistance. Also, Japanese aid should make the maximum possible use of multilateral institutions. For this to take place, power-sharing must follow from burden-sharing to the extent that it accords with Pax Americana Phase II.

NOTES

The author gratefully acknowledges constructive comments made by Shafiqul Islam and Brian Woodall on an early draft of this chapter. Another version of this chapter appeared in International Affairs, *65, no. 1 (Winter 1988/1989), 15–28.*

1. Takashi Inoguchi, *Tadanori to ikkoku haneishugi o koete* (Beyond free ride and prosperity-in-one-country-ism) (Tokyo: Toyo keizai shimposha, 1987); and ——— "Tenkanki Nihon no kadai" (Japan's tasks at a time of transition), *Nihon keizai shimbun*, November 1, 8, 15, 22, and 29, 1987. Also see "The Ideas and Structures of Foreign Policy: Looking Ahead with Caution," in Takashi Inoguchi and Daniel I. Okimoto, eds., *The Political Economy of Japan: The Changing International Context* (Stanford, California: Stanford University Press, 1988), 23–63, 490–500; ——— "Japan's Images and Options: Not a Challenger, but a Supporter," *Journal of Japanese Studies* 12, no. 1 (1986), 95–119; and "Foreign Policy Background," in Herbert J. Ellison, ed., *Japan and the Pacific Quadrille* (Boulder, Colorado: Westview Press, 1987), 81–105.

2. Department of Public Relations, Office of the Prime Minister, *Gaiko ni kansuru yoron chosa* (Opinion poll on diplomacy) (Tokyo: Printing Bureau, Ministry of Finance, 1988).

3. Watanuki Joji et al., *Nihonjin no senkyo kodo* (Japanese electoral behavior) (Tokyo: University of Tokyo Press, 1986).

4. Sigeki Nisihira, *Yoron ni miru dosedai shi* (Contemporary history through opinion polls) (Tokyo: Buren shuppan, 1987).

5. Inoguchi, "Tenkanki Nihon no kadai."

6. Stephen Krasner, ed., *International Regimes* (Ithaca, New York: Cornell University Press, 1983); Robert O. Keohane, *After Hegemony: Cooperation and Discord in the World Political Economy* (Princeton, New Jersey: Princeton University Press, 1984); and Kenneth A. Oye, ed., *Cooperation under Anarchy* (Princeton, New Jersey: Princeton University Press, 1985).

7. Bruce M. Russett, "The Mysterious Case of Vanishing Hegemony: Or Is Mark Twain Really Dead?" *International Organization* 39, no. 2 (1985), 207–231; Susan Strange, "The Persistent Myth of Lost Hegemony," *International Organization* 41, no. 4 (1987), 551–574; and Paul Kennedy, *The Rise and Fall of the Great Powers* (New York: Random House, 1987).

8. Naohiro Amaya, *Nahon wa dokoe ikunoka* (Whither Japan?) (Tokyo: PHP Institute, 1987); and Yasusuke Murakami, "After Hegemony," *Chuokoron*, November 1985, 68–89.

9. Murakami, "After Hegemony."

10. Robert Gilpin, *War and Change in World Politics* (Cambridge, England: Cambridge University Press, 1981); and———*The Political Economy of International Relations* (Princeton, New Jersey: Princeton University Press, 1987).

11. Inoguchi, "The Legacy of a Weathercock Prime Minister," *Japan Quarterly* 34, no. 4 (1987), 363–370.

12. Kennedy, *Rise and Fall.*

13. Kuniko Inoguchi, *Posuto haken sisutemu to Nihon no sentaku* (An emerging post-hegemonic system: choices for Japan) (Tokyo: Chikuma shobo, 1987).

14. Shinji Fukukawa, *21 seiki no Nihon no sentaku* (Japan's choice in the 21st century) (Tokyo: TBS Britannica, 1990), 130–131.

15. Inoguchi, *Tadanori to ikkoku haneishugi o koete.*

16. Ezra Vogel, "Pax Nipponica?" *Foreign Affairs* 64, no. 4 (1986), 752–767; and Ronald A. Morse, "Japan's Drive to Pre-eminence," *Foreign Policy,* 69 (1987–1988), 3–21.

17. "Beikoku deno Tokkyo shutoku" (Obtaining patents in the United States), *Nihon keizai shimbun,* March 26, 1988.

18. Masamitsu Negishi, "Gakujutsu kenkyu ronbun su no kokusai hikaku chosa" (International comparison of academic articles), *Gakujutsu geppo* (Monthly Bulletin of Academic Affairs), 41, no. 7 (1988), 40–47.

19. "*Beikoku ga Nihon datta koro*" (When the United States was like Japan), *Asahi shimbun,* evening edition, March 24, 1988, 15.

20. Toyoko Yamazaki, "Shimidarake no shidosha" (The leader full of stains), *Bungei shunju,* May 1985, 230–236.

21. John W. Sewell and Anne Dixon, "Africa, Japan, and America Can Work Together," *International Herald Tribune,* August 11, 1989, 4.

22. Robert Orr, Jr., "Long on Yen, Short on Experts," *International Herald Tribune,* March 11–12, 1989, 4.

23. Susumu Awanohara, "Many East Asian Countries Want the U.S. to Remain," *Far Eastern Economic Review,* April 21, 1988, 26–28.

COMMENT

William H. Gleysteen, Jr.

Takashi Inoguchi has produced a very thoughtful and balanced analysis of the kind of international regime that may embrace Japan and the United States over the next few decades. His four scenarios—Pax Americana Phase II, Bigemony, Pax Consortis, and Pax Nipponica—cover all possibilities, and I share most of his conclusions. His abstract approach, however, presumes rather than highlights changes in the context of U.S.–Japan relations that prompted the Council on Foreign Relations to undertake this study of Japan's potential role in Third World development. His approach also tends to understate the practical, political, and psychological problems that plague practitioners in both Washington and Tokyo as they wrestle with adjustment of global roles.

Whatever the exact nature of the regime that will govern U.S.–Japan relations in the early 21st century, it is already quite clear that the relative power between Japan and the United States has undergone a fundamental shift, that the currently emerging international order reflects a diffusion of power away from the superpowers of the Cold War era, that economic prowess now weighs far more heavily in the calculus of national power than it did in the past, but that, nevertheless, certain inherent American strengths and Japanese liabilities are working against a radical switch in global influence from the United States to Japan in the foreseeable future. Complicating thoughts of cooperation in finding new roles for Japan, competition between the world's two greatest economic powers will almost certainly grow, perhaps causing relations to be more fractious and emotional than they have been in past years. In any event, the data and attitudes Inoguchi cites, together with the past fifteen years of experience, suggest that development assistance is the only promising area for any large expansion of Japan's global role.

Changes in the world order have become increasingly apparent in the decade and a half since Americans, Japanese, and others began to talk of Japan's picking up some of the economic and security burdens the United States was no longer willing or able to carry. By 1975, the proposed shift was a reasonable proposition for Americans, because any lingering vision of Pax Americana had faded by the end of the Vietnam War, and they widely acknowledged, if not always welcomed, Japan's swift rise. Americans were weary of foreign burdens and convinced that Japan was enjoying a "free ride" from the United States in defense matters and taking unfair advantage of the international free trade regime. Since the Cold War remained a powerful consideration and Third World needs for assistance continued to grow, "burden-sharing" with Japan seemed an obvious answer.

The concept of having Japan as an "almost equal" ally picking up ever growing amounts of the international burden was politically appealing in the United States. American political leaders competed with ideas for shifting expensive burdens to Japan, while a somewhat grudging Japan responded by steadily increasing defense expenditures and within a few years greatly expanding its aid efforts, in both cases stressing its adherence to continuing American leadership. Arguing that Japan was not spending a sufficient proportion of gross national product for security compared with expenditures by the United States and other members of the North Atlantic Treaty Organization (NATO), the Carter administration pressed Japan to spend more and enlarge its self-defense role. Pressure for military expansion eased in the 1980s as the relative size of the Japanese effort became better understood—and as Americans began to appreciate the unwillingness of other Asians to see Japan take on a regional defense role.

In the assistance area, Japan not only raised its aid levels but, partly in response to constant American urging, also undertook an economic expansion, leading to sustained growth of its market and significant increases in imports. Throughout the decade, and despite severe periodic tension over trade issues, Japan accepted this burden shifting without much challenge to its junior status in the partnership.

If only because of the continued shift in the relative power of the United States and Japan, burden-sharing remains an understandable, if hard to achieve, goal of American policy. But the process of sharing, which Americans never analyzed very thoroughly, has taken on new complexity with changes in the U.S.–Japan bilateral relationship and the international environment.

Whether or not Japan ever becomes a superpower in the comprehensive sense of economic, political, and military power, its world importance is already second only to that of the United States in the minds of most people. Within East Asia, where economic considerations have for some time overshadowed military ones, Japan has become a second center of relationships, in some cases complementing the American role, in others rivaling it. Japan has largely replaced the United States as the region's creditor and provider of assistance, as the source of the most useful technology, and as an appropriate model for economic development. With a huge market no longer so dependent on exports, Japan is also becoming a major market for other East Asian states, increasingly for manufactured items produced in the region by Japanese or foreign firms. For the region, the yen has become a safer, if less convenient, currency than the dollar. Moreover, the influence of Japan's economic and technological prowess, combined with its massive capital accumulation, is spreading rapidly beyond East Asia to most parts of the world.

In contrast to this burgeoning of Japan's importance, American competitiveness has eroded in a damaging process long apparent to foreigners and increasingly understood at home. Although the symptoms (particularly, excessive consumption, budget deficits, short time horizons, and deteriorated education) are so well known as to be part of conventional wisdom, lack of national resolve stymies almost all efforts at reform. Even when such resolve finally manifests itself, the reform process will be protracted, and domestic weakness will likely handicap American foreign policy for much of this decade.

Along with these changes in relative strength, U.S.-Japan relations are more consciously competitive than they were in the past, more quarrelsome, and less reinforced by common concern over the threats of the Cold War. For Americans, the difficulties and frustrations of finding ways to reinvigorate their economy have compounded the inherent discomforts of accommodating to a relatively diminished status in the world. Some Americans have, in effect, developed an inferiority complex about U.S. ability to compete against a vigorous Japan. With the fading of any sense of military threat from the Soviet Union, this powerful economic challenge has reintroduced an adversarial quality into American perceptions of Japan lacking since World War II.

These trends in American attitudes, which do not bode well for the kind of cooperation required for burden-sharing, parallel changes in Japan, where rising status and generational shifts are affecting attitudes toward the United States. Although extreme American behavior occasionally provokes extremist Japanese reactions, Japanese generally restrain displays of their annoyance, if only because they have a greater sense of the two countries' interdependence. Nevertheless, Japanese are puzzled and concerned by evidence that Americans fear Japan. Growing numbers of them feel their accomplishments warrant more equal treatment from the United States, and at least some are beginning to question the value of so close an alliance in today's conditions. The United States no longer seems such a dominating consideration when neither the Soviet Union nor the People's Republic of China poses a foreseeable military threat, when communism is in retreat, when new coalitions of power are developing in Europe, and when economic dynamism seems a sounder basis on which to project national power than sheer military strength.

These are the new realities that Inoguchi might have discussed at greater length. These issues, not speculation about the largely imponderable question of how powerful Japan will be in the 21st century, form the context for contemplating any practical effort at burden-sharing in this decade. In addition, Americans and Japanese must have a clearer understanding than they did in 1975 about the burdens that might be shared. Beyond development assistance, few possibilities exist for sharing.

In security matters, for example, the limits are fairly clear, given domestic and foreign constraints stemming from Japan's policies of the 1930s and 1940s. Neither Japan nor the United States will contemplate any shifting of the nuclear defense burden to Japan in the foreseeable future, even though the "nuclear shield" may become a progressively less important issue. Similarly, Japan cannot realistically share the stabilizing role U.S. forces have played in East Asia, because other Asian countries are wary of a resurgent Japan and would be deeply concerned were it not for the military presence of the United States and cooperative U.S.–Japan military ties. Japan's self-defense and possibly peacekeeping are the only security-related functions that can be shifted to Japan. Moreover, a rapid assumption of the entire self-defense effort by Japan would probably arouse concern in China and other parts of Asia, while peacekeeping activities involving dispatch abroad of military personnel remain beyond public tolerance within Japan.

In the political sphere, Japan and the United States could presumably benefit from the former's playing a greater role within East Asia and in some other parts of the world, bringing new resources, energy, and a degree of detachment that might be effective. If Japan were to greatly increase its economic stake in Europe, some political role might also follow, as it has in East Asia. But Americans (and the others involved) are less likely to welcome these developments as burden-sharing than to see them, and sometimes resent them, as unwarranted expansion of Japanese influence.

Thus, Third World economic development remains the only area with much scope for burden-sharing, or, in some instances, for "burden transfer," since the United States has virtually abdicated assistance efforts in many parts of the world. Japan will almost surely confirm its place as the foremost source of capital, and it will face pressure to be more generous in the transfer of competitive technology in Asia, Eastern Europe, Latin America, and Africa. If current trends continue, Japan will be the unchallenged leader in the assistance field. Less certain but also likely is the possibility that Japan's market will absorb increasing amounts of imports, with the result that trade may eventually dwarf assistance efforts for economic development.

For many reasons, of course, one must be cautious about making linear projections regarding Japanese economic growth. Nonetheless, even assuming some slowdown and many problems, Japan will almost surely gain more prominence in the international economic system and acquire substantially greater influence in political matters than it has today. If Japan is to avoid resentment from others as this process occurs, it will have to dramatically step up its efforts to liberalize its economic policies and adapt its political behavior to global concerns. To the extent this difficult adjustment succeeds, the opinion poll data Inoguchi cites suggest that a majority of Japanese may be satisfied that this expanded economic and political role is the best way to channel their national wealth and energy.

Yet it is hard to envisage Japan's taking on so much of the world's development needs without getting a far greater share of the economic and, to some extent, political leadership than the United States and the Europeans have so far granted it. Japanese would have to head many international economic organizations, and inevitably Washington and European capitals would have to share the limelight with Tokyo as the forum for many decisions—an adjustment that would be slow and painful for Americans and Europeans.

Finally, such a shift of the development assistance burden to Japan could not possibly take place to the mutual benefit of all concerned unless Japan and the United States maintained the fundamentally cooperative ties that have bound them together in increasing interdependence for the past 45 years. Obviously, Japan would not cooperate if Americans foolishly convinced themselves that they needed a new adversary in the post–Cold War era and that Japan was the natural candidate. Nor would Americans be gracious in yielding the necessary portion of their international authority to a rising Japan if Japanese were patronizing and stridently nationalistic. Certainly, both nations are capable of managing this challenge successfully, but considering the experience of the last few years, the risk of drifting mindlessly into failure is not to be dismissed.

II

Official Development Assistance

AN OVERVIEW OF
JAPAN'S FOREIGN AID

Toru Yanagihara & Anne Emig

In the 1980s, Japan emerged as a more important and visible player in the world economy than it had ever been before. It ranked first among the eighteen Development Assistance Committee (DAC) members in total net financial flows to developing countries in 1987–1988. While comparable data for 1989 on total resource flows are not yet available, Japan surpassed the United States to become the number one donor of official development assistance (ODA) that year, with net disbursements of $8.9 billion. Although this represents a 2 percent decline from the 1988 total of $9.1 billion, U.S. aid fell by 27.5 percent to $7.6 billion.[1]

As Japan's economic assistance has expanded, and as Tokyo has adjusted to its new role, both the quantity and the quality of its aid have faced increasing expectations, pressures, and criticisms. In what follows, we review the evolution of Japan's official development assistance. We examine the composition and distribution of Japanese aid, assess shifts in quality, describe Japan's aid policymaking process, and identify administrative capacity as a major limiting factor. We end this overview with a brief look at two other topics of interest: strategic aid and the so-called Japanese Recycling Plan.

BRIEF HISTORY

Japan's economic assistance effort began on a small scale in 1954 with technical aid within the framework of the Colombo Plan for economic development in South and Southeast Asia. Though Japan was itself still an aid recipient at the time, participation in this widely supported international cooperation scheme helped Tokyo regain acceptance into the family of nations after the war.

Financial assistance began in 1955, when Japan entered into reparations agreements with Southeast Asian countries, both to fulfill outstanding international obligations and to develop the export potential of industries rebuilding from the war. Providing for payment of wartime indemnities in the form of services and capital goods, the accords—with the governments of Burma, the Philippines, and Indonesia—effectively opened markets to Japanese suppliers in Southeast Asia and thus attracted substantial business interest. Reparations programs also established the pattern of geographic concentration in Asia that has characterized Japanese aid ever since.

The Japanese government made its first yen loan as part of a World Bank consortium for India in 1958; other early government loans went to Paraguay, South Vietnam, Pakistan, and Brazil. In making yen loans, too, Japan kept the needs of its economy in the forefront.

In this early period, the Japanese government used the term "economic cooperation," rather than "aid," to describe a range of efforts to promote mutually beneficial economic relations with developing countries, including official aid, but also export credits and private capital flows. It was not until late in the 1960s that Tokyo separated official and nonofficial aid flows in its discussions of foreign aid.

Early government statements of aid policy made no attempts to hide the high priority assigned to developing Japanese industry and fostering Japanese economic prosperity through aid. Tokyo justified this approach on the basis of the extensive needs and limited capability of the nation's economy. Ironically, Ministry of International Trade and Industry (MITI) reports on economic assistance at the time reflected doubts that Japanese products would succeed in advanced country markets and encouraged the targeting of developing-country markets instead. The rationale was that aid should go toward increasing purchasing power, thereby opening markets to Japanese products. In addition, Japan aimed to contribute to the political, economic, and social stability of its Asian neighbors.

The chief implementing agency for concessional yen loans in the early days of Japanese aid was the Export-Import Bank of Japan (Exim Bank). Though not all of the bank's lending was of a concessional nature, all its loans were explicitly aimed at promoting Japanese trade interests, in the form of exports of plant and equipment or imports of raw materials. The early 1960s witnessed the establishment of two principal aid agencies, the Overseas Economic Cooperation Fund (OECF) and the Overseas Technical Cooperation Agency (OTCA). Established in 1961, OECF was supposed to take over responsibility for soft lending from Exim Bank, though in reality it functioned as a weak junior partner to the bank for nearly a decade. Initially, OECF made loans and equity contributions to facilitate private business activities in developing countries. In 1966, it started loans to governments of developing countries and to public institutions. In 1975, a set of government guidelines clarified the demarcation between OECF and Exim Bank; OECF became clearly oriented toward ODA and assumed responsibility for implementing all loans with a grant element of 25 percent or above.

OTCA, established in 1962, integrated organizations involved in technical assistance to promote a comprehensive and efficient framework for technical assistance efforts. In 1974, OTCA took up additional functions and became the Japan International Cooperation Agency (JICA), the implementing agency for technical assistance and subsequently also for a large part of grant aid.

The early 1960s reaffirmed the preeminence of domestic interests in aid policy and witnessed the institutionalization of a number of traits still characteristic of the aid program. Japan increased yen loans sharply relative to technical assistance, thus establishing the pattern of low share of grant aid to total ODA that has persisted over the years. Official appraisals of aid were framed in terms of quantitative growth rather than qualitative achievement, a characteristic that began to show signs of change only in the late 1980s.

Japan formally joined the club of aid donors as a founding member of DAC in 1961; however, the motivation was more a determination to win early admission to the Organization for Economic Cooperation and Development (OECD) than a willingness to submit the Japanese aid program to the test of international standards or to be part of the mainstream aid debate. In 1964, Japan achieved its goal: the country graduated from the status of aid recipient and joined the club of advanced countries when it shifted to article 8 status at the International Monetary Fund (IMF).[2]

The concentration of Japan's ODA in Asia became a systematic feature of the aid program at this juncture, as the Sato administration pursued an activist aid policy in Asia. The initial foci of this policy were Taiwan, South Korea, and Indonesia. Tokyo concluded an economic cooperation agreement with Taiwan and normalized diplomatic relations with Korea in 1965. It pledged substantial economic assistance to the new Suharto government of Indonesia and joined the Inter-Governmental Group for Indonesia, a donor aid consortium. It also played an instrumental role in founding the Asian Development Bank in 1966. These decisions reflected not only economic motivations such as trade and investment promotion, but also a response to political pressure by the United States and security concerns related to political stability in the region.

During the late 1960s and the early 1970s, Japan recorded large and continued current account surpluses. As the surpluses became a stable feature of the economy, the United States and other DAC members, as well as the developing countries, exerted increasing pressure on Japan to expand the volume and improve the quality of its aid. Tokyo responded with multistep economic policy programs. Expanding economic assistance constituted an important component both of an eight-point comprehensive external economic policy issued in September 1971 and of a five-point set of external economic measures announced in October 1972.

The 1973–1974 oil crisis sent the Japanese economy into a recession and briefly led to stagnation in the aid program. The geographic scope of aid broadened in this period as Japan sought to strengthen relations with the oil-exporting countries of the Middle East and to establish ties with African states it had previously left out of the aid program. Ensuring stable supplies of energy and other natural resources formed an important motivation for this diversification. Thus, the link of Japanese aid with export promotion gave way to more varied objectives, such as resource availability. Later, security concerns and the expanded responsibilities of global economic power also came to play an increased role in the aid program.

By the middle of the decade, the economy had returned to health and the ODA program had recovered as well: disbursements in 1978 amounted to twice the 1973 total. During 1976–1977, when Japan again recorded a large current account surplus, pressure from foreign governments for an improved aid policy returned. In response, Tokyo adopted a new eight-point external economic policy toward the end of 1977. At the Bonn Summit in 1978, the Japanese government announced a plan to double ODA volume over the 1977 level of $1.4 billion within three years. It surpassed this so-called first medium-term target for ODA in 1980, when net disbursements totaled $3.3 billion. Nevertheless, pressure on Japan to expand aid volume and improve aid quality intensified. The government responded according to its standard pattern, setting a series of concrete quantitative targets while skirting issues of quality.

The second medium-term target, for 1981–1985, called for doubling the 1976–1980 ODA total of $21.4 billion. With a rapidly rising dollar during the five-year period of the plan, the total reached no more than 85 percent of the target level in dollar terms ($18.1 billion), though in yen terms the ODA budget achieved the committed doubling.

The terms of the third medium-term target, covering 1986–1992, were more comprehensive than those of the previous programs, establishing quantitative goals for both the final year and the period total. The targets included doubling the 1985 net ODA disbursement level to $7.6 billion per year by 1992 and making total disbursements in excess of $40 billion for the period. Another target was to raise the ratio of ODA to gross national product (GNP), although the government failed to translate the increase into a percentage figure. The plan also recognized the need to improve the quality of Japan's aid through the expansion of grant aid and technical assistance.

This time around, the exchange rate shifted in favor of the yen, and the quantitative targets were reached earlier than pledged. At the Venice Summit in June 1987, Japan announced it was moving the target for net ODA disbursement of $7.6 billion up two years, to 1990. Even this accelerated target was achieved by 1988, forcing Japan to formulate a new set of meaningful targets.

Thus, Prime Minister Takeshita announced the fourth medium-term target at the Toronto Summit in 1988. The new plan committed Japan to make total net ODA disbursements in excess of $50 billion over the 1988–1992 period, doubling the performance of 1983–1987. The government plans to realize this target by increasing net disbursements at an average annual rate of 10 percent (in dollar terms). In addition, Tokyo expressed its objective of raising the ratio of ODA to GNP to the DAC average level of 0.35 percent in 1992. Qualitative targets include expansion of grant aid and technical assistance, promotion of untying, and increased assistance to the least-developed countries.

At the 1989 Paris Summit, Japan once again focused its commitments on aid quality, pledging $600 million in grant aid to the least-developed countries over three years, beginning in 1990. In addition, the government pledged roughly $2 billion in environmental aid over three years.

DISTRIBUTIONAL SHIFTS

During 1980–1989, total financial flows, in U.S. dollars, from Japan to developing countries increased over threefold, and Japan's ODA nearly tripled (Table 1). Over the same period, Japan's share in the total flows of DAC countries rose by a large margin (Table 2). But as a share of GNP, Japan's contributions to development finance have not shown a rising trend: total financial flows moved inconsistently, and ODA registered the same 0.32 percent share at the end of the decade as it had in 1980

TABLE 1. NET DISBURSEMENT OF FINANCIAL RESOURCES FROM JAPAN TO DEVELOPING COUNTRIES (*in millions of dollars*)

Type of Resources	1975	1980	1985	1987	1988	1989
ODA	1,148	3,304	3,797	7,454	9,134	8,965
Bilateral assistance	850	1,961	2,557	5,248	6,422	6,779
Grants	202	653	1,185	2,221	2,908	3,037
Grant assistance	115	375	636	1,154	1,483	1,556
Technical assistance	87	278	549	1,067	1,425	1,481
Loans	649	1,308	1,372	3,027	3,514	3,741
Contributions to multilateral institutions	297	1,343	1,240	2,207	2,712	2,186
ODA AS % OF GNP	0.23	0.32	0.29	0.31	0.32	0.32
OTHER OFFICIAL FLOWS	1,370	1,478	− 302	− 1,808	− 639	1,544
Export credits (over one year)	339	823	− 152	− 2,047	− 1,838	− 1,245
Direct investment & others	1,016	767	− 1	287	1,410	1,892
Multilateral institutions	15	− 112	− 148	47	− 211	897
PRIVATE FLOWS	363	1,958	8,022	14,723	12,822	13,502
Export credits (over one year)	83	74	− 994	1,081	219	687
Direct investment	233	906	1,046	7,421	8,190	11,290
Bilateral portfolio investment & other	40	660	5,138	4,357	2,830	1,289
Multilateral portfolio investment	7	318	2,832	1,865	1,583	236
GRANTS BY PRIVATE VOLUNTARY AGENCIES	10	26	101	92	107	122
Total net flow	*2,890*	*6,766*	*11,618*	*20,462*	*21,423*	*24,133*
Total net flow as % of GNP	*0.58*	*0.65*	*0.87*	*0.86*	*0.75*	*0.85*

Source: Ministry of Foreign Affairs, *Waga Kuni No Seifu Kaihatsu Enjo, 1990* (Japan's official development assistance: 1990 annual report) (Tokyo: 1990).

TABLE 2.   NET FINANCIAL FLOWS FROM DAC TO DEVELOPING
COUNTRIES AND MULTILATERAL AGENCIES

	Billions of Dollars				Percentage of GNP			
Donor	1977–1979 Avg.	1980	1987	1988	1977–1979 Avg.	1980	1987	1988
Japan	7.9	6.8	20.3	21.4	0.24	0.66	0.85	0.75
U.S.	13.8	13.9	13.2	17.5	0.23	0.52	0.29	0.36
France	7.3	11.6	8.7	na	0.59	1.76	0.99	na
W. Germany	7.0	10.6	8.8	11.8	0.39	1.30	0.79	0.98
Italy	3.1	4.0	2.0	5.1	0.11	0.88	0.27	0.62
U.K.	9.9	12.2	3.4	3.0	0.48	2.29	0.50	0.36
Canada	2.4	3.2	2.5	na	0.50	1.30	0.62	na
Total DAC	66.1	75.4	65.7	69.1	1.15	1.03	0.55	na

Source: Development Assistance Committee, *Development Cooperation in the 1990s: Efforts and Policies of the Members of the Development Assistance Committee* (Paris: Organization for Economic Cooperation and Development, 1989), 225.

na = not available.

(Table 3). Japan's contribution is above the DAC average in terms of the ratio of total financial flows to GNP, but its ratio of ODA to GNP has been persistently lower than the DAC average (Tables 2 and 3).

Contributions to Multilateral Institutions

In 1989, slightly less than 25 percent of Japan's ODA (on a net disbursement basis) consisted of contributions to multilateral institutions. Japan is thus in the top half of DAC member-countries as to the proportion of ODA channeled through multilateral institutions. In terms of the volume of these contributions, Japan surpassed the United States in 1987, becoming the largest single donor of ODA to multilateral agencies, and has alternated with the United States in the top donor position since then.

Strong commitment to multilateral development institutions has been an ongoing characteristic of Japanese aid. Tokyo

TABLE 3.   NET ODA FROM DAC COUNTRIES TO DEVELOPING COUNTRIES
AND MULTILATERAL AGENCIES

	Billions of Dollars				*Percentage of GNP*				
Donor	*1977– 1979 Avg.*	*1980*	*1987*	*1988*	*1989**	*1977– 1979 Avg.*	*1980*	*1987*	*1988*	*1989**
Japan	2.1	3.6	7.3	9.1	9.0	0.24	0.32	0.31	0.32	0.32
U.S.	5.0	7.1	8.9	10.1	7.7	0.23	0.27	0.20	0.21	0.15
France	2.8	4.2	6.5	6.9	7.5	0.59	0.63	0.74	0.72	0.78
W. Germany	2.5	3.6	4.4	4.7	5.0	0.39	0.44	0.39	0.39	0.41
Italy	0.3	0.7	2.6	3.2	3.3	0.11	0.15	0.35	0.39	0.39
U.K.	1.6	1.9	1.9	2.6	2.6	0.48	0.35	0.28	0.32	0.31
Canada	1.0	1.1	1.9	2.3	2.3	0.50	0.43	0.47	0.49	0.44
Total DAC	*19.5*	*27.3*	*41.4*	*48.1*	*46.5*	*0.34*	*0.37*	*0.34*	*0.36*	*0.33*

Sources: Development Assistance Committee, *Development Cooperation in the 1990s: Efforts and Policies of the Members of the Development Assistance Committee* (Paris: Organiza-tion for Economic Cooperation and Development, 1989), 225; and Organization for Economic Cooperation and Development, "Financial Resources for De-veloping Countries: 1989 and Recent Trends," press release, Paris, 1990.

* Preliminary figures.

recognizes the limitations bilateral donors confront owing to recipient concerns about external intervention in domestic af-fairs. Japanese officials appreciate the leverage that political neutrality gives multilateral development agencies in discussions with developing countries on structural adjustment and eco-nomic reform, and they seek to support the multilaterals' func-tioning in global debt relief and development efforts.

Japan shares the top quota (and therefore top voting rights) with the United States in the Asian Development Bank, and a Japanese has served as president of that organization since its founding in 1966. In 1988, Japan was the largest contributor to the bank. Japan is the second-largest shareholder in the World Bank, and in the IMF it will formally rise in 1991 from the fifth position to jointly occupy the second position with Germany.

In 1987, Japan moved ahead of the United States to become

the top contributor to the International Development Association (IDA) and the African Development Fund. However, the United States reclaimed the number-one position in 1988. These shifts reflect multilateral contribution cycles, but it is also true that Japan is fast catching up with the United States in multilateral aid.

Allocation by Purpose

One characteristic distinguishing Japan's ODA from that of other DAC members is its allocation pattern. Most conspicuous is the high proportion of ODA allocated to economic infrastructure, in particular to transport and communication. In 1988, nearly half of Japanese aid went to economic infrastructure projects, compared with just over one-fifth of total DAC aid. Also high, although not uniquely so, is the proportion Japan allocates to industry, mining, and construction. Together, economic infrastructure and industrial production accounted for nearly 55 percent of Japan's ODA in 1988, twice the 27 percent DAC average. The other side of the coin is the below-average proportions of Japan's ODA allocated to social and administrative infrastructure and to program assistance: social infrastructure aid accounted for 15 percent of Japanese ODA but for 25 percent of ODA overall; program aid accounted for 22 percent and 32 percent, respectively. Similarly, technical assistance receives only a small share of Japan's ODA (11 percent, as against the DAC average of 25 percent).

This allocation pattern stems partly from a Japanese preference for focusing on the real sector of the economy in economic development. Officials argue that adequate infrastructure is a precondition for sustainable growth and development. Plainly, Japanese expertise is greater in this area than it is in technical cooperation or the basic human needs side of development aid. Because Tokyo's emphasis on infrastructure and industrial production in aid allocation often has clear benefits for Japanese private industry, the aid seems self-serving. It raises the question of whether the philosophical preference for "real economic ingredients" results from a well-studied analysis of competing devel-

opment approaches or represents rather an ex post facto justi-
fication for the program as it developed in the 1950s and has
served Japanese interests well ever since.

Geographic Distribution

Another characteristic of Japan's ODA is the large share allocated to Asia (Table 4). This feature reflects not only geographic
proximity, but also close historical, cultural, and economic relations, as well as Tokyo's recognition of Asia as its logical sphere of
responsibility in global burden-sharing. East Asia alone receives
46 percent of Japan's bilateral ODA, and when South Asia is
included the figure jumps to 63 percent. Likewise, Asian countries rank high on the list of individual recipients of Japanese aid.

TABLE 4. GEOGRAPHIC DISTRIBUTION OF JAPAN'S BILATERAL ODA,
1980–1989

Region	Millions of Dollars				Percent Share in Total			
	1980	1987	1988	1989	1980	1987	1988	1989
Asia	1,383	3,416	4,034	4,240	70.5	65.1	62.8	62.5
Northeast Asia	82	577	725	919	4.2	11.0	11.3	13.6
Southeast Asia	861	1,866	2,197	2,226	44.0	35.6	34.2	32.8
South Asia	435	970	1,109	1,091	22.2	18.5	17.3	16.1
Other Asia	5	3	4	3	0.3	0.1	0.1	0.0
Memo: ASEAN*	703	1,680	1,920	2,132	35.9	32.0	29.9	31.5
Middle East	204	526	583	368	10.4	10.0	9.1	5.4
Africa	223	516	884	1,040	11.4	9.8	13.8	15.3
Latin America & the Caribbean	118	418	399	563	6.0	8.0	6.2	8.3
Oceania	12	68	93	98	0.6	1.3	1.4	1.4
Europe	−1.5	2	4	11	−0.1	0.0	0.1	0.2
Unclassified	22.5	302	425	458	1.2	5.8	6.6	6.8
Total	1,961	5,248	6,422	6,779	100.0	100.0	100.0	100.0

Source: Ministry of Foreign Affairs, *Waga Kuni No Seifu Kaihatsu Enjo, 1990* (Japan's
official development assistance: 1990 annual report) (Tokyo: 1990), 60.

*ASEAN (the Association of Southeast Asian Nations) includes Brunei, Indonesia,
Malaysia, the Philippines, Singapore, and Thailand.

In 1989, Indonesia and China led all recipients; Thailand, the Philippines, Bangladesh, India, Sri Lanka, Pakistan, Nigeria, and Kenya completed the top ten. The concentration of Japanese aid in this area matches that of U.S. aid in the Middle East, and of French aid in Sub-Saharan Africa. The share of Japan's ODA directed to Asia recorded an 11 percent decrease over the 1980s; meanwhile, the shares directed to Africa and to Latin America and the Caribbean showed significant increases. The Asian focus of Japanese aid is likely to continue, however, for the above reasons and because of the high proportion of the region's population living in poverty.

The renewed focus of the world development community on poverty alleviation in the late 1980s sparked new Japanese efforts to increase contributions to the least-developed countries. The efforts began with the Special Joint Financing with the Special Facility for Sub-Saharan Africa of IDA. Introduced in 1985, this contribution is designed to provide resources to Sub-Saharan African countries that have agreed on programs of policy and institutional reforms with IDA. Japan is the largest contributor to the facility, having provided $304 million over a three-year period.

Another measure, also focusing on Sub-Saharan Africa, is the program of $500 million nonproject grant assistance announced as one item in the Urgent Economic Measures package in May 1987 and extending over three years. Introduced on a bilateral basis as a new aid scheme, the plan aims to support goals similar to those of the Special Joint Financing with IDA, and prospective recipients are expected to have an agreement with IDA on a structural adjustment program before they can receive funds. All of the funds pledged under this plan are untied. About $300 million of the total had been committed to nineteen African countries by the end of 1988. At the Paris Summit in July 1989, the Japanese government further pledged to extend $600 million in nonproject aid to Africa over three years beginning in 1990.

A third type of measure is debt relief for the poorer members of the developing world in accordance with resolution 165 of the Trade and Development Board of the United Nations Conference on Trade and Development (UNCTAD). Passed in March 1978, the resolution aims to relieve the debt burden of the least-developed countries most seriously affected by the first oil crisis by easing the terms of previously disbursed ODA. Tokyo introduced a scheme for target countries in 1979 that replaced debt incurred through official yen loans prior to 1977 with bilateral grant aid. At the 1988 Toronto Summit, Prime Minister Takeshita announced an expansion of the plan to cover debt incurred through 1987. The expansion will add $5.5 billion to debt relief for the neediest countries over ten years. Tokyo is considering additional measures for debt relief, under which Sub-Saharan Africa would be the main beneficiary.

The fourth measure to increase financial flows to the least-developed countries is a loan of SDR 2.2 billion from Exim Bank to the IMF's Enhanced Structural Adjustment Facility, which provides assistance on very concessional terms to low-income countries undertaking comprehensive macroeconomic reform programs. Furthermore, the Japanese government's subscription of SDR 3 billion to the IMF also increased the Fund's resources directed to Sub-Saharan Africa. These two contributions formed part of Japan's $30 billion Recycling Plan.

QUALITATIVE CHANGES

As noted earlier, Tokyo has repeatedly faced criticism for the quality of its assistance efforts. Whereas the Japanese government clearly is reluctant to compromise certain of its long-held philosophies, noticeable changes are under way in other areas. Trends in the grant element and tying status of ODA are important indicators of qualitative change.

Grant Element

In discussions of ODA terms, it is necessary to distinguish between the grant element of aid and grant aid. Grant element is a measure of aid concessionality, combining interest rates, grace period, and repayment period. Grant aid has a grant element of

100 percent because it does not have to be repaid. Loan assistance, on the other hand, can vary considerably in its grant element.

Although the proportion of Japan's ODA total made up of grant aid increased from 41 percent in 1980 to 61 percent in 1986, it remained considerably lower than the DAC average of 84 percent (Table 5). Moreover, the share of the overall aid effort represented by grants plunged back to 47 percent in 1987, and to 36 percent in 1988 (commitment basis), partly because of massive increases in bilateral loans and a tapering off in special contributions to multilateral development banks under the Recycling Plan. These figures rank Japan last among the eighteen DAC member-countries, although Ministry of Foreign Affairs figures for 1989 suggest marked improvement in the grant aid ratio.

The grant element of Japan's ODA rose steadily from 70 percent in the late 1970s to 82 percent in 1986 before slipping back to 73 percent in 1988 (Table 5). Although the grant element of ODA also declined for DAC as a whole after 1986, the Japa-

---

TABLE 5.   GRANT AID AND GRANT ELEMENT AS PERCENTAGE OF
TOTAL ODA (*Japan and DAC average*)

Degree of Concessionality	1977	1980	1983	1986	1987	1988	1989
GRANT AID							
Japan	38	41	55	61	47	36	50
DAC average	72	75	80	84	78	na	na
GRANT ELEMENT							
Japan	70	74	80	82	75	73	82
DAC average	89	90	91	93	90	na	na

Sources: Various issues of DAC's annual report, *Efforts and Policies of the Members of the Development Assistance Committee* (Paris: Organization for Economic Cooperation and Development); and Ministry of Foreign Affairs, *Waga Kuni No Seifu Kaihatsu Enjo, 1990* (Japan's official development assistance, 1990 annual report) (Tokyo: 1990).

na = not available.

nese figure remained some 15 percentage points below the 90 percent average. Actually, Japan is the only DAC country that fails to meet the committee's norm of 86 percent for grant element. Its low share of grant aid in total ODA is the biggest factor accounting for the low overall grant element. Another factor is the low grant element of Japan's ODA loans.

In the early and mid-1980s, other donors often criticized Tokyo for the relatively high interest rates on its ODA loans. OECF, however, lowered the interest on yen loans considerably in 1987 and again in 1988, bringing the grant element of yen loans more in line with the DAC average.

The terms of Japanese aid will soften somewhat as disbursement to least-developed countries in Sub-Saharan Africa and South Asia increases. Overall, however, Japanese aid will probably continue to lag behind DAC averages in grant element for the foreseeable future. While Tokyo has made significant progress in softening the terms of aid, it retains a philosophical preference for loans over grants, arguing that the former promote self-help and enforce discipline on the recipient country.

Tying

ODA falls into one of three categories on the basis of conditions attached to sources of procurement: generally untied, partially untied (also called LDC, or less-developed-country, untied), and tied. Generally untied aid allows bidding by all interested suppliers; partially tied aid limits bids to suppliers from the donor country and developing countries; and tied aid restricts bidding to suppliers from the donor country.

Critics have long viewed Japanese aid as thinly veiled export promotion. Even though Tokyo claims its aid is now largely untied, they argue, Japanese firms win a disproportionate share of contracts through informal tying techniques. Two culprits commonly cited are the exclusive use of Japanese consultants to conduct feasibility studies and provide engineering services, and the "on-request" basis for aid project identification.

The use of Japanese consulting firms for feasibility studies and engineering services, critics charge, results in informal tying, as connections between consulting firms and suppliers create an incentive for project designs to specify materials and equipment that can be supplied only by friendly firms. Japanese consulting firms have lobbied to maintain the generally tied arrangements for these activities, claiming that the consulting industry in Japan is still in its infancy and therefore is unable to compete with established foreign rivals. They further assert that their intermediary role is essential for successful transfers of technology from Japan. Nonetheless, in 1988, Tokyo decided to untie the engineering services component of ODA loans gradually and to allow foreign consultants to participate in development surveys financed through Japanese grant aid.

According to official statements, the stipulation that Japan's ODA will fund only projects requested by potential recipients promotes self-help; specifically, it helps ensure that the aid will fund projects with high priority in the recipient country's own economic development plan. Critics claim that reliance on recipient requests in developing countries where administrative capacity is already strained leaves a vacuum that Japanese trading companies are happy to fill. A trading company finds a project that is attractive to its own business interests and then suggests it to developing country officials as an appropriate ODA project. Having expended the resources to locate and design a proposal, the trading company, like the consulting firm, will naturally seek to maximize its profit from the project by specifying materials that its own contractors can best supply. Here, too, the Japanese government has begun to realize the need for change, as expansion of project identification activities by JICA and OECF in the late 1980s indicates.

In 1978, Tokyo declared its intention to untie its aid in principle, and Japan's ODA has indeed steadily shifted toward untying (Table 6). From early on, Japan's multilateral ODA has been generally untied, and since 1978 this has been the principle of newly pledged bilateral loans. In terms of international comparison, the 72 percent of Japan's ODA falling into the generally untied category is a much higher proportion than the DAC average of 55 percent. Japan ranked third among the eighteen

TABLE 6. TYING STATUS OF JAPANESE ODA (*in percent*)

Status	1974	1977	1980	1983	1987	1988	1987 DAC Average
Untied	34	44	53	70	72	73	55
Partially tied	6	20	17	16	17	14	13
Tied	60	36	29	14	11	13	32
Total	*100*	*100*	*100*	*100*	*100*	*100*	*100*

Sources: Various issues of DAC's annual report, *Efforts and Policies of the Members of the Development Assistance Committee* (Paris: Organization for Economic Cooperation and Development).

Note: Based on gross disbursements.

DAC members in the proportion of generally untied ODA in 1988, and last in the proportion of tied ODA.

Despite considerable progress, suspicion lingers that Japan's de jure untying has not been translated into de facto untying because of covert arrangements between government agencies and private companies in Japan. Although Japan is not the only country to use aid to promote the commercial interests of private business, a common and strongly held impression in business circles, as well as in the international development community, is that Tokyo is unusually systematic and aggressive in promoting exports through aid. Intensified Japanese government efforts to increase the transparency of competitive bidding and procurement procedures have begun to yield results: while 67 percent of procurement contracts for yen loans went to Japanese suppliers in 1986, only 38 percent went to Japanese firms in 1989 (Table 7).

MAJOR ACTORS

Four ministries share responsibility for policies on official aid: the Ministry of Foreign Affairs (MOFA), the Ministry of Finance (MOF), MITI, and the Economic Planning Agency (EPA). In

TABLE 7. PROCUREMENT SOURCES FOR JAPANESE YEN LOANS
(*in percent*)

Source	All Yen Loans				Generally Untied Yen Loans			
	1986	1987	1988	1989	1986	1987	1988	1989
Japan	67	55	43	38	48	37	27	25
U.S.	2	3	4	5	3	4	5	7
Other OECD Members	7	7	12	16	14	11	17	20
Developing Countries	24	35	41	41	35	48	51	48
Total	*100*	*100*	*100*	*100*	*100*	*100*	*100*	*100*

Source: Ministry of Foreign Affairs, *Waga Kuni No Seifu Kaihatsu Enjo, 1990* (Japan's official development assistance: 1990 annual report) (Tokyo: 1990), 60.

addition to their separate aid-related responsibilities, the four jointly administer lending policy for OECF; all OECF yen loans require the unanimous approval of a committee made up of representatives of each of these ministries. Needless to say, the so-called four-ministry system at times requires substantial compromise to accommodate the disparate interests that representatives bring to the table.

Ministry of Foreign Affairs

MOFA places and evaluates economic assistance in the context of diplomacy and foreign policy. Since international public relations are its chief concern, MOFA is sensitive to pressures from advanced countries, particularly the United States. Its efforts to ensure that Japan's aid policy conforms to the expectations of the United States and other Western countries have particular relevance in determining the geographic distribution of economic assistance; the result often is higher aid flows to countries the United States has targeted as priority recipients. The ministry also works to erase views of Japan as a mere economic power or as a free rider in the global system. On the one hand, this leads to an emphasis on the cultural and human aspects of international exchange. On the other hand, it leads to an implicit recognition of political responsibilities based on security or humanitarian considerations.

More specifically, MOFA has been influential in encouraging measures to bring the quantity and quality of Japan's assistance into line with DAC standards. These initiatives have involved untying and increasing grant aid over loans, shifting the allocation of aid away from loans to grants and technical assistance, and diversifying geographically, especially to Sub-Saharan Africa.

MOFA is arguably the most important among the four ministries in setting the tone and direction of aid policy. In addition to sharing authority over yen loans, MOFA, which supervises JICA, is solely responsible for decisions on technical assistance, grant aid, and contributions to UN agencies, and it administers half of the general account budget for ODA. MOFA officials head delegations for intergovernmental negotiations with recipient countries and for consultations with other donors. MOFA is the only ministry with an entire bureau dedicated exclusively to implementing economic cooperation; by contrast, the other three ministries assign aid-related issues to divisions within bureaus that have broader responsibilities. MOFA also has by far the largest number of staff assigned full-time to economic cooperation issues of all the ministries.

Ministry of Finance

Three Ministry of Finance bureaus have divisions involved in official aid: the International Finance Bureau, the Budget Bureau, and the Financial Bureau.

The International Finance Bureau has exclusive jurisdiction over issues related to multilateral financial institutions. It has constant communications and negotiations with its counterparts in other advanced countries and is always cognizant of Japan's responsibilities in international financial affairs. Since 1982, the debt problem of the less-developed countries has been one of the most pressing concerns for the bureau.

The Budget Bureau's principal concerns are to maintain a sound fiscal balance and to make expenditures as efficient and cost-effective as possible. It has the formal authority to set an aggregate ceiling and to scrutinize individual budget items. The Japanese government has recorded sizable fiscal deficits since the mid-1970s (as much as 5.5 percent of gross domestic product in fiscal year 1979 and 1980), and MOF has been campaigning for fiscal austerity. While the Budget Bureau has succeeded in reducing the government deficit, it has become increasingly concerned with efficiency in the use of official aid as Japan's ODA budget has rapidly expanded.

The Financial Bureau is responsible for the Fiscal Investment and Loan Program (FILP) and government bonds.[3] In fiscal year (FY) 1990, the general account budget financed 51 percent of the operating budget for ODA, FILP financed 37 percent, and government bonds financed 14 percent.[4]

As actual and expected ODA expenditures have steadily grown, MOF has emphasized efficient use of budgetary resources allocated to official aid. The notion of efficiency has failed to be translated into any systematic method of evaluation, but it seems to serve a useful purpose as a general criterion by which MOF officials can examine budgetary requests from other ministries and agencies. In practice, the ministry is particularly critical of staff increases and new programs, since these are difficult to cut once in place, and therefore takes a conservative position in the allocation of budgetary resources. In some sense, MOF's attitude may appear detrimental to a quick and flexible response to emerging needs, thereby creating inefficiency in the allocation of ODA. Nevertheless, MOF is capable of taking decisive steps in directing overall orientation of aid policy if and when a high-level political decision has been made, as was the case with the Recycling Plan.

MOF supervises Exim Bank; consequently, as the bank has become active in Third World debt-related financing, the ministry's influence has grown. MOF is also co-responsible for yen loans administered by OECF under the four-ministry system. MOF gains further influence over Exim Bank and OECF because the presidents of both agencies are retired high-ranking MOF officials.

Ministry of International Trade and Industry

MITI approaches official aid from the perspective of private business and sees it in relation to international trade and investment. The interests of the business community are of two types: specific industry-level interests in aid-generated business opportunities; and general interests in economic security, stable external relations, and a healthy global economy. While specific business interests seek mercantilist policies of export promotion, notably through the tying of aid, the enlightened self-interest of the business community as a whole leads to an internationalist stance on economic assistance, similar to the position of MOFA.

MITI exerts influence as one of the four ministries responsible for the yen loan program. The ministry seems to have been effective in having specific business interests reflected in decisions over individual yen loans. As a matter of general principle, MITI favors an increase in the quantity of aid and improvement in the quality. In terms of distribution of aid, it assigns high priority to countries that have close economic relations with Japan. MITI promotes a comprehensive approach to economic cooperation, combining official aid, direct investment, and market access. The New Asian Industrial Development Plan, proposed in 1987, represents a recent and systematic application of MITI's initiative. Similarly, MITI has proposed expanding its investment insurance facility with ODA funds to promote greater private-sector capital flows to developing countries through foreign direct investment. In the late 1980s, the ministry also devoted increased attention to promoting the transfer of Japanese-style management know-how to developing countries.

Economic Planning Agency

EPA is technically responsible for supervision of OECF; that assignment was a consequence of indecision arising from the other three ministries' rivalry for control of OECF when it was established. In effect, however, the agency's role has been limited. Although theoretically it serves as a coordinator, differences in opinion among MOF, MOFA, and MITI typically are resolved by appealing to higher political authorities. Since the late 1980s, EPA has promoted policy-based nonproject assistance and has been trying to contribute to official aid design on the basis of its expertise in the analysis and formulation of economic policy.

Other Actors

The general public in Japan widely shares a vague support for economic assistance, but no citizens organizations exist that are well organized and influential enough to be a factor in political and administrative decision making on aid. In contrast, private business can influence the orientation of aid policy, as well as administrative procedures.

Meanwhile, external actors serve as a countervailing force to domestic economic interests. ODA constitutes a focal point of Japan's diplomacy not only in relation to recipient developing countries, but also in the context of burden-sharing among and public relations efforts toward advanced countries. Tokyo thus makes its ODA decisions with these two groups of external actors in mind.

The Diet plays virtually no role in the process of decision making on aid. It is empowered to pass the annual budget allocation for aid, though the legislature has never used this authority to examine aid plans and programs or to evaluate aid outcomes. About the only exception to this general rule is the Diet's questioning of cases of fraud and abuse; the Marcos scandal represents the most highly publicized instance in this category.

For high-profile economic cooperation issues, top-level political involvement establishes the framework for policy, and the bureaucracy fills in the specifics. However, even in such cases, it is not the Diet but the Policy Affairs Research Council of the ruling Liberal Democratic Party that makes policy decisions. As Japan's ODA budget ballooned in the late 1980s, certain Diet members attempted to establish legislation increasing the role of the Diet in aid policy, but with no noticeable consequences.

PROBLEMS OF PROCESSING CAPACITY

While the volume and diversity of ODA operations have been multiplying rapidly, the institutional and human infrastructure for administering ODA have failed to keep pace. Japan urgently needs to strengthen its institutional capacity to administer ODA.

Whereas the United States and most other donor countries have substantial numbers of aid staff in the field, Japan's aid staff are concentrated in Tokyo in administrative positions and maintain a very limited presence in the field. Despite growing recognition within the aid bureaucracy that processing capacity must be enhanced, MOF is reluctant to approve permanent staff increases.

As the types and geographic distribution of Japan's ODA have diversified, lack of expertise has become increasingly clear. First, staff are unfamiliar with the regions outside of Asia. This problem is particularly serious with regard to Sub-Saharan Africa. Second, a lack of expertise is acute in the area of policy-based lending. Aid specialists in Japan and elsewhere have repeatedly called for the formulation of country economic assistance strategies, but the Japanese aid agencies' capacity to conduct macroeconomic and sector studies is very limited. Since 1988, both OECF and Exim Bank have taken steps to address this shortfall by initiating country economic analysis efforts, but they have a long way to go before they can establish adequate research capacity.

MOFA has been actively promoting the establishment in Japan of an international development university, which would train high-level aid experts at the graduate level. Evaluations of the feasibility of this proposal suggest stimulating aid-related education in existing universities while further studies assess the merits of a dedicated development university. In a related measure, MOFA and private resources joined in April 1990 to establish the Foundation for Advanced Studies on International

Development. The foundation offers a variety of research and educational programs designed to raise understanding of development and improve the effectiveness of ODA programs in Japan.

Japan has introduced a number of innovations to fill the gap between increased demands for quick disbursement and the aid agencies' capacity to meet them. For example, Tokyo has called upon the Crown Agents—the implementing arm of the British Overseas Development Administration—to provide expertise in processing Japan's $500 million nonproject grant aid to Sub-Saharan Africa. The possibility of greater cooperation with the U.S. Agency for International Development (AID) is also under exploration. More systematically, Japan has relied on the World Bank for the formulation of policy-based lending and the IMF for negotiating structural adjustment programs, providing funds on the basis of cofinancing and parallel lending.

An added factor, project identification, makes building up government capacity even more urgent. Although Tokyo has long adhered to the on-request principle for identifying aid target projects, Japanese consulting firms and trading companies have traditionally played a major role in the process, as discussed above. They have their own business-oriented motivations for project finding and formulation insofar as their preparatory work leads to business opportunities in the implementation stage. To the extent that Japan truly conforms to the principle of untying, incentives for private enterprises to engage in the preparatory stage of project identification will diminish. Recognizing this need, Japanese implementing agencies have begun to take a more active role in discovery and formulation of suitable projects, though MOFA continues to adhere in general to the on-request principle.

Aid administering agencies, pressured by the need for rapid disbursement of financial resources to meet both recipient-country needs and Japanese aid targets, are exploring two avenues. First is the expansion of nonproject assistance. Policy-based loans have begun to supplement the traditional scheme of commodity loans, initially through cofinancing with the World Bank, but with a view to launching a similar facility on a bilateral basis as well. Second is the promotion of project assistance through provision of local cost financing and through stepped-up efforts in project identification and formulation. One example of increased attention to project finding is the use of ODA loans in combination with technical assistance to rehabilitate existing equipment, plants, and infrastructure. Rehabilitation loans have an immediate effect on productive capacity and are highly cost-effective. Another example is the use of the grant fund portion of the Japan Special Fund at the World Bank, totaling 30 billion yen, to finance project feasibility studies.

STRATEGIC AID

Strategic considerations in Japan's aid decisions comprise two aspects: economic and political-military. Narrowly defined, the first addresses Tokyo's concerns about secure access to food, raw materials, and energy resources. More broadly, this motive arises from Japan's desire to maintain friendly economic relations with recipient developing countries and with fellow donor states.

Japan's concern with political and military stability in the neighboring Asian region affects the overall "interdependence" calculation in aid decisions. Aid serves as material and symbolic support to the governments of recipient countries, though the ideological element so prominent in U.S. aid is absent from Japan's ODA.

U.S. demands for burden-sharing from a global security viewpoint add another element to the security-motivated economic assistance equation. Japan introduced this type of more overt strategic aid in the late 1970s in Thailand, Pakistan, and Turkey under the rubric of "aid to countries bordering areas of conflict." Subsequently, U.S. demands came to cover Egypt, Oman, North Yemen, Sudan, and Jamaica. Most recently, U.S. officials have requested that Japan increase strategic aid to the Philippines, Egypt, Turkey, and Jordan. In addition, Eastern Europe has come to the fore as a target area for aid to support democratization. As political and economic opening moves forward in Poland, Hungary, and other countries in the region, some Japanese funds will be forthcoming, although Tokyo will expect Western Europe and the United States to take the lead.

In the late 1980s, the United States shifted the central focus of demands on Japan for increased burden-sharing from military-related expenditures to strategically motivated economic assistance. The U.S.–initiated Multilateral Assistance Initiative, also known as the mini–Marshall Plan for the Philippines, is a typical example of such aid. Generous Japanese government pledges to the initiative at the July 1989 donors meeting suggested that Tokyo would not oppose U.S. requests for strategic aid so long as such assistance was not officially linked to military bases or other clearly military-strategic concerns. Similarly, the halting process by which Tokyo arrived at its package of measures responding to the Iraqi invasion of Kuwait indicates the difficulty Japan faces in providing strategic aid when the possibility of direct military linkage is high.

The issue of strategic aid places in relief the critical role that the United States plays in directing Japan's economic assistance. For Japan, maintaining a harmonious relationship with the United States is an overriding concern of national security policy, broadly defined. With so many bilateral issues threatening the harmony between the two nations, it is imperative for Japan not to create another bone of contention with the United States on issues involving third countries. The hope is that cooperation in aid policy will ameliorate other frictions between the two nations.

RECYCLING PLAN

The $65 billion Recycling Plan is another instance of Japan's efforts to respond to international expectations and pressures. The plan, in reality three measures announced between late 1986 and mid-1989, emerged from a series of political decisions in the face of mounting pressure from Western countries in general and from the United States in particular. It reflects both Japan's recognition of its responsibility as a major economic power and Tokyo's increasingly active effort to make a significant contribution to improving economic circumstances in the developing world, especially in heavily indebted countries. It is true that a large current account surplus forced Tokyo to act and may explain the timing of recycling initiatives. Nevertheless, Japan will remain obliged to actively participate in development finance even if its current account situation changes.

The original three-year $30 billion plan was actually two programs, a $10 billion initiative oriented toward multilateral development agencies and a $20 billion program combining bilateral and multilateral financing. It is significant that former Prime Minister Nakasone announced the latter during his final official visit to Washington, in April 1987, after several months of rising economic friction in the U.S.–Japan relationship. The Japanese government then revealed details of the plan as part of Japan's Urgent Economic Measures package, just in time for the Venice Summit.

Similarly, the Venice Summit served as the forum for Japan's pledging to expand its recycling efforts. At the Arche Summit in July 1989, Tokyo pledged to recycle $65 billion over the five-year period from 1987 to 1992, giving special attention in the additional $35 billion component to support for the new debt strategy U.S. Treasury Secretary Nicholas Brady had announced earlier that year.

The Recycling Plan pulls together ODA, other official flows, and private flows into one package. ODA takes the form of contributions to the multilateral financial institutions and OECF loans. Other official flows are Exim Bank loans, at market-related terms, while private flows are funds raised in financial markets and commercial bank cofinancing with Exim Bank and, possibly, with multilateral development banks.

Official financial flows through the program were expected to serve as catalysts for increased private flows to developing countries, particularly heavily indebted countries, either through multilateral financial institutions or through cofinancing arrangements with Exim Bank. However, Japanese commercial bank reaction to the recycling effort has been lukewarm at best, and the government has pledged to examine options for reducing barriers to greater flows of Japanese private capital to the Third World.

Multilateral financial institutions play a critical role in the scheme, channeling the whole of the $10 billion portion, $8 billion out of the $20 billion portion, and at least $14.5 billion of the $35 billion expanded commitment. In particular, the World Bank is crucial as a senior partner in the cofinancing arrangements with OECF and Exim Bank.

One characteristic of the Recycling Plan is that all types of funds included in the package are untied. This is appropriate insofar as the plan's primary purpose is to "recycle" Japan's large current account surplus, not to generate new business opportunities for Japanese firms.[5]

The specific allocation of funds under the three recycling measures reflects Japan's response to demands from various recipient countries, as well as from the United States. It also reflects an effort to respond to these external pressures within the context of an overburdened, understaffed aid implementing infrastructure that lacks the expertise required for country and regional economic analysis. The high proportion of multilateral financing in the plans, for example, demonstrates both Tokyo's conviction that international financial institutions should take a leading role in resolving the debt crisis and the need to supplement Japan's severely limited economic analysis capacity with the expertise of multilateral institutions.

It is useful to summarize the main features of the recycling measures. The *$10 billion component,* announced in the fall of 1986, receives most of its funding (80 percent) from official resources. It consists of the following major elements:

- Financing of approximately $2 billion for the World Bank, including establishment of the Japan Special Fund within the World Bank, with 30 billion yen in Japanese government grant aid and 300 billion yen in additional fund-raising authority in Japanese capital markets. The Special Fund covers a three-year period and will support technical assistance for project feasibility studies and design of adjustment programs.

- A $2.6 billion contribution over three years to the eighth replenishment of IDA.

- A $1.3 billion contribution over four years to the fourth replenishment of the Asian Development Fund.

- SDR 3 billion (about $3.6 billion) in government loans to the IMF over four years.

The *$20 billion component*, announced in April 1987, contains the following four elements:

- Establishment of Japan Special Funds at the Asian Development Bank and the Inter-American Development Bank, plus expansion of the earlier scheme at the World Bank.

- Nonproject loans from OECF over three years, both on a bilateral basis and through cofinancing with multilateral development banks.

- Loans from Exim Bank, with two-thirds channeled through cofinancing with multilateral development banks and, in some cases, involving Japanese commercial banks; the rest involves direct bilateral financing, as well as cofinancing with Japanese commercial banks.

Of the total $20 billion in this part of the program, the $1 billion government contribution to the multilateral development banks and the $3 billion in OECF loans count as ODA, while the rest is made up of other official flows and private flows.

The expanded $65 billion program, announced in July 1989, aims not only to increase and improve Japan's recycling efforts, but also to support the debt strategy initiated in March 1989 under the Brady Plan. It combines the two original recycling plans with pledges of an *additional $35 billion* in funding by the end of FY 1992. The program has three principal aspects:

- Exim Bank loans totaling $23.5 billion, of which approximately $13.5 billion is additional to the bank's contribution in the first two recycling measures. A new feature of Exim Bank's participation is the initiation of parallel lending with the IMF in support of structural adjustment in major debtor countries. Parallel lending will represent $4.5 billion of Exim Bank's commitment, while cofinancing with the World Bank and other multilateral financial institutions will account for the remaining $9 billion. At least $8 billion of Exim Bank's new recycling responsibility will be committed to countries the Brady Plan targeted for debt relief. Indicative of the importance the Japanese government attaches to the success of the Brady Plan, Exim Bank committed $2.05 billion to the Mexican package in the 1989 debt negotiations—$1 billion in parallel lending with the IMF and $1.05 billion in cofinancing with the World Bank.

- Yen loans by OECF totaling $12.5 billion, of which roughly $7 billion is additional. At least $2 billion of these concessional funds will be directed to Brady Plan target countries.

- Contributions and subscriptions to the World Bank and other multilateral financial institutions totaling $29 billion, of which $14.5 billion is additional.

One may wonder to what extent the Recycling Plan is actually a program, rather than just a series of disjointed components. The plan encompasses a number of schemes for channeling Japan's surplus, some of which are new, and some of which merely repackage or expand on existing programs. Within the initial $10 billion plan, contributions to IDA ($2.6 billion) and the Asian Development Fund ($1.3 billion) were nothing more than a repackaging of previously pledged funds. On the other hand, the remaining elements of the $10 billion plan and the whole of the $20 billion plan can be considered additional to ongoing schemes of economic assistance. The July 1989 recycling commitments are also largely additional. Overall, however, Japan's assistance program contains an element of double counting: OECF's disbursements and capital contributions to multilateral development banks are counted toward both the recycling and the fourth medium-term ODA targets.

A review of the geographic distribution reveals that Asia and Latin America have been the principal beneficiaries of the recycling effort, receiving roughly equal shares of funds committed to date. Asia's prominence in recycling totals reflects Japan's broad and deep relations with its regional neighbors, as well as Tokyo's recognition of Asia as its logical sphere of responsibility in global burden-sharing. Within Asia, Indonesia ranks as the number-one recipient, a position explained not only by its substantial trade and investment ties with Japan, but also by its status as the primary recipient of Japanese ODA and Exim Bank credits over the postwar period. Indonesia borrowed heavily in yen in the 1970s and early 1980s, and its external obligations have ballooned with yen appreciation.

Latin America's sizable share reflects Tokyo's commitment to contribute actively to resolving the debt crisis. Not surprisingly, Mexico heads the list of Latin American recipients. Given the low volume of Japanese ODA to Latin America, the Recycling Plan represents Tokyo's effort to increase Japanese official capital flows to the region.

Though often presented as Japan's response to the debt crisis, the Recycling Plan includes a number of elements that address Japanese political interests rather than debt issues. For example, under the $20 billion component, the Japanese government has established a $2 billion fund to provide financial support, through concessional loans and equity investment, to private-sector development in the six economies of the Association of Southeast Asian Nations (ASEAN). This ASEAN–Japan Development Fund is funded by OECF and Exim Bank concessional loans and is available to all ASEAN member-countries, regardless of their level of development. There are two facilities. One is a scheme of so-called two-step loans whereby national development banks obtain loans and then on-lend funds to private-sector enterprises. The other facility is an equity investment fund established and managed by the Japan–ASEAN Investment Corporation. Half of the equity contribution came from OECF, and half from private business. Finally, in the fall of 1987, Japan set up a $200 million line of untied credit on concessional terms from Exim Bank for Oman, in support of U.S. efforts to secure oil tanker passage through the Persian Gulf.

One final remark is in order. The assumption behind the Recycling Plan seems to be "the more, the better." This assumption needs to be examined critically, especially in relation to heavily indebted countries. Perhaps the biggest lesson of the 1980s was that financial flows per se are not sufficient to improve economic fundamentals in recipient countries; indeed, generous financing may result in weakened incentives for structural adjustment. The Japanese government has attempted to minimize this moral hazard by relying heavily on joint financing with the international financial institutions to support developing country adjustment efforts. However, in the case of bilateral loans, the possibility that financing will substitute for rather than support adjustment is a serious risk.

CONCLUSION

Japan's official aid will continue to expand under ever increasing expectations and pressures, though at a less dramatic pace than it did in the late 1980s, when exchange rate adjustment exaggerated growth in the dollar value of Japanese economic assistance spending. Foreign aid will continue to be an important component of the burden-sharing equation, since Tokyo finds it easier to respond to external expectations and take an active role in this area than in trade or defense issues.

In the 1990s, aid quality issues will gain increasing attention as Japan struggles to adjust to the responsibilities of an aid superpower. The most serious constraint on the expansion of Japan's aid is the processing capacity of its aid agencies. In this regard, the case for collaboration with the United States and other donors is obvious. AID seems to be abundantly endowed with the kind of expertise in project or program formulation and evaluation that the Japanese aid agencies urgently need to make Japan's official aid more systematic and coherent. At the same time, since the objectives of Japanese ODA do not coincide completely with the policy goals of other donors, collaboration is no more than a partial solution to the capacity problem.

As Japan gains experience and confidence as an aid superpower, we can expect it to have a greater input into aid and development policy debate. Tokyo's traditional approach to economic development and assistance, based on lessons drawn from Japan's own development experience, has focused almost exclusively on "real economic ingredients" of development. Japanese aid's lopsided emphasis on production-oriented projects reflects this orientation. In contrast, the U.S. orientation in development and aid is primarily toward "framework"; emphasis is on abstract principles, such as sound economic management, deregulation, and privatization.

Successful development and effective assistance require both the right ingredients and the right framework. The challenge for the two aid superpowers, and the donor community in general, will be to find a new, integrated approach that will meet the development needs of the coming decades.

NOTES

1. Two factors account for the decline in 1989 ODA figures: yen depreciation and multilateral institution funding cycles. DAC records international statistics on ODA in U.S. dollar terms; a stronger dollar erased a 5.7 percent increase in Japan's yen-dominated aid for 1989. Multilateral aid dropped sharply in 1989 after large capital subscription payments to the International Development Association, the concessional lending arm of the World Bank Group, the previous year.
2. Article 8 status indicates that a country agrees not to use foreign exchange restrictions for balance-of-payments adjustments.
3. Funded primarily through the postal savings and postal pension systems, FILP is frequently referred to as the second budget. The economic cooperation budget is one of the items FILP funds supplement. The requirement that FILP and government bond money be repaid with interest affects the terms at which certain types of Japanese development assistance can be extended.
4. The proportions total more than 100 percent because the FY 1990 budget also included a net negative contribution of paid-in capital to aid implementing agencies. See Ministry of Foreign Affairs, *Waga Kuni No Seifu Kaihatsu Enjo, 1990* (Japan's official development assistance: 1990 annual report) (Tokyo: 1990), 253.
5. The Recycling Plan constitutes the first time Exim Bank has provided financing unrelated to Japanese exports, imports, or overseas direct investment. The bank has had the legal authority to make untied loans since the early 1970s; however, until 1986, it made such loans only for natural resource exploration and development.

A U.S.–JAPAN AID ALLIANCE?

Julia Chang Bloch

Since the mid-1960s, the relative positions of the United States and Japan in the world economy have undergone a fundamental shift as Japan has evolved from a major recipient of World Bank aid to the largest source of development assistance—a position held by the United States for some 25 years. This shift has created rising tensions between the two allies as each tries to adapt to the new order. While many of these tensions have culminated in open disputes, the area of development assistance still offers the hope for collaboration rather than conflict. Despite their differences in origin and purpose, aid efforts of the two nations have enjoyed relative harmony and cooperation in an era in which trade disputes have increasingly dominated U.S.–Japan bilateral relations.

Although a collaborative alliance is feasible, numerous problems impede its realization. Many of the barriers are attitudinal, rooted in outdated perspectives on the evolving aid programs. American development professionals, for instance, continue to view Japanese aid through 30-year-old lenses, seeing it as no more and no less than a mercantilist instrument for commercial gain. At the same time, the Japanese interpret U.S. efforts at aid cooperation not as interest in real collaboration but only as interest in tapping Japanese resources to further U.S. objectives.

To forge an effective U.S.–Japan aid alliance, Americans and Japanese will need a much better understanding of each other's aid approaches and systems. Whether such an alliance is possible will depend upon the willingness of the United States to share power with the emergent number-one donor. Japan, for its part, will need to decide whether it is willing and able to lead and to assume the responsibilities of being number one.

The road to a new aid relationship between America and Japan will be rough but worth traveling. This chapter reviews the major issues along that road, beginning with an analysis of the common criticisms of Japanese aid. The discussion then turns to a review of development aid's role in the current debate over burden-sharing. It closes with an analysis of the prospects for a U.S.–Japan aid alliance and specific recommendations to make that alliance develop and succeed.

PHILOSOPHIES AND PURPOSES OF JAPANESE AID

U.S. and Japanese aid have been driven by forces unique to each country's circumstances, culture, and values. Japanese aid has been conditioned by the policy formula that produced Japan's own economic miracle, while U.S. aid has derived its prescription for development primarily from America's hegemonic role as defender of the free world and its democratic institutions. Inevitably, U.S. and Japanese aid philosophy and purpose exhibit striking divergences. In many cases, critics rightly view these differences as problems that the Japanese official development assistance (ODA) system must address. In some cases, however, differences are merely that—differences—and are unfairly stigmatized as errors on the part of Japan.

Commercial Nature

Foremost among U.S. criticisms of Japanese aid is that Japan uses aid as a predatory instrument for unfair commercial gain. This perception manifests itself in open disputes over three related issues: tied aid, mixed credits, and capital projects.

Tied Aid. Although all donors tie certain aid expenditures to the procurement of domestic goods and services, the Development Assistance Committee (DAC) member-countries, particularly the United States, have been critical of Japanese tied aid practices since the 1970s. Japanese aid has had to live down its image as an arm of Japan, Inc., using virtually 100 percent tied aid in the 1960s and 1970s to push exports for the Ministry of International Trade and Industry (MITI). Statistically, for what it is worth, Japan has responded to criticism and untied over 70 percent of its ODA, qualifying its aid as one of the most untied in DAC.

Criticisms, however, have not stopped, as practice belies the statistics. Grant-aid projects through the Japan International Cooperating Agency (JICA—the government body responsible for implementing technical assistance) are strictly tied. Project loans through the Overseas Economic Cooperation Fund (OECF—the agency responsible for loan implementation), which cover the procurement of construction material and supplies and the financing of engineering consultancy services, are either "generally untied" or "LDC (less-developed-country) untied." While the construction portions of OECF project loans have been generally untied, all engineering consultancies were LDC untied until May 1988. As one might expect, Japanese firms invariably outmaneuver their competitors from less-developed countries and corner the consultant services contracts. As one might also expect, Japanese consultants often tailor their feasibility studies to specifications that suit Japanese construction firms.

According to an article in the *Far Eastern Economic Review*, Japan's OECF representative in Bangkok noted with pride that of six 1987 projects, OECF awarded four to Thai contractors in joint ventures with Japanese firms, one to a Chinese group, and the sixth to a British company. However, local contractors insisted that Japanese firms, through their "shopfront partners," were using OECF projects to establish bases to take over the Thai construction industry. The Chinese group, critics also pointed out, was totally dependent on Japanese subcontractors.[1]

However, Japan continues to make progress in untying its aid. Until 1988, industry links with the ruling party, various ministries (particularly MITI), and important Diet members made engineering consultancy loans a virtual political "sanctuary," immune to change. Before the aid bureaucracy could make even modest moves on engineering consultancies, it had to overcome "violent" opposition from the construction and consultancy industries, which resulted in the creation of a special Diet committee to oversee tied aid policy. Since May 1988, OECF lending to Korea and Malaysia has become wholly untied; OECF financing of engineering consultancies to Thailand, the Philippines, Brazil, and Papua New Guinea was generally untied by 1990, and the list is likely to grow over time. Opposition, however, has succeeded in keeping China and Indonesia, Japan's two major yen loan recipients, out of the untying process, at least for the time being.[2]

Japan's aid bureaucracy also has stepped up the opening of Japanese aid procurement to international bidding. Working with British consulting firms and the U.S. Agency for International Development (AID), the Ministry of Foreign Affairs (MOFA) has supported seminars designed to educate non-Japanese on how to do business with Japanese aid, demystifying, in particular, the Japanese bidding process. These efforts seem to be having effect. The proportion of yen loan contracts going to Japanese companies went down 15 percentage points from 1981 to 1987.

Tied aid is likely to persist as a point of conflict between the United States and Japan. For whatever reason, of all companies winning bids, the proportion that is American-owned appears to have dropped by half since 1983. American criticism of Japanese tied aid, therefore, is likely to continue. At the same time, the untying of Japanese aid and the dramatic rise of the yen since 1985 are squeezing Japanese construction and engineering consultants. Japanese companies won only 1 percent of contracts tendered by the World Bank in 1986, a reflection of their high costs of doing business.

Mixed Credits. The practice of sweetening export financing with aid grants, known in the aid business as mixed credits, is related to, but also different from, tied aid. In American eyes, it differs little from tied aid, but is more egregious. Because of traditional American support for free trade and aversion to export subsidies, the United States, in contrast to every other major donor, does not use aid to directly promote exports or support specific industries.[3] Beginning in the mid-1970s, as other donors increased the use of mixed credits and tied or partially tied low concessional loans to promote their exports, the United States launched diplomatic efforts to reach an agreement in DAC to eliminate, or at least limit, the use of such practices.

Arguing that unfair competition results when government export financing is supplemented by aid grants to persuade foreign purchasers to buy products, the United States sought to discourage the use of mixed credits by making such joint financing packages more costly for governments. The U.S. proposal would raise the minimum aid levels required in any mixed credits package from 25 percent to 50 percent. It also would change the formula for calculating the aid component of such packages, so as to raise the cost for countries that traditionally maintain unusually low interest rates, as Japan does.

Japan, considering the U.S. proposal unreasonable and feeling itself unfairly singled out, adamantly opposed the plan. France, whose mixed credits record is possibly worse than Japan's, was hardly affected, since it does not maintain low interest rates. Negotiations took three years, during which the United States pulled out all the stops, by lobbying DAC member countries aggressively, and Japan conceded partially when talks reached the DAC-determined deadline for settling the issue. U.S. tactics, however, did nothing to persuade Japan that mixed credits are wrong in any respect. With increased ODA levels, Japan will adjust to the new mixed credits rules with very little pain, while the United States, with declining ODA levels, will find itself even less able to play the mixed credits game.

Capital Projects. Another important difference between U.S. and other donor aid programs has provoked criticisms from U.S. business. Among the major donors, the share of bilateral ODA committed to capital projects ranges from roughly 60 percent to 70 percent for Canada, the European Economic Community, and Japan, to over 30 percent for Germany and France. By comparison, capital projects constitute only 3 percent of U.S.

bilateral ODA. Except in Egypt and Pakistan, capital projects and infrastructure have disappeared from AID's portfolio because, among other reasons, the United States can no longer afford them.

U.S. exporters have complained that they face an implicit disadvantage compared with competitors whose countries' aid programs are heavily involved in capital projects. U.S. aid, spent largely in cash transfers and basic human needs projects in sectors such as agriculture, health, and education, requires very little in the way of procurement of commercial interest. Capital projects, on the other hand, require equipment, machinery, and other goods of significant commercial value, and often involve sectors in which export competition is intense. Where the construction of industrial infrastructure—such as telecommunications and power generation—is involved, the establishment of engineering and technical specifications based on one or another supplier country's standards can have enormous multiplier effects on future private—as well as public-sector export markets.

The U.S. trade deficit is further fueling the complaints, placing Japan once again at the center of criticism. Japan makes a fair target because it puts more ODA into capital projects than any other donor and concentrates its resources in the highly export-sensitive sectors of power, transportation, and telecommunications, as well as in middle-income countries where commercial returns are the highest. This pattern of ODA spending reinforces the American perception that Japanese ODA remains an arm of Japan, Inc.

Lack of Strategic Focus

The importance of security, or strategic, interests in U.S. aid is equaled by Japanese aversion to linking strategic objectives to aid. Protected by the U.S. security umbrella and armed by its Peace Constitution, Japan has shunned direct military aid, and remained unwilling until the 1980s to use aid for overt strategic purposes. The government's extreme sensitivity stems from its fear of eroding the broad domestic consensus supporting aid. It is also a reflection of caution in the face of potential trouble. The opposition parties, often disregarded and seldom united, managed in April 1987 to codify restrictions against military aid in the form of two resolutions by the House of Representatives Foreign Affairs Committee. The resolutions contained the following prohibition: "the Government should take effective measures to forestall any attempt to divert Japan's aid to military purposes or any purpose which would intensify international conflicts."[4]

Charity versus Self-Help

The humanitarian motivations that have driven large portions of U.S. aid are not readily apparent in the Japanese aid tradition. Japan's preference for loans over grants and for keeping hard aid terms are symptomatic of its antipathy to giveaway programs and its strong belief that less-developed countries can advance only through hard work, efficiency, frugality, self-reliance, and private initiative—hallmarks of its own development experience.

International reaction to Japan's "hard" aid stance has ranged from skepticism to demands for Japan to improve the quality of its aid. What critics too often overlook is that Japan, the only Asian member of DAC and the only major donor to have risen from the ranks of the developing world, may hold a view of development that differs from that of its Western DAC colleagues. Japanese aid, vague in its public face, is founded, like all donor aid, on fundamental beliefs and historical experiences.

Whereas the distinctive characteristic of U.S. aid has been its global reach and its strategic use "in assisting other nations to attain economic, military, political and social conditions that will contribute to a world order conceived to serve the ultimate interests of the free world,"[5] Japanese aid has had a much narrower scope. For reasons of history, geography, and politics, Japan has always concentrated its aid on Asia; almost all of its bilateral ODA went to the region in the early years. Despite the "globalization" efforts of the 1980s, 70 percent of Japanese ODA still goes to Asia; the remainder is allocated about evenly to

Africa, Latin America, and the Middle East. As recently as 1987, the top ten recipients of Japanese aid were Asian.

Implementation Constraints

The most valid criticisms of Japanese aid revolve around what is known as Japan's processing-capacity problem. From conceptualization of its aid program to the final implementation of specific projects, the Japanese aid system is woefully short on direction, leadership, and implementation skills. It lacks both a political and an administrative center, and it suffers at the cabinet level from not having a unified or consistent advocate.

Major problems arise due to the lack of qualified staff to oversee Japan's fast-expanding aid expenditures. Severe understaffing in its aid bureaucracy, coupled with the government's request-based approach to aid-giving, have given Japanese private consulting firms practically a free hand in drawing up project proposals, shepherding them through both the Japanese and recipient governments' approval processes and directing the lucrative contracts to related Japanese companies. It is, therefore, not surprising that Japanese aid is too often the captive of commercial interests.

It is also not surprising that today's conventional wisdom regarding Japanese aid results in an abundance of criticisms and few kind words. In reality, however, the conventional wisdom is outdated. In response to external and domestic criticism—and in recognition of its own lessons learned from aid programs to date—Japan is beginning to make changes in its aid administration. While many of the problematic areas still exist, Japan's stance is evolving; and the United States should recognize, encourage, and support such changes. It is equally important to remember, however, that not all differences represent errors. As the U.S. and Japanese aid systems individually evolve, and the two governments explore collaborative areas, the United States must take into account the distinctive histories, cultures, values, and philosophies that define each donor's approach to development. The result should be cooperation, not necessarily conformity.

SHARING BURDENS AND POWER

Symptomatic of the changing roles and responsibilities, a ground swell of resentment has built up in the United States against Japan. Billionaire Donald Trump's October 1987 full-page advertisement in the *New York Times* was a sign of the times. Addressing himself "to the American People," Trump declared that "over the years, the Japanese, unimpeded by the huge costs of defending themselves (as long as the United States will do it for free), have built a strong and vibrant economy with unprecedented surpluses. . . . It's time for us to end our vast deficits by making Japan, and others who can afford it, pay."[6]

Aid burden-sharing, however, is nothing new. As early as 1958, the United States began to pressure the Marshall Plan beneficiaries that had become aid donors, particularly Germany, to pick up a fair share of the aid burden. It singled out Japan because that country spent relatively little on defense.

Initially, aid burden-sharing was hardly controversial. But as Japan takes over the number-one aid donor's position from the United States, both nations must confront burden-sharing's mirror image—power-sharing. Neither is quite ready to do so: while the United States is ambivalent about sharing power, Japan is reluctant—although decreasingly so—to take on the responsibilities of leadership.

As U.S. aid declines and Japanese aid continues to rise by leaps and bounds, America will inescapably lose influence to Japan. In fact, the United States and Japan already have clashed at the Asian Development Bank, where Japan has always been a key player, traditionally holding the presidency. Although Japan is neither ready nor inclined to challenge U.S. dominance in the international financial institutions, the leadership question becomes more urgent, particularly as the United States presses the issue of burden-sharing. As a prominent former Ministry of Finance official put it, "Japan will not continue to increase its ODA contributions and maintain a small voice. There needs to be a harmonization of money and voice."[7]

In the United States, pressure for burden-sharing is indeed increasing. Congressional resentment over Japan's "free ride" defense posture runs particularly deep, fueling demands that Japan increase its military spending to reflect its current economic power.

However, these congressional sentiments are shifting toward the idea that Japanese aid burden-sharing would be better for the world than defense burden-sharing. Former Secretary of Defense Richard Armitage exemplified this position when he testified for the Reagan administration against a congressional resolution urging Japan to spend 3 percent of its gross national product (GNP) on defense. Instead, he suggested, "Why not encourage Japan to increase its foreign economic assistance?"[8]

A September 1987 Senate amendment to the Defense Department authorization bill would have Japan increase its ODA to 3 percent of GNP by 1992. A growing consensus is building behind an idea advanced by Sam Nunn, chairman of the Senate Armed Services Committee, that the Japanese should combine increased defense spending with much-increased overseas development spending. Nunn favors a 4 percent combined figure—1.5 percent for defense and 2.5 percent for strategic aid.[9] Such an increase would leave Japanese ODA substantially higher than the combined ODA of the other 17 DAC countries.

Without going to such extremes, Japanese, too, are calling for ODA increases. According to former Foreign Minister Saburo Okita, many Japanese believe that by the year 2000, their government should raise ODA to approximately 1 percent of GNP, a level that prevails in most Scandinavian countries. Okita himself has proposed a comprehensive national security plan, based on a budget of 5 percent of GNP—1 percent allocated to defense, 1 percent to aid, and 3 percent to scientific and technological research and development.[10]

While the above proposals may be attractive means to balance a politically sensitive equation, they are neither feasible nor desirable. First and foremost, Japan has been unable to expend its existing $10 billion annual aid budget, and the rush to merely disburse has led to unacceptable sacrifices in aid quality. Before

Japan embraces plans to double or triple its existing aid levels, it must secure the administrative capacity to effectively design, implement, and evaluate quality aid programs.

Second, the absorptive capacity for aid levels that would immediately double the current DAC total is not sufficient. Donors are already having difficultly programming conventional aid moneys in many parts of the world. Even the countries of Eastern Europe—currently requesting large amounts of immediate assistance—would be hard-pressed to expend effectively the levels generated by an aid program pegged to 1 percent to 2.5 percent Japanese GNP. The economic dislocations of massively increased aid infusions are easy to imagine, as is the likelihood of waste, corruption, and abuse if administrative capacity does not keep pace. It is even doubtful if the multilateral financial institutions could absorb the amounts being discussed—and the concomitant programming responsibilities. And if they tried, the United States and Japan would run headlong into the power-sharing issues described above.

Finally, it is hard to believe that the Japanese public—recently faced with increased taxes—would willingly support a threefold, fourfold, or fivefold increase in foreign aid. Domestic private-sector support has already suffered as ODA has untied its procurement for foreign competition. Expanded coverage of ODA issues in the popular press, particularly stories covering criticisms and scandals, has softened general public support, as well.

Even if Japan were willing to massively increase ODA to offset the perception of being a free rider, the result could be counterproductive. Throwing money at development problems has seldom proven to be the most effective solution. Using aid to address conflicts in trade and defense may end up sacrificing development at the altar of burden-sharing.

PROSPECTS FOR A U.S.–JAPAN AID ALLIANCE

As Japan enlarges its role and influence in aid, conflicts with the United States may multiply. However, the two countries share interests in maintaining global peace, prosperity, and security—goals that effective development assistance programs help support. The complementarity of goals and the comparative strengths of each system make a U.S.–Japan aid alliance necessary and achievable.

History

U.S.–Japan aid collaboration is not a new concept; discussions toward this end began once the emerging role Japan was charting for itself became apparent. Since 1978, when the two countries held their first aid consultation in Shimoda, the AID administrator and the director general of MOFA's Economic Cooperation Bureau have met more or less annually. And as a result of the January 1985 Reagan-Nakasone summit, the under secretary of state for political affairs and one of Japan's two deputy foreign ministers have held yearly meetings, focusing on the strategic aspects of aid and overall U.S.–Japan bilateral relations.

DAC, too, has attempted to coordinate donor efforts. Since 1979, DAC members have actively formed like-minded groupings, but according to DAC's own assessment, "Of all the problems in DAC's field of primary concern, none remains more thoroughly unsolved than that of inter-donor coordination."[11] Not unexpectedly, U.S.–Japan aid coordination has gone the way of general DAC aid coordination: a great deal of information has been exchanged, but next to no cofinancing or viable joint ventures have emerged.

The United States and Japan took a tentative step toward real coordination at what Robert M. Orr has characterized as the most significant and substantive aid dialogue between the two.[12] In May 1988, at the East-West Center in Honolulu, U.S. and Japanese aid professionals began working out pioneer joint strategies and methods for improving aid programming, management, and implementation in selected Asian countries. This dialogue has continued. Honolulu II took place at the East-West Center on October 16–18, 1989. Most notably, the process initiated at Honolulu I undoubtedly contributed to the successful launching of the Philippines Multilateral Aid Initiative in Tokyo, which Richard Solomon, assistant secretary for East Asian and Pacific Affairs, subsequently called "an important precedent for aid coordination . . . and a model for such programs in the future."[13]

Despite the Honolulu meetings, most collaborative efforts to date can be classified only as discussions, with few concrete actions to show as results. To turn from talks into an active alliance will require increased commitment, effort, and understanding on the part of both governments.

Conditions for Collaboration

The essential conditions for collaboration are so straightforward, they are often overlooked. First, because the two countries have very different historical and cultural perspectives, the United States needs to understand that Japanese aid cannot be shaped in the image of U.S. aid. Second, although the United States and Japan share commitments in Third World development, their aid priorities will not always coincide. The United States needs to accept that differences do not necessarily spell wrongheadedness or inferiority in aid philosophy. Finally, before true bilateral aid cooperation can occur, the United States needs to shed the notion that cooperation should be founded on "Japanese money and U.S. brains." Both countries need to focus on existing complementarities of interest that would make cooperation worth the effort and mutually beneficial.

Recommended Areas of Collaboration

Among the areas highlighting the striking complementarity of U.S. and Japanese aid strengths and weaknesses, consider first personnel. Although long on cash, Japan is woefully short on development know-how. While Japan's ODA increased more than fivefold between 1977 and 1987, the number of aid personnel hardly changed at all; as a result, the volume of ODA administered per staff jumped 350 percent. The United States, at the same time, may be short on cash but is long on knowledgeable and experienced aid personnel. Collaboration in the training of development personnel could enhance Japanese staffing capabilities. An agreement between MOFA and Harvard University offers one model: in exchange for Japan's commitment to build a development studies infrastructure at Harvard, the university will help to train Japanese personnel both at Harvard and in Japan.

AID has extensive experience in administering development training programs; the Development Studies Program, a soup to nuts course for development professionals, is one example. The agency should invite Japanese aid personnel to participate in this and other such programs; likewise, AID, JICA, and OECF should also develop exchanges of personnel. AID-MOFA collaboration in joint training initiatives and the design of a Japanese development training curriculum would be useful in helping Japan deliver on its commitment to improve the quality of its aid. It would also improve the balance between what Toru Yanagihara & Anne Emig, elsewhere in this volume, call the framework and the ingredients approaches to aid, a balance that neither donor has achieved.

Meanwhile, Japanese expertise has the advantage in other areas. For instance, Japanese aid has more experience working with the private sector than U.S. aid has. Collaboration could improve U.S. capacity to involve commercial enterprises in development activities, with a suggested focus on providing appropriate technologies and know-how to developing countries. Collaboration also could strengthen U.S.–Japan interest in maintaining a global economic system free from protectionism and based on free enterprise.

On the other hand, the United States has learned many valuable lessons regarding the variety of aid delivery modes. AID has extensive experience working with nongovernmental organizations (NGOs), universities, and cooperatives to design and deliver a wide range of development services. Japanese aid officials have periodically expressed interest in exploring such mechanisms as a way of addressing delivery constraints. Japan could well tap the wealth of U.S. experience by using American NGOs to help strengthen the administrative, financial management, project design, and implementation capabilities of its NGOs.

In development, most lessons are learned only the hard and expensive way—through long-term experience and trial and error. Given its rapid rise to number-one donor, the scrutiny from the international donor community, and its well-recognized distribution constraints, Japan cannot afford the luxury of taking the time to learn these lessons for itself. By extrapolating AID's experience, Japan can shorten the learning curve. Areas that offer particular promise include evaluation, monitoring, and accountability systems; environment; food aid; and regional expertise in Africa and Latin America.

Recommended Actions

Given the importance of U.S.–Japan bilateral relations and the Third World countries' need for quality aid, collaboration between the two largest donors in the world is worth priority attention. Specifically, each government needs to establish collaboration as a clear-cut foreign policy priority. Clarity of policy will prevent the bureaucratic caprice and inertia that may otherwise hamper effective collaborative action.

Furthermore, for the United States, aid collaboration is too important to leave solely to the aid technicians, who see the difficulties but not the opportunities inherent in collaboration. At the same time, nonaid personnel normally do not understand how aid works and cannot, by themselves, effectively enforce cooperation within the aid bureaucracy. Consequently, the program must include both policymakers and aid implementers, and must reward successful cooperative activities.

Another necessary step for the United States is development of a national security directive on aid collaboration that clearly lays out the objectives, responsibilities, and lines of authority. Given the numerous agencies involved in U.S. aid decision making, an interagency group will need to be established, with the deputy secretary of state as chair, to oversee the implementation of the directive. AID would handle day-to-day operations. The periodic U.S.–Japan consultations described earlier could continue, but with more coherent and integrated agendas, flowing from the policies developed by the interagency group coordinated at the working-group level. Likewise, the working-level meetings, such as the 1988 and 1989 sessions in Honolulu, should also continue.

Finally, the United States and Japan must recognize that developing countries have a valuable role to play in this collaborative process; they know best what their development needs are. To set the proper tone and to allay developing countries' fears that the two largest donors will "gang up" on them, U.S.–Japan aid collaboration might publicly launch itself with a multiparty symposium (involving recipient countries) on the emerging development problems of this decade. Participants could jointly identify the problems ahead and the types of assistance required. Specific products could involve collaborative ventures in selected priority countries and sectors.

Roadblocks and Concerns

U.S.–Japan aid cooperation lacks for neither interest nor opportunities, but the obstacles—not the least of which is the uncertainty of where aid cooperation fits in U.S. policy toward Japan—are formidable. Exacerbating this uncertainty, AID appears to be beating a retreat on the effort.

After more than a decade of consultations, the staff of AID's donor coordination office has no one who speaks Japanese or knows Japan. Three years after the retirement of its chief official responsible for U.S.–Japan aid coordination, AID has not replaced him. The unit in the agency's Bureau for Asia and the Near East responsible for the East-West Center meeting has been disbanded. AID's office of International Trade and Investment Promotion, after mounting two successful seminars on Japanese procurement, has lost its one officer with any knowledge about Japanese aid and has no plans for a replacement. The agency has abandoned an initiative to assign an officer to the U.S. Embassy in Tokyo. Receiving mixed signals, Japan is unsure how to react—whether to treat aid cooperation with the United States as a priority or not. Meanwhile, Japan is moving ahead on aid cooperation with Canada and the Europeans.

Differing expectations also make aid cooperation an elusive objective. It is yet unclear what exactly the United States or Japan hopes to achieve from aid cooperation. On the U.S. side, as aid levels decline, aid professionals see cooperation with Japan as a way to stretch resources. However, they are notorious for their criticism of Japanese aid and convey an arrogance that translates into the idea that collaboration will be based on "Japanese money and U.S. brains."

On the Japanese side, aid cooperation appears to mean learning from the United States, gaining exposure to American know-how and techniques. Yet AID's field missions have grown tired of responding to Japan's seemingly insatiable appetite for information, with no visible returns for their trouble.

Recipient countries are also wary of U.S.–Japan aid cooperation, and may impede implementation-level progress unless their concerns are addressed. While receptive to coordination that improves the effectiveness or increases the volume of aid flows, recipients nonetheless have a decided preference for multilateral aid coordination, in which they also participate.

CONCLUSION

As the 1990s begin, U.S.–Japan aid appears stalled between conflict and cooperation: while conflict has not gotten out of hand, cooperation has taken one step backward for every step forward.

One critical test for the two economic powers will be whether they can find sufficient resilience and incentive in shared interests and values to emerge as partners rather than rivals. The extraordinary importance of the U.S.–Japan relationship behooves the partners to make the marriage work. Amid disputes over market access, unfair trade practices, and burden-sharing, foreign aid stands out as a potential area for cooperation. As both the United States and Japan adjust to a fast-changing world, aid cooperation can facilitate each nation's accommodation to the attendant changing roles and responsibilities. Ulti-mately, the future of a U.S.–Japan aid alliance will rest on the ability of each nation's leadership and aid professionals to better understand the other's interests and promote mutual trust and respect.

NOTES

I would like to acknowledge Lori Forman, whose long distance help and support made this chapter possible.

1. Paul Handley, "Thailand Remains Wary of Japan Inc.'s Generosity," *Far Eastern Economic Review*, March 10, 1988, 70.
2. Taken from discussions at the U.S.–Japan ODA Management Confer-ence, East-West Center, Honolulu, Hawaii, May 10–12, 1988.
3. The exception is the Food for Peace program under Public Law 480. The legislation specifically states export promotion as one of the program's four goals.
4. Ministry of Foreign Affairs, *Japan's Economic Cooperation* (Tokyo: February 1, 1988), 17–19.
5. John D. Montgomery, *Foreign Aid in International Politics* (Englewood Cliffs, N.J.: Prentice Hall, 1967), 19–20.
6. As cited in Morton M. Kondracke, "Make 'em Pay," *New Republic*, October 12, 1987, 15.
7. Interview with former Ministry of Finance official, Tokyo, Japan, May 1989.
8. Kondracke, "Make 'em Pay," 15.
9. Ibid., 16.
10. Saburo Okita, *The Developing Economies and Japan* (Tokyo: University of Tokyo Press, 1980), 259.
11. See Chairman of DAC, *Development Cooperation: 1981 Review* (Paris: OECD, 1981), 37–54.
12. Robert M. Orr, *Collaboration or Conflict? Foreign Aid and U.S.–Japan Rela-tions.* (Paper presented at the annual Association for Asian Studies Confer-ence, Washington, D.C., March 17–19,1989), 15.
13. Richard Solomon, "U.S. and Japan: An Evolving Partnership," speech before the Foreign Correspondents Club of Japan, Tokyo, April 10, 1990.

A JAPANESE PERSPECTIVE ON
AID AND DEVELOPMENT

Masamichi Hanabusa

The most remarkable characteristic of Japan's assistance to the
Third World in the past three decades is the official view that the
main purpose of foreign aid is development: to provide financial
resources and technical knowledge to developing nations in response to their own assessments of their development needs.[1]
For better or worse, the Japanese government has maintained
the position that Japan's role as a donor is to support self-help
efforts toward social and economic development by the aid recipients. It has refrained, in the main, from tying its aid to the
pursuit of political goals or to ethical values; rather, the Japanese
government's primary reason for giving aid derives from a general desire to maintain good relations with developing countries
once they have achieved political independence following the
collapse of colonial rule.[2]

While this basic belief has remained the principle underlying Japanese aid, the modality of aid has undergone many
changes, owing to the steady increase in Japan's aid-giving capacity and the changing needs of recipients. Over the years, the
outright commercial elements that once colored Japanese aid
have steadily given way to the recognition that Japan can best
contribute to the international community in the area of aid.

The instruments of Japan's bilateral aid today cover a wide
gamut, from project loans to policy support loans, from food aid
to untied nonproject grants, from vocational training to transfers of pollution prevention technology, and from donations of
fishing boats to the construction of cultural centers.

Throughout the 1980s, Japan's official development assistance (ODA) budget grew at an average annual rate of 9.6
percent, while the ODA budget of the United States has leveled
off. Japan became the world's largest aid donor in 1989, provid-

ing nearly $9 billion in ODA to developing countries. The United States ranked second, with a $7.7 billion contribution.

Where does Japanese ODA go? Nearly $3 billion of the total is channeled through international or regional aid agencies. During fiscal 1988, the Overseas Economic Cooperation Fund (OECF), Japan's loan implementing agency, concluded 133 loan agreements on highly concessionary terms totaling over 1 trillion yen, mostly with lower-middle-income countries (those with per capita gross national products, or GNPs, of between $700 and $1,300 in 1987). Japan's loan funds financed an estimated 200–300 ongoing economic and social infrastructure building projects. At the end of fiscal 1988, outstanding accumulated lending by the OECF reached 4.7 trillion yen.

Under Japan's technical assistance programs during fiscal 1987, about 3,400 technicians and experts and 1,600 youth volunteers worked in the field, and over 7,300 individuals received technical training in Japan. About 150 technology transfer projects were in operation, and 250 development-related studies for regional master planning, project feasibility, basic data gathering, and detailed project designing were undertaken.

In the same fiscal year, Japan's grant programs concentrated mainly on basic human needs (including the provision of foodstuffs and materials for food production), as well as on needs for human resources development in low-income countries (those with per capita GNPs of less than $700 in 1987) all over the world. Japan also provided balance-of-payments support grants to the poorest countries, mostly in Sub-Saharan Africa.

Such is the present-day scale of Japan's ODA. Contrary to the widely prevalent perception that Japan's aid activities are commercially motivated, the program is a professional operation geared solely to economic and social development. Its geographic scope has become global, though the main part of aid is still directed to the Asian region. And while it has both strengths and weaknesses, it is an aid program uniquely influenced by Japan's efficiency, frugality, self-reliance, and private initiative.

PHILOSOPHY AND CHARACTERISTICS OF JAPANESE AID

An emphasis on "self-help" runs through Japan's aid planning and implementation. This focus derives in part from Japan's own experience of climbing to modernity in rapid strides. Japanese economic development in the years after the Meiji Restoration of 1868 and, later, in the postwar period depended relatively little on foreign capital and substantially on Japan's own national will. So Japanese tend to feel that others should follow similar routes. In the Japanese view, developing countries should manage or regulate their economies with the objective of achieving self-reliance as soon as possible.

While Japan recognizes that external economic assistance is clearly necessary for developing countries as they start on the road to prosperity, it does not want to see recipient nations develop a mentality or an economic structure that takes aid for granted. Rather, such countries should strive to generate domestic resources and capital for sustained growth, and to earn foreign exchange so they can import necessities and repay foreign debt. Needless to say, such requirements have made Japanese aid somewhat unpopular among recipients.

Also deeply embedded in Japan's philosophy of development is the idea that the public and private sectors must work not as adversaries, but as partners in development. Indeed, the countries that have succeeded in Asia have all embraced a policy of partnership between government and the private sector. Entrepreneurs know how to create capital fast; their business skills are crucial for the expansion of exports and investment in all developing countries. The role of the recipient government, meanwhile, is to foster an environment that encourages the private sector to grow and flourish in a way that is good for the nation as a whole.

For the same reason, the private sector of the donor nation should be involved in the aid process. The donor government should not hesitate to create opportunities for its business community to participate in aid programs, as long as such activities are conducive to the recipient's steady economic development. Undeniably, private-sector participation in Japan's aid process has made Japanese aid suspect of commercial promotion. The latest departures from mercantilist tendencies in Japan's external economic policies, which started in the mid-1980s, have already had a positive influence on Japan's aid policies. Today there are more untied loans[3] and program aid has expanded.

Foreign aid can make no long-term progress if the recipient is not seriously committed to imposing discipline on its own economy. However, the reality in many parts of the Third World is that discipline is lacking and corruption is prevalent. An overly puritanical approach would make it very difficult for aid efforts to continue, but closing one's eyes to misuse and mismanagement of aid funds would surely erode public support for aid in donor countries. Japan's answer to the tough question of how to impose discipline on aid recipients has been to look to international agencies to impose macroeconomic discipline. To minimize the misuse of funds, Japanese procurement guidelines require competitive bidding procedures similar to those used by international lending agencies.

Nevertheless, with Japan's foreign aid encountering mounting criticism in print media and Diet debates, it is becoming increasingly difficult for the government to place most of the responsibility for how aid funds are used in the hands of recipient governments. It will be incumbent on the Japanese aid authorities to devise ways of balancing the self-help credo they have hitherto upheld with the disciplinary requirements the public demands.

A distinctive feature of the Japanese aid experience is manifest in its success in maintaining a national consensus in favor of aid giving. This support may be due to the involvement of wide segments of Japanese society in aid activities. Government departments with varying interests participate in aid planning and implementation; for example, in technical assistance, all relevant departments supply experts to be sent on various missions abroad, as well as receive trainees from abroad. The close working relations between the government and private sector have already been noted. This multisectoral approach has enabled Japan to undertake massive aid operations without building a huge aid administration.

Perhaps, this approach is not unrelated to Japan's basic attitude that its aid activities should respond to individual requests from recipients. In responding to those requests, Japan has used existing domestic mechanisms of decision making and available resources in both the government and the private sectors. For instance, rather than independent aid missions abroad, Japanese embassies in developing countries channel aid to the recipient government departments. In formulating projects and scrutinizing their feasibility, Japanese trading firms and consulting firms have played significant roles both within and outside of the aid process.

Japan's aid system is effective and efficient, although with its pragmatic approach and lack of central coordination it may seem a little unwieldy and confusing. As the volume of Japan's aid expands, more macro-level socioeconomic analysis of recipient countries and more planning and priority setting will be required to maximize its effectiveness. The fourth medium-term target of ODA, covering 1988–1992, emphasizes strengthening aid implementing agencies.

In the fiscal 1989 and 1990 budgets, the government addresses these needs more effectively than before. Japan apparently has reached the stage where it will no longer be able to maintain a national consensus in favor of aid without convincing the general public that its taxes are being put to useful aid purposes and without ensuring the transparency of both the decision-making process and the implementation of aid.

LOPSIDEDNESS IN THE AID DEBATE

From the Japanese perspective that aid is meant to support self-help efforts toward social and economic development, many debates on aid policy and activities in various international forums appear lopsided, or at least off the mark. Comparative analyses of the aid performance of Development Assistance

Committee (DAC) members have relied heavily on quantitative yardsticks in accordance with the various criteria set down by DAC and the United Nations Conference on Trade and Development (UNCTAD). This is particularly so in DAC, which the United States created to achieve more comparability among donors and promote a greater sharing of the "aid burden." As American enthusiasm for aid has waned, the most important criterion for assessing performance has become greater comparability in terms of grant element, tying status, and so forth. UNCTAD has supported the "magic" criterion of the ratio of aid to GNP as the most important measure to gauge the sincerity of the North in its efforts to make amends for colonial exploitation.

The Japanese have never been comfortable with the approach that the developed countries should increase ODA as narrowly defined by DAC or UNCTAD, as if this were the only way to promote the social and economic development of the Third World. Japan prefers a broader framework and speaks in terms of "economic cooperation." Economic cooperation is predicated on the principle that the relationship between donor and recipient is a cooperative and mutually beneficial one between equals. Moreover, it covers wider financial, technological, trade, and investment relations than does ODA alone. From the Japanese point of view, many non-ODA activities have valuable development effects.

ODA, as DAC defines it, includes some activities with little or no bearing on economic development, such as grant aid for food or grants for salaries of expatriates in administrative branches of recipient governments. In addition, ODA excludes such important financial flows as untied recycling loans from the Export-Import Bank of Japan (Exim Bank) to consolidate debt restructuring.

When the requirement of financial resources is vast, is it better to provide a small amount in grant aid or a larger amount in the form of both grants and loans? If the recipient takes on debts that it can repay, why make a fuss about whether aid comes in the form of grant or loan? The long-term debt-servicing capacity of the given developing country must determine the aid mix. Such capacity can be generated and strengthened only by fast economic development accompanied by rapidly increasing export capability. Capital projects financed by loans to increase long-term productive capacity can be more beneficial than grants of surplus foodstuffs or strategically motivated funds for general consumption. The argument that donors should refrain from capital projects goes sharply against the Japanese aid philosophy. Furthermore, given the role of the private sector in economic development, remarkably high levels of Japan's private flows to the Third World could be appreciated more positively.[4] Comparing ratios of ODA to GNP among DAC members misrepresents the real contributions those nations make to economic development in the Third World. The true test is in the substantial transfers of financial resources and technology, which effectively contribute to economic and social development.

The effectiveness of aid in promoting development has seldom been the subject of serious discussion. The failure of past aid analyses in this regard stems from the difficulty of establishing a meaningful causal relationship between aid efforts and actual development. Social and economic development depends on many complex variables: aid is but one, probably marginal, factor in successful development. Work ethics, mobilization of indigenous resources, and the degree of acceptance of market mechanisms often play much more important roles in promoting effective development.

However, difficulty in establishing a causal relationship between aid and development should not minimize the importance of aid. Studies on the effectiveness of aid are very much in order. In DAC's early days, this topic was a major area of study for the committee. Later, DAC turned its focus to peripheral issues, such as the propriety of mixed credits or how to limit the financing of capital projects. Some of the discussion going on in DAC had little relevance to the interests of the developing world.

What, then, are the key ingredients for effective development? They are massive financial resources to build economic and social infrastructure; local efforts to educate and provide vocational training to the population; an active private sector; control of foreign exchange requirements, including control of capital flight and nonproductive capital imports, promotion of exports, and manageable debt policy; and mitigation of the adverse effects of development by implementing social welfare programs and protecting the environment.

How effective have Japan's aid efforts been in promoting Third World development? In East Asia, substantial amounts of aid, largely from Japan, massive foreign investments, access to world markets, and the sweat and ingenuity of indigenous entrepreneurs have combined to create a formula of spectacular success. Cultural traits have also played a role. As scholars have attributed the success of capitalism in Western Europe to the Protestant work ethic, by the same token, Confucianism is said to be an important element in the economic development of East Asia. Loyalty to authority, frugality, hard work, self-discipline, close family ties, and other Confucian values certainly seem to be making important contributions to the success of Japan and other countries in East Asia.

Can the formula that brought success in East Asia serve as a model for development in a non-Asian context? In this area, Japan should, and can, make intellectual contributions to the global aid community in years ahead by undertaking studies on East Asian success in development.

The Cold War has distorted the allocation of aid resources. For instance, the United States directs substantial amounts of aid to security-related assistance. In fiscal 1990, the U.S. foreign aid budget allocates $4.8 billion to finance arms sales to other countries and $3.7 billion for economic support funds. That means $8.5 billion is going to security-related assistance—over three times the $2.4 billion allocated to development assistance. While American interests lie in security, Japan's are in development. Various differences between Japan and the United States on aid matters—including strategic focus, aid tying, mixed credits, and geographic distribution—will likely come under new scrutiny in the post–Cold War period.

JAPAN'S AID DECISION-MAKING PROCESS

The generally reactive nature of Japan's external policies, wide support among the public for involvement in Third World development, and a history of improvisations have led the Japanese authorities to neglect creating transparency in their aid decision-making and implementation activities. As a result, aid decision making is shrouded in mystery and suspicion. However, the recent rise in the volume of public funds available for ODA and the concomitant increase in public attention to, and scrutiny of, the effectiveness of those activities have obliged aid authorities to undertake greater efforts to disclose their activities. To this end, the publication of various annual reports began in the late 1980s.[5]

Apart from the continuing lack of transparency, conceptual issues have confounded analysis. Very few individuals, even in the aid officialdom, can tell what constitutes ODA and what does not. Bureaucratic rivalry often aggravates the confusion, as the various offices are tempted to paint better and larger pictures of the roles they play. Against this background, analyzing the roles of the many actors in the aid decision-making process is no easy task. Broadly speaking, aid decisions are made at three levels, as described below.

Level One—Total volume of ODA in terms of multiyear plans and annual levels, as well as their breakdown into various categories.

Decisions at this level are for certain political: they take into consideration such factors as the desired degree of Japan's contribution to the international community, budgetary concerns, and the implementing capacity of aid institutions. Politicians at the highest level in both the government and the ruling party arbitrate the tug-of-war between the Ministry of Foreign Affairs (MOFA) and Ministry of Finance (MOF) with regard to aid volume.

Normal processes of budgetary formulation determine how aid is broken down into categories (grant, loan, etc.). Each government department submits its ODA-related budget proposal to MOF. In the general account budget, nearly 90 percent of aid funds are appropriated to MOFA and MOF. The budget is subject to approval by the Diet.

Level Two—Geographic distribution of grant and technical assistance, and eligibility and concessionality criteria of loans.

Broadly speaking, MOFA decides the distribution of grant and technical assistance at the beginning of each fiscal year, taking into account past distributional patterns, plus shifting regional emphasis based on diplomatic policy objectives. Loan eligibility criteria, concessionality criteria, and other policies pertaining to loans (e.g., the degree of untying, changes in modality of loans) are decided by consensus among MOFA, MOF, the Ministry of International Trade and Industry (MITI), and the Economic Planning Agency.

Level Three—The nuts and bolts of aid going to recipients.

Japanese embassies in developing countries maintain close contact with various branches of the host governments, which, in turn, are well aware of the potential for aid from Japan. Aid occupies a substantial and important part of relations with many developing countries. Japan was the largest donor in 29 countries in 1987.[6]

The Japanese government receives aid requests (often in the form of "shopping lists") through diplomatic channels, and then determines their feasibility, desirability, and suitability. This process is arduous, but the Japanese penchant for the meticulous pursuit of congruity in details minimizes the risk of accepting unwarranted requests. The process includes consultations with recipients and evaluations in Tokyo. In relying more on dispatches of missions from headquarters than on resident missions, Japan has followed a similar methodology to the one employed by the World Bank/International Development Association. Missions from headquarters are staffed by government officials from relevant departments and agencies that implement the aid. In the case of grant and technical assistance, MOFA is the decision maker. In the case of loans, the four aforementioned government departments make decisions collectively on the basis of MOFA proposals. The loan program is global in its scope. For major loan recipients in the Asian region, annual aid levels are usually kept stable. For countries in other regions, the volume of loan aid is decided on an ad hoc basis, keeping in mind eligibility criteria. As a result, the geographic distribution of loan aid varies annually more than that of grant or technical assistance.

Decision making based on consensus among all aid agencies concerned is surely cumbersome. But decision by consensus is normal in Japan, be it in private firms or in the affairs of government. Since agencies such as the Japan International Cooperation Agency (JICA) and OECF implement ODA activities—with the active involvement of various government departments—their involvement during the planning and decision-making stages is the most effective way of ensuring fast and effective implementation of aid.

Ultimately, without exception, it is the two governments concerned that conclude aid agreements. Thus, development assistance forms an integral part of Japan's diplomatic relations with developing countries. This system makes it possible for the Japanese government to ensure consistency in foreign affairs. Sometimes diplomatic objectives require the government to participate in joint international actions involving the withholding of ODA from certain countries. Vietnam presented such a case. When it invaded Cambodia, Japan completely suspended its aid flows, with very minor exceptions for humanitarian assistance. Similarly, after the Tiananmen incident, Japan subjected new aid to China to judicious diplomatic considerations. It is because of such foreign policy considerations and MOFA's integral role in the decision-making mechanism of Japanese aid that in the Diet and elsewhere (general public, media, academia, etc.) the MOFA is held responsible for aid activities.

The role of the Diet in aid decision making is not direct, except insofar as it must approve proposed budgets. Nonetheless, the Diet does exert some influence over Japan's ODA. By posing questions (raised mainly by opposition party members) about aid activities as they regard diplomatic issues, the Diet exercises a critical surveillance role.

For ODA, the Diet has performed a basically similar part. In one very important area, the legislature exercises a significant restraining role. It has clearly indicated its sense that military aid, or aid that would intensify international conflicts, should be prohibited. The Foreign Affairs Committee of the House of Representatives adopted resolutions to this effect in 1978, 1980, and 1981. The Audit Committees of both Houses of the Diet, on the basis of Board of Audit findings, have been intensifying their scrutiny of ODA activities in recent years, in particular after the Marcos scandal of 1985. The special Research Committee of the House of Councillors has taken up ODA as an important subject since 1986. The committee held a series of hearings with aid officials and produced reports that set out unanimous views of its members on aid policies and activities. Active debates on environmental aspects of ODA activities in various Diet committees have substantially influenced government positions and practices.

INTERNATIONALIZATION OF JAPAN'S ODA AND U.S.–JAPAN AID COOPERATION

With such enormous leaps in scale and variety, Japan's development assistance program is bound to further internationalize in the years ahead. It must be more open both in involving non-Japanese elements and in interlacing itself with the aid activities of other major donors and international and regional aid agencies. Progress in this direction is already under way, as Japan unties procurement sources of its loan programs, invites non-Japanese into its development survey program, involves non-Japanese agents to oversee procurements under its nonproject grant program for Sub-Saharan Africa, provides grant assistance to small-scale projects undertaken by either local or international nongovernmental organizations (NGOs), and includes non-Japanese experts in its aid evaluation activities. Because of language constraints and chronic understaffing in the Japanese aid structure, those openings are still modest in scale, but they clearly indicate the direction Japan intends for its aid policy to follow.

Internationalization is inevitable for other reasons, as well. First, heavy indebtedness for an increasingly large number of developing countries calls for balance-of-payments support. This unavoidably involves Japanese aid officials in macroeconomic analysis of, and structural adjustment requirements for, recipient economies. Recycling loans by Exim Bank, program loans to promote structural adjustments and sector loans by OECF, and nonproject grants for Sub-Saharan Africa require close coordination with the activities of the International Monetary Fund and World Bank.

Second, as Japan's aid expands, the necessity and importance of coordinating it with aid activities of other donors grow. Such coordination will improve the effectiveness of Japan's aid. Small recipient countries especially need major donors to coordinate aid activities, as their aid-absorbing capacity and aid-receiving administrative structures are often limited and overburdened. Aid to island nations—particularly, aid in such areas as transportation and telecommunications in the Pacific region—calls for coordination with aid coming from other sources. In the 1980s, Japan gradually increased aid coordination efforts with the United States, the United Kingdom, France, Australia, New Zealand, and the World Bank.[7]

Third, as Japan's aid programs globalize, Japanese aid personnel will be working in unfamiliar environments. Coordination with aid agencies and personnel from donors with long histories and associations with these regions will help aid staff acclimate to new sites.

Fourth, growing concern about environmental issues both at home and in recipient nations demands great care and attention to the adverse effects of development. This is an area in which respect for local knowledge is particularly important. Already, new guidelines on environmental consideration for undertaking studies of project feasibility have opened the way for employing local experts in such studies.

What are the prospects for greater aid cooperation between Japan and the United States, given this internationalization of Japan's aid activities in the 1990s? The easing of East-West tension in the Third World may lessen hitherto heavy security considerations in the U.S. aid program. If a significant change takes place and the U.S. aid philosophy returns to placing emphasis on economic and social development, Japan and the United States will share many goals and activities in the Third World.

At the moment, substantial increases in U.S. development aid do not seem imminent. Rather, increasing concern among U.S. manufacturers and construction firms about the possible loss of business opportunities to Japanese competitors in the developing world may sharpen differences between the two donors. The United States may continue to view Japanese aid activities with suspicion. If true collaboration is to develop between the two countries in the aid field, the Americans must first understand, without preconceptions, what the Japanese have been doing in the Third World. They also must refrain from basing such cooperation on the assumption that Japanese money and American knowledge can do things better.

Some elements of Japan's aid philosophy—such as private-sector involvement, export promotion, and the belief that material progress is the surest way to democracy—may go against the American grain. But it seems necessary, above all, for the United States to reorient its aid goals and clearly ascertain the place for economic development in its aid strategy. Such a change is not only long overdue but also inescapable if the United States is to remain a major donor in the 1990s. Public sentiment toward aid in the United States is negative.[8] Without a new push by the U.S. administration to help the developing countries in the changed international situation, American involvement in the Third World will substantially weaken and American influence there will inevitably decline.

At the same time, as the Cold War between the two military superpowers recedes, regional conflicts may become more frequent. The Third World itself must shed its Cold War mentality and ask itself what is the best allocation of scarce resources for its billions living in economic plight. If developing countries believe that they may, over time, reap the benefits of peace dividends, it is incumbent on these countries not to divert resources to non-development purposes.

In this connection, it is relevant that substantial military expenditures by some countries of the Middle East and the Indian subcontinent effectively disillusion even ardent supporters of aid to the Third World. Here again, Japan and the United States can jointly exert a positive influence. Without basic changes in the American stance, the Third World will remain the forgotten world, and the 1990s may become another wasted decade for those poor nations. U.S.–Japan cooperation should include a new Western philosophy toward the developing world in the 1990s.

While it may take some time before such a needed turn-around occurs, a good measure of collaboration may still be feasible and useful in certain concrete areas.

First, environmental protection can be an area for fruitful U.S.–Japan aid cooperation. Japan has already made a commitment to emphasize environmental protection in its aid program; in 1989, it decided to allocate 300 billion yen for the coming three years for this purpose. Since environmental problems transcend national borders and require a coordinated approach among major donors, Japan and the United States should explore areas for cooperative endeavors in this field.

Second, the worsening debt problem in the Third World will pose challenges for Japan as the world's largest creditor nation. Since Latin American middle-income nations suffer most seriously from accumulated debts, the United States will increasingly look to Japan as an effective partner for the resolution of the issue in the 1990s. The Miyazawa/Brady Plan for the alleviation of private bank debt burdens of developing countries is probably only a precursor to further endeavors.

Third, on the supply side, growing collaborations between Japanese and American corporations may present novel opportunities for joint project implementation in Japan's untied aid financing of economic infrastructure projects in developing countries.

Elsewhere in this volume, Julia Chang Bloch has made a number of concrete suggestions for aid collaboration between the United States and Japan. I would like to stress the following items she has described: collaborative training efforts on the model of MOFA's program with Harvard University; joint work between fledgling Japanese NGOs and experienced American NGOs; and sharing of the U.S. Agency for International Development's (AID's) experiences in evaluation, monitoring, and accountability systems. These hold great promise for success in aid cooperation between the two donor nations.

CONCLUSION

Japan's ODA, though presently subject to intense criticism at home, will remain one of the cornerstones of Japanese foreign policy. Criticism is in a sense understandable, considering that not until the mid-1980s has the government undertaken to publicize details of Japan's aid activities, decision-making process, and guiding principles. Nor has it attended to the understaffing of the aid apparatus and implementing agencies, or to other institutional deficiencies. The five-year period under the present fourth medium-term ODA target is an important one for readjustments.

Asia's economic situation is undergoing profound change. Market-oriented Asian economies are growing fast, and major Japanese aid recipients may achieve the economic self-reliance to which they aspire before the century is over. If present trends persist, the nature of Japanese aid to East and Southeast Asia will change, with emphasis gradually moving from financial resource transfers to technology transfers. With such changes in the 1990s, geographic distribution of Japan's aid may be more globally dispersed. Upper-middle-income nations in Latin America and Eastern Europe (those with a per capita GNP exceeding $1,300 in 1987) probably will require a new approach. Given the urgency of financial need due either to heavy indebtedness or to political necessity, these areas may require more than the usual private flows.

As the world's greatest creditor, supported by a high savings propensity, Japan is bound to play an important role in financing global needs. The United States is likely to remain hamstrung in providing financial resources to the needy. West German resources may be tied up in Eastern European financing. Under the circumstances, Japan and the United States must stop looking at each other as adversaries and must find, as partners, a modus vivendi to work out a global program of financing priority needs, particularly development needs in the Third World.

NOTES

The views expressed herein are those of the author and do not necessarily represent those of the government of Japan.

1. Ministry of Foreign Affairs, *Japan's Official Development Assistance: 1988 Annual Report* (Tokyo: 1989), 19–23.
2. The Japanese government refrained, in a very limited number of instances, from providing aid to countries that the international community condemned for certain internationally unacceptable acts.
3. About two-thirds of Japanese ODA loans are untied for worldwide procurement and the remainder are untied for procurement in developing countries. DAC, *Development Cooperation in the 1990s* (Paris: OECD, 1989), 166.
4. Net non-ODA financial flows from Japan to the developing countries amounted to $14.7 billion in 1987, accounting for 78 percent of the total of such flows from all DAC members. Ibid., 226.
5. MOFA published the first full-fledged ODA annual report, in both Japanese and English, in 1987. The Japan International Cooperation Agency (JICA) (which implements technical assistance) and OECF published their first English annual reports in 1988.
6. Ministry of Foreign Affairs, *Japan's Official Development Assistance*, 13.
7. Ibid., 30.
8. The *New York Times*/CBS News poll conducted in May 1990 found that 83 percent accepted the reduction of foreign aid if spending had to be cut. Michael Oreskes, "Grudging Public Thinks Tax Rise Must Come," *New York Times*, May 27, 1990, 1, 24.

COMMENT

Shinji Asanuma

In their contributions to this collection, Toru Yanagihara & Anne Emig, Julia Chang Bloch, and Masamichi Hanabusa touch on a number of important aspects of Japan's foreign aid and offer insights into its nature, possible directions of its evolution, and implications thereof. By way of commenting on these chapters, I would like to offer my view on the nature and the future of Japan's foreign aid policy. My focus is on foreign aid as an instrument of Japan's international economic policy in the context of its international economic relations and its position in the world economic community. This view is of necessity an oversimplified one, but I believe it captures the essence of the structural characteristics, broad historical trends, and possible directions of further evolution.

JAPAN'S AID: PHILOSOPHY, ECONOMICS, AND POLICY

How has Japan's foreign aid policy evolved in the postwar period? Former Japanese Minister of Foreign Affairs Saburo Okita's view—also reflected in Yanagihara & Emig's chapter—is that Japan has used its aid policy to further its international economic interests and that, through disparate periods, the objective of foreign aid changed. Thus, in the immediate postwar period of economic reconstruction, foreign aid took the form of war reparations to Asian countries, the objective being to foster Japan's reintegration in the international economic community. In the period of rapid economic growth through the 1960s, Japan used foreign aid to enhance export market development. With the oil shocks in the 1970s, the focus broadened to cover Japan's concerns over the growing dependence on imported natural resources, and the concept of comprehensive international security emerged. This concept clearly indicated Japan's choice of international economic aid over defense buildup as a means of protecting its economic security. More recently, the enunciated policy of foreign aid has emphasized Japan's contributions to the international economic community and the management of the world economy, as well as the resolution of world economic problems.

This summary of Japan's foreign aid history, though it depicts correctly the shifts of policy emphasis, is somewhat misleading: it gives the impression that the Japanese government took the initiative in formulating its foreign aid policy to further Japan's economic development, that Japan's aid policy was based on some grand design. The fact was that there never was any grand design and that Japan's aid policy has been essentially reactive to specific situations. A number of observations are necessary to complete the story.

First, throughout the postwar period, the objective of Japan's aid policy has been the rather vague notion of maintaining and enhancing "good" relationships with nations of the world, and Japan's policymakers have perceived this objective as essential to the reestablishment and development of Japan as a viable industrial and trading nation in the world community. But the aid policy did not lead the development of relationships. Rather, exporters and importers initiated economic relationships with other countries. After the trading volume reached a certain threshold, financiers (banks) came on the scene; manufacturers followed, attempting to secure market outlets or natural resources by way of direct investments and industrial relocation. In the case of a developing country, imbalances in the economic relationship would emerge, and the country would demand Japanese government aid in maintaining a "good" and "harmonious" economic relationship. Invariably, this was the stage at which Japan would introduce foreign aid. Foreign aid was thus a reactive policy instrument under the pressures brought upon Japan to accommodate the emerging and ever changing problems in various bilateral economic relationships.

Second, this course of development explains the geographic pattern of Japan's foreign aid activities. The key is the nature and level of preexisting trading and investment activities between the recipient country and Japan. It is thus not surprising that initially East Asian countries and subsequently South Asian countries were major recipients of Japan's foreign aid, while South American countries became significant recipients only later, and African countries were left out until fairly recently. One might postulate that the magnitude of Japan's aid is a rather simple function of a composite volume of exports, imports, and investments. The picture is one of a series of concentric waves of trading, investment, and aid activities spreading through the Third World as Japan's economic power in the world economy has grown.

This view of Japan's aid policy brings out a number of its structural characteristics, particularly as they contrast with those of U.S. aid policy. First, Japan is predominantly an economic power, and its world strategy and policy are rooted in economics and underlying economic relationships. This is quite natural. But Bloch's characterization of Japan's aid policy as primarily "mercantilist" and "commercial" is perhaps too narrow. The Japanese perceive foreign aid less as an instrument of export promotion than as a tax on international trade and investment, imposed voluntarily, but collectively, by and on industrialized, high-income trading nations.

Second, specific aid policy decisions in Japan take into account the context of the total economic relationship with the recipient. This is in sharp contrast to what one can observe of U.S. aid policy. Since the immediate postwar period, when Max Milikan and Walt Rostow argued that economic aid to developing countries would contribute to economic stability and development of the Third World, thereby fostering political stability and reducing political vulnerability,[1] U.S. aid policy has been based largely on geopolitical orientation. The current distribution pattern of U.S. economic aid—the bulk of which goes to a select number of countries where the United States has strong geopolitical interests—shows this clearly. It is difficult to argue that the major objective of U.S. aid is economic development of the Third World. Thus, an important question asked in the U.S. aid policy decision is, What would be the right mix of security and economic aid? In the Japanese context, the question is, What would be the right mix of exports, imports, and investments, on one hand, and economic aid on the other? Geopolitical consideration is a rather alien element in Japanese aid policy formulation.

Finally, the reactive and passive nature of Japan's aid policy also explains the composition of aid. The wishes of recipient governments and of Japanese traders and manufacturers strongly influence aid decisions. Hence the criticism that Japanese aid is often biased toward capital projects and large infrastructure projects, at the expense of projects with direct orientation toward basic human needs, social development, poverty alleviation, or humanitarian objectives. However, one may argue that Japan's aid, if taken together with other aspects of its international economic activities, is better integrated with the total development process of recipient economies than U.S. aid. Japan's aid may not be driven exclusively by development concerns (see Hanabusa), but it is fairly responsive to—and at the same time constrained by—the preoccupations of recipient governments, whether the concern is for industrialization drive or infrastructure development.

By contrast, within the limits of basically geopolitical considerations, U.S. aid policy is driven by the dominant development ideology of the time, which often varies according to the changing intellectual fads and the ideological leanings of the incumbent administration. At different times, then, U.S. aid policy is rather narrowly concerned with development issues of the times, and takes a fairly purist approach toward technical assistance aimed at indigenous institutional development, human resources capacity building, private-sector development, poverty alleviation, basic human needs, and so forth. The periodic shifts in U.S. aid policy reduce its reliability from recipients' point of view and intrude on recipient governments' development policies. One outcome of these swings is that U.S. aid policy has become an exclusive domain of the government; it has lost a broad constituency in the domestic political arena, such as manufacturers and exporters, and this loss of support will eventually contribute to a sense of aid fatigue.

FUTURE EVOLUTION OF JAPAN'S AID POLICY

The above observations do not mean that we should be content with the reactive tendencies of Japan's foreign aid policy in the future. Undeniably, Japan has emerged as an economic superpower, and its donor role requires that its aid policy be guided by more than the vague notion of maintaining and enhancing economic relationships with other nations, ultimately Japan's bilateral concerns. As such, Japan has a vital national interest in participating more proactively than it has in the collective efforts of the industrialized countries toward resolution of global economic problems.

Indeed, Japan's foreign aid policy has been moving in that direction. Japanese contributions to multilateral aid agencies have been increasing substantially. Japan's aid to Africa has grown at a pace and to a level that Japan's preexisting economic relationships with African countries cannot explain. Japan has come up with new facilities for financial assistance for the middle-income debtor Latin American economies and the Philippines. It is gearing up for the needed economic assistance for Eastern Europe, as well as for global environmental matters.

While a wholesale change in Japan's aid policy is neither feasible nor desirable, to enhance its future effectiveness, the Japanese government must attend to two requirements. First, it must consider how effectively and by what institutional framework it could participate in the resolution of world economic problems. Multilateral institutions alone will not provide adequate channels. The government must make conscious efforts to establish its coordinating machinery capable of interacting with other donor governments and aid agencies.

Second, Japan must expand its institutional capabilities for carrying out its foreign aid activities. Foreign aid is not simply a matter of financial contribution; the process of development assistance requires substantial involvement of aid personnel with the right mix of skills. Expansion of aid personnel is thus imperative, and the past tendency on the part of the Japanese government to maximize aid volume with the minimum number of aid personnel must change. In the past, nongovernmental participants in the aid process—be they recipient government officials, Japanese trading companies, or manufacturers—carried a considerable part of the required technical skills. For the Japanese government to take a more proactive policy approach, however, it must strengthen its aid agencies, as well as relevant parts of the relevant ministries.

U.S.–JAPAN AID ALLIANCE?

Could a U.S.–Japan aid alliance be an important element of the future evolution of Japan's foreign aid policy, as Bloch suggests? If such an alliance means more than a closer coordination of two countries' aid policies and programs for specific countries' development issues, or of approaches to global issues, and if it therefore means formulation of commonly owned programs of aid activities, it will yield little.

In the postwar period, two objectives have driven much of Japan's foreign policy. I have already mentioned one: that of maintaining and enhancing good and harmonious—and primarily economic—relationships with other nations. The second has been the steering of the U.S.–Japan relationship, and it has assumed an increasing importance in the 1980s amid the mounting tensions between the two countries over trade issues. Given this setting, it would not be hard for the United States to pressure the Japanese government to formulate some collaborative aid programs along the lines of the proposed alliance. However, the scope for such an alliance is limited, and Japan is likely to regard it more as a concession to the United States in the bilateral context than as an important trilateral element of its foreign aid policy.

As the above observations make abundantly clear, the aid

policies of the two countries have totally different orientations. To begin with, the geographic areas where the United States has strong geopolitical interests are generally not the ones the current Japanese aid policy emphasizes. The Philippines and, possibly, Mexico are exceptions. Caribbean and Central American countries are often cited as possible subjects of collaborative efforts, but Japan does not have enough economic interests in these areas. Collaborative possibilities may exist in China, Indochina, and Eastern Europe, but these are not major recipients of U.S. aid at the moment. Furthermore, as Bloch points out, a durable collaborative aid policy cannot be based on the idea of "Japanese money and U.S. brains." From Japan's viewpoint, such a policy would be nothing more than Japanese foreign aid to U.S. foreign aid programs.

CONCLUSION

Japan's foreign aid policy has developed around the notion of maintaining and enhancing its economic relationships with Third World nations, in line with Japan's evolving economic status in the world economy. To forcibly change its basic nature will be neither possible nor desirable, as the policy appears to have served well the development needs of recipient countries. However, Japan's aid capacity—and, indeed, Japan's position in the world economy—has created considerable room for the government to adopt a more proactive aid policy for the resolution of global economic problems. Doing so would also be in line with Japan's growing willingness and capacity to participate in the collective management of the world economy. To this end, the multilateral donor coordination mechanism and Japan's aid machinery require strengthening.

NOTES

The views expressed herein are those of the author and do not necessarily represent those of the World Bank.

1. Max F. Milikan and Walt W. Rostow, *A Proposal: Key to an Effective Foreign Policy* (New York: Harper and Brothers, 1957).

COMMENT

Ernest H. Preeg

The three chapters describing the key features of Japan's foreign aid and the U.S.–Japan aid relationship are most useful and complement each other nicely. Toru Yanagihara & Anne Emig's and Masamichi Hanabusa's essays present as clear and concise a summary of Japanese development assistance as I have seen anywhere, and Julia Chang Bloch gives a balanced critique of the Japanese program from the American point of view. The authors also provide timely suggestions for improvements in the Japanese program, including closer collaboration between the United States and Japan.

My comments are directed at sharpening some key points made in the chapters, and drawing out the implications for change into a somewhat broader perspective. This involves, to some extent, an extended critique of U.S. economic assistance programs, since the prospects for a more balanced, cooperative approach will require significant change on both sides. More precisely, I would like to comment on five key aspects of the U.S.–Japan aid relationship, which I address in descending order of importance.

A COMMON APPROACH TO BILATERAL ECONOMIC AID

Difficulties in the U.S.–Japan aid relationship spring from the substantial differences in the two countries' rationales and objectives for providing bilateral economic aid. The Japanese program rightly receives criticism for its commercial orientation and its insufficient attention to helping the poorest people, such as through small-scale agriculture and rural health projects. However, as Hanabusa explains, underlying the Japanese program is a well-defined development assistance strategy based on the

Japanese postwar experience and the more recent success of the East Asian newly industrialized economies (the so-called NICs). It stresses the need to motivate people to work hard, save, and educate their children. The key to modernization is the application of advanced technologies through the private sector. The process requires high levels of public- and private-sector investment that can be met, in large part, through external development finance and technical assistance such as the Japanese government provides. Japanese companies play a central role in transmitting applied technologies and management skills through direct investment and, with respect to economic infrastructure, official capital project contracts. The Japanese approach, demonstrably successful in East Asia, is now spreading to Southeast Asia, Mexico, and elsewhere. The strategy fully and appropriately integrates trade, private investment, and development finance. Because it is clearly effective and it provides widespread benefits to domestic business interests, the program enjoys a high level of public support in Japan.

In the U.S. program, by contrast, two-thirds of bilateral economic aid goes for balance-of-payments support for a small number of countries of strategic importance to the United States, and the remainder is predominantly direct assistance to the poorest segments of society in recipient countries. A rationale thus based on foreign policy and humanitarian interests manages to obtain budget appropriations each year, but aid is declining, and public support is waning. Moreover, U.S. bilateral assistance plays only a small role in major regions of the developing world, including South America and almost all of Asia. The close interface of trade, investment, and development finance, basic to the Japanese development strategy, is largely absent from the U.S. strategy. Recent critical assessments of the U.S. aid program by former U.S. Agency for International Development (AID) Administrator Alan Woods and a congressional task force chaired by Representatives Lee Hamilton and Benjamin Gilman highlighted its lack of tangible development impact and loss of public support.[1] Senator Robert Dole's initiative in January 1990 to reduce the earmarked concentration of U.S. aid dedicated to the largest recipients is another symptom of the problem, but it was put forward in terms of new, competing short-term foreign policy interests, in Panama and Poland.

What is needed urgently, as we move from the era of Cold War U.S.–Soviet rivalry in the military sphere to more diversified and predominantly economic global relationships, are updated development assistance strategies in both countries that are responsive to the rapidly changing circumstances in the developing world. Such strategies should be the priority objective of official U.S.–Japan consultations, and existing consultative mechanisms should be strengthened to provide the analytical depth and follow-through capability that, unfortunately, have been lacking. The United States and Japan are at the forefront of new technology development, are the principal trade and investment partners of most developing countries, and are the two largest aid donors. It is time to update our respective aid strategies, aiming toward a more common approach based on the momentum of private-sector, export-driven economic growth in many parts of the developing world, now including Eastern Europe. The four points that follow encompass specific objectives.

UNTIED AID

This is the crux of widespread criticism in the United States that the Japanese aid program adversely affects U.S. export interests. As long as Japanese aid remains concentrated in commercially sensitive infrastructure projects—particularly in the power, telecommunications, and transport sectors—and this aid is tied, directly or indirectly, to Japanese exports, substantial adverse impact on U.S. exports is inevitable. The tied aid problem for U.S. exporters is not just with Japan. Other aid donors also provide substantial aid and mixed credit financing for infrastructure capital projects, while the United States has decided, for policy reasons, not to enter this area of development assistance. Nevertheless, Japan is the largest provider of capital project assistance and, therefore, the principal target of U.S. concern.

In this context, all three chapters provide only partial explanations of the current circumstances of Japanese aid-tying and underestimate the problem. Japanese capital project assistance amounts to several billion dollars per year and routinely ties the engineering portion of loans to Japanese firms. By all reports, this leads to de facto tying of almost all commercially sensitive equipment purchases, even though the latter are officially untied. In May 1988, after long debate within the Japanese government, the engineering portion of loans was untied for South Korea and Malaysia, but these countries are basically aid graduates that should no longer be receiving subsidized credits for commercially sensitive capital projects. Japanese projects in all other countries are still tied, at least for the engineering portion.

Two sets of potentially misleading statistics obscure this situation and should be clarified. Japan reports a high proportion of its aid as "untied" to the OECD's (Organization of Economic Cooperation and Development's) Development Assistance Committee (DAC) even though this includes projects whose engineering portion is tied. Since DAC members, including Japan, have long agreed that if any part of a project is tied, the entire project is considered tied, the figures greatly overstate the extent of Japanese untied aid. Yet the DAC figures are the ones authors often cite—as Yanagihara & Emig do in their Table 6, and Hanabusa does in his Note 3.

The second set of statistics are for procurement sources on an aggregate basis for all Japanese aid projects. They indicate substantial non-Japanese procurement, most of which is from developing countries. However, the figures are based not on actual procurement but on "primary contractors," who undertake procurement, including from Japan. Many Japanese aid projects, particularly in the transportation sector, have primary contractors that are indigenous joint ventures; they are thus "developing country contractors," but are controlled by Japanese interests. This arrangement would normally lead to a large amount of procurement in Japan, especially for technology-intensive equipment, although the official figures given do not reflect such procurement. In any event, Japanese procurement for trade-sensitive capital projects is probably much higher than that for the aid program in the aggregate.

Direct figures for procurement are the solution. Unfortunately, Japan does not make public who wins the bidding on procurement open to international competitive bidding and at what price. Japanese officials say that such disclosure is the responsibility of the recipient government, but this is not an adequate response. As with the World Bank and other donors, if aid is untied, the donor is responsible for ensuring that competitive bidding actually takes place. Public disclosure of the winning bid and price is fundamental to that responsibility.

Three concrete steps could help Japan truly untie economic aid, as is its oft-quoted official objective: first, Japan should untie the engineering portion of loans for all recipient countries, if possible; if this is not feasible, the government should properly report the entire project as tied. Second, the Japanese government should adopt transparent procedures to ensure that de jure untying leads to de facto untying. Full disclosure should be standard procedure for selection of engineering firms and procurement in terms of who wins the bidding and at what price. Japan could perhaps contract this whole process to the World Bank or some other technical body. The implementing agency in the recipient country may well resist such intrusion to ensure international competitive bidding, but this is a legitimate requirement for receiving highly concessionary aid funding. Third, the United States and Japan could jointly adopt these first two steps for all large projects of commercial sensitivity on an open-ended basis. In other words, they would be initially untied to each other but with other donors welcome to join if they are also willing to fully untie such projects.

FUNCTIONAL DISTRIBUTION OF AID

In addition to untying capital project assistance, Japan should shift its overall aid resources somewhat from capital project assistance to direct help to the poorest people. This is because capital project assistance has such strong commercial underpinning that it tends to get a larger share of overall aid resources than development priorities would justify. Perhaps a ceiling could be put on the share of aid for such projects. A more controversial question is whether Japan should increase or decrease the share of aid devoted to fast-disbursing balance-of-payments support. Such immediate financial support clearly is necessary for the most distressed, poorest countries, such as those in Sub-Saharan Africa, but a good case can be made that project-oriented support is preferable for other countries. Bilateral balance-of-payments support is often motivated by political considerations and can allow recipient governments to delay necessary economic reforms.

In any event, Japan should work out such shifts in the structure of aid and the establishment of broad parameters for particular sectors in close consultation with the United States and, more broadly, with other bilateral donor countries in the DAC. The United States could provide Japan timely assistance in developing a greater capability to deliver management-intensive projects in the agriculture and health sectors. At the same time, a shift of Japanese aid resources to the humanitarian and balance-of-payments support sectors would permit the United States to reestablish a capability for providing technology-intensive infrastructure projects. Such greater balance between the United States and other donors in the capital projects field would, in addition to providing the most efficient and low-cost project assistance, help to reduce the existing adverse impact of such assistance on U.S. exports.

GEOGRAPHIC DISTRIBUTION OF AID

A broader geographic distribution of Japanese aid is not likely to be as important as many analysts portray it to be. Some diversification of Japanese aid to regions other than Asia is appropriate, but most of the people in the developing world are, in fact, in

Asia, and that is the region where Japan has its most direct interests, which is always a factor in allocating bilateral aid programs. Similarly, West European aid is predominant in Africa, and U.S. aid in the Caribbean basin.

In any event, diversification of Japanese aid should be a subject of deliberate consultation among donors and of clearly established priorities. For example, the Japanese initiative to provide fast-disbursing grant aid to Sub-Saharan Africa in 1987 was a welcome support for multilateral efforts coordinated by the World Bank. In contrast, the announcement in February 1989 of Japanese capital project assistance of $500 million for Brazil, presumably with engineering services tied to Japanese companies, produced a mixed reaction in the United States. U.S. companies were legitimately concerned that such concessionary financing would enable Japanese firms to supplant their American counterparts in traditional South American markets, while the U.S. government has never clearly stated whether it favors Japanese-financed infrastructure projects in Brazil in which the engineering portion remains tied.

A more balanced approach to geographic distribution of aid has implications for the United States as well as for Japan. In this context, I would disagree with Bloch that "the distinctive characteristic of U.S. aid has been its global reach." In fact, over two-thirds of U.S. economic aid is concentrated in six countries, and although Japan sometimes sometimes comes under criticism for allocating only 10 percent of its overall aid to Sub-Saharan Africa, this still accounts, in absolute terms, to an aid level comparable to that of the United States in that region.

BURDEN-SHARING

As Bloch points out somewhat diplomatically, this issue is a nonstarter in terms of balancing out in a significant way U.S. military expenditures through increased Japanese economic aid. As Yanagihara & Emig show (see their Table 3), Japanese economic aid more than quadrupled from 1977–1979 to 1988, while as a proportion of gross national product (GNP), it increased only from 0.24 percent to 0.32 percent, because of the growth in Japanese GNP and the strengthening of the yen in dollar terms. Those who advocate an increase in Japanese official development assistance (ODA) to 2–3 percent of GNP, over several years, imply an increase in disbursements ten to fifteen times current levels, taking account of continued growth in Japanese GNP. Among other implications, this would mean a Japanese aid level two to three times that of all other aid donors combined.

The reality is that even with a further rapid increase in Japanese ODA, the level is unlikely to rise more than a couple of tenths of a percent of GNP—perhaps to the 0.5 percent range—over the next several years. This would not constitute a significant dent in the military versus economic aid burden-sharing equation.

The confusion in the burden-sharing debate is not so much a lack of communication between the United States and Japan as between military-oriented and economic-aid-oriented interlocutors. The two groups seldom meet, and each tends to feel that the burden-sharing solution lies in the other camp.

The solution to the burden-sharing issue is, in fact, finally at hand, but it lies on the U.S. side of the equation. The United States is in the process of reducing its military budget, which should soon drop below 5 percent of GNP and may decline considerably further if the Soviet threat indeed greatly diminishes. If a small part of that reduction—a couple of tenths of a percent of GNP—were shifted to ODA, the result would be a more balanced overall burden of military and economic aid commitments. Far more important, such a shift in resources within the international sector of the U.S. budget would be very much in keeping with the reordered set of U.S. interests underway in the post–Cold War world. It would also provide the basis for a truly balanced and cooperative U.S.-Japanese leadership in support of successful economic development throughout the world.

NOTE

1. *Development and the National Interest: U.S. Economic Assistance into the 21st Century* (Washington, D.C.: U.S. Agency for International Development, February 1989); and *House Committee on Foreign Affairs, Report of the Task Force on Foreign Assistance* (Washington, D.C.: 1989).

JAPANESE AND U.S. AID TO THE PHILIPPINES: A RECIPIENT-COUNTRY PERSPECTIVE

Filologo Pante, Jr. & Romeo A. Reyes

In assessing the impact of official development assistance (ODA), it is necessary to consider not only donors' perspectives and the global economic context, but also the perspectives of recipient countries. What types of assistance best meet a recipient's needs? Which sectors require assistance, and is appropriate aid available to them? What mechanisms are most effective in planning aid objectives and goals? These are among the questions that color a recipient country's evaluation of an aid program.

This chapter presents a Philippine perspective on U.S. and Japanese ODA to the Philippines. Several factors make the Philippines a suitable choice for this type of study. Both the United States and Japan have a long history of involvement with, and continuing security interests in, the Philippines. Furthermore, they offer substantial—and comparable—amounts of ODA to the Philippines. Yet their aid programs differ in important ways that bring to light the strengths and weaknesses of ODA from the recipient country's viewpoint.

In light of the pitfalls and difficulty of impact assessment, this chapter does not attempt to quantify the contribution of ODA to development. Rather, it reviews the quantity and quality of ODA flows and indicates possible directions for the role of U.S. and Japanese development assistance to the Philippines. It provides a brief historical background of the two donors' ODA; offers a comparative analysis of their aid programs; and discusses a number of measures that could enhance the contribution of U.S. and Japanese ODA to Philippine development.

HISTORICAL BACKGROUND

U.S. development assistance to the Philippines began during the postwar period of the 1940s. The Rehabilitation Act (Tydings Act) of 1946 provided financial and technical assistance for the reconstruction and rehabilitation of roads, bridges, and public buildings. It awarded the Philippine government a sum of $400 million for war damage, and $120 million for the rebuilding of public works and highways in 1946–1948.

On November 14, 1950, the Quirino-Foster Memorandum of Agreement was signed. This pact created the legal framework establishing economic and technical ties between the United States and the Philippines, and formally assured U.S. assistance to the Philippine efforts toward economic reconstruction. Among the agreement's provisions were the creation of the U.S. Economic Survey Mission to the Philippines and formation of the Philippine Council for U.S. Aid (PHILCUSA); the latter represented the Philippine government in its transactions with the U.S. Economic Cooperation Administration (ECA). ECA had the responsibility for overseeing, advising, and guiding the Philippine government in the use of American funds and for providing assistance in the implementation of the general aims and recommendations of the Economic Survey Mission to the Philippines. ECA later became the U.S. Agency for International Development (AID). As for PHILCUSA, its tasks vis-à-vis ECA are now being performed by the National Economic and Development Authority (NEDA), the central planning and policymaking body in the Philippines.

Japanese development assistance to the Philippines commenced in 1956 with the reparations payments, or *baisho*. Under the reparations agreement, Japan committed $550 million in capital goods and technical services to the Philippine government during the period 1956–1976. From 1959 to 1969, the bulk of reparations was devoted to public works, transport and communications, education, and health facilities. The reparations program came primarily in the form of purchase of Japanese machinery, such as spare parts and raw materials.

It is clear that Japanese and U.S. development assistance to the Philippines sprang from the need to rebuild the Philippine economy after World War II. This objective set the stage for the more significant role these two sources of ODA would subsequently perform in the development of the economy.

COMPARATIVE ANALYSIS OF JAPANESE AND U.S. ODA

Comparison of U.S. and Japanese ODA requires examination of several characteristics of the aid programs: aid volume, types of assistance involved, composition of ODA flows, structure of loans, allocation by sector, planning and programming, procurement, and policy conditionalities.

Amount of Development Assistance

ODA flows to the Philippines from multilateral and bilateral sources amounted to $10.8 billion in 1952–1986 on a commitment basis. Of this total, 78 percent came in the form of loans; the balance came in the form of grants.

For the whole period, Japan contributed about 20 percent of ODA, while the United States contributed 17 percent. However, these figures do not tell the whole story. In the 1950s and the 1960s, the United States was clearly the major source of development assistance to the Philippines, while Japan was only a minor donor (Table 1).

With the transition from reparation payments to yen loans in the 1970s, Japan's share of total ODA to the Philippines, which had been 6 percent in the 1960s, leapt to 15 percent in the 1970s and 23 percent in the 1980s. While U.S. development assistance continued to increase in absolute terms, its overall share dropped from 40 percent in the 1960s to 13 percent in the 1970s and 14 percent in 1980–1986. In 1986, the Japanese contributed 36 percent of total ODA, whereas the United States contributed 26 percent.[1]

TABLE 1. U.S. AND JAPANESE TOTAL ODA TO THE PHILIPPINES
(*in millions of dollars*)

Period	United States		Japan	
	Amount	As % of total ODA to the Philippines	Amount	As % of total ODA to the Philippines
1952–1961	230.54	86.8	0.08	0.0
1962–1970	216.46	40.2	34.02	6.3
1971–1979	357.86	13.0	422.42	15.3
1980–1986	1,828.99	14.1	1,652.27	22.8
1952–1986	2,633.85	16.9	2,108.79	19.5

Source: Data provided to the authors by the external assistance staff of the National Economic and Development Authority of the Republic of the Philippines, Manila.

Types of Assistance

The United States and Japan each offer several types of ODA. U.S. assistance comes in the form of grants and loans. The former primarily finance the costs of technical assistance, training, and commodity procurement to support institution building; the latter cover the requirements of public investment projects. U.S. assistance consists of development assistance, the Economic Support Fund (ESF), Public Law (P.L.) 480; and Section 416 of the Agricultural Act of 1949.

Development assistance is project-oriented, and it has the basic aim of promoting the recipient country's economic development and welfare. The U.S. Congress determines specific priorities for identifying projects qualifying for assistance.

ESF (assistance provided for special economic, political, and security reasons), in the Philippine case, is largely tied to the agreement for continued American access to the facilities at Clark Air Base and Subic Naval Base. Under the 1979 amendment to the Bases Agreement, the U.S. government provided $200 million in ESF grants from 1979 to 1984. In 1983 the

United States agreed to provide an additional $475 million in economic support for 1985–1989.

Through the Agricultural Trade Development and Assistance Act of 1954 (P.L. 480), the United States extends support in the form of proceeds from the sale of U.S. surplus agricultural commodities, to be either loaned or donated to developing countries, including the Philippines. P.L. 480 assistance comes under four titles: Title I commodities can be sold for foreign currencies; Title II supplies famine relief and other emergency assistance; Title III commodities are donated to nonprofit voluntary organizations; and Title IV commodities can be sold for dollars under long-term credit agreements. Most of the excess agricultural commodities made available to the Philippines fall under either Title I or Title II.

Section 416 of the Agricultural Act of 1949 specifically provides that the U.S. secretary of agriculture may furnish "eligible commodities" for carrying out programs of assistance in developing countries.

Japanese economic cooperation with the Philippines falls into three categories: loan assistance, grant aid, and technical cooperation.

Japan extends a major portion of its ODA to the Philippines in the form of loans through its Overseas Economic Cooperation Fund (OECF). From 1971, when OECF began providing loans to the Philippines, to 1986, Japan's cumulative loan commitment to the Philippines amounted to 515 billion yen, or approximately $2.3 billion.

To a lesser extent, Japan offers assistance to the Philippines in the form of capital grants for building construction and equipment supply. Japan's cumulative grant aid commitment to the Philippines has amounted to about $385 million in yen.

Between fiscal years 1954 and 1985, the Japanese government provided about $130 million in yen to the Philippines in the form of expert services, training, master plan and feasibility studies, and equipment. In 1985–1986, assistance extended under technical cooperation amounted to over $30 million. A major portion of this total went to financing various projects and development surveys. The rest went for training local counterparts, expert dispatch, and limited provision of equipment.

Composition of Development Assistance Flows

Table 2 shows a breakdown of U.S. and Japanese ODA in terms of loans and grants. Two facts are worth noting. First, while the

TABLE 2.   U.S. AND JAPANESE ODA TO THE PHILIPPINES: DISTRIBUTION OF LOANS AND GRANTS (*in millions of dollars*)

	United States			
	Loans		Grants	
Period	*Amount*	*As % of total ODA to the Philippines*	*Amount*	*As % of total grants to the Philippines*
1952–1961	19.8	51.8	210.7	92.6
1962–1970	9.8	4.0	206.7	71.4
1971–1979	109.5	4.7	247.8	56.8
1980–1986	226.3	3.9	797.8	56.2
1952–1986	*365.5*	*4.3*	*1,462.9*	*61.7*

	Japan			
	Loans		Grants	
Period	*Amount*	*As % of total ODA to the Philippines*	*Amount*	*As % of total grants to the Philippines*
1952–1961	0.0	0.0	0.1	0.0
1962–1970	30.0	12.1	34.0	11.7
1971–1979	365.0	15.7	57.5	13.2
1980–1986	1,451.4	24.9	200.8	14.2
1952–1986	*1,846.4*	*21.9*	*292.4*	*11.1*

Source: Data provided to the authors by the external assistance staff of the National Economic and Development Authority of the Republic of the Philippines, Manila.

United States was a principal source of ODA loans in the 1950s, it became quite a minor provider of this type of assistance in the following decades. In contrast, Japan's share of ODA loans began to increase sharply in the 1970s. Second, whereas the United States is the principal source of grants among all ODA donors, Japan performs only a modest role in this respect; its contribution became significant only in the 1970s and remains far behind the U.S. contribution in terms of both absolute amount and share in total grants.

In the 1950s and 1960s, grants accounted for over 90 percent of U.S. ODA to the Philippines (Table 3). Though this proportion declined in the 1970s and 1980s, it remained substantial—69 percent in the 1970s and 78 percent in 1980–1986. In comparison, Japanese assistance since the 1970s has consisted mainly of loans; grants have made up only about 18–20 percent of Japanese ODA to the Philippines since OECF loans began in 1971.

Term Structure of ODA Loans

U.S. ODA loans carry an annual interest rate of 2 percent during the first ten years (grace period), and 3 percent thereafter for 30

TABLE 3.   U.S. AND JAPANESE ODA TO THE PHILIPPINES: PERCENTAGE DISTRIBUTION BY TYPE OF ASSISTANCE

Period	United States		Japan	
	Loan	Grant	Loan	Grant
1952–1961	8.6	91.4	0.0	100.00*
1962–1970	4.5	95.5	0.0	100.00*
1971–1979	30.6	69.4	81.8	18.2
1980–1986	22.1	77.9	80.2	19.8

Source: Data provided to the authors by the external assistance staff of the National Economic and Development Authority of the Republic of the Philippines, Manila.

*Japan provided assistance in the 1950s and 1960s through reparation payments in the form of grants. Loan assistance through OECF started only in 1971.

years. Japan's interest rate and loan-term structure vary according to the recipient's economic situation. For the Philippines, the interest rate has generally been 3.0–3.5 percent annually, with a repayment period of 27–30 years, inclusive of a ten-year grace period.[2]

Sectoral Allocation

The project destination of assistance differs markedly between the two donors. Most U.S. assistance is of the institution-building type, while Japanese aid focuses largely on infrastructure support. Moreover, the United States provides much more support to social services than does Japan. Domestic policies, of course, strongly influence the direction of ODA from Japan and the United States. While the orientation of Japanese ODA has by and large remained unchanged, that of the United States has undergone a number of shifts.

During the early 1950s, the thrust of U.S. assistance was geared toward the rebuilding of national institutions and the training of administrative and technical personnel to respond to the growing development efforts of the Philippines, particularly in the areas of agricultural production and education. Toward the latter half of the 1950s, U.S. ODA's emphasis shifted to investment for industrial development and the improvement of management skills in government. The passage of the U.S. Foreign Assistance Act of 1961 resulted in a gradual move toward agricultural production, community development, and a variety of social programs. Since 1973, the thrust of U.S. assistance has been aimed at improving the conditions of the rural poor.

ODA Planning and Programming

Planning and programming of assistance funds vary according to composition and source. Japan dispatches annual missions to formally discuss with the Philippine government the programming of grant assistance. For the United States, programming takes place through informal consultations between AID and NEDA, as the former maintains a fairly large mission in the Philippines. The AID staff in Manila includes 98 technical personnel. For Japan, the number of technical personnel engaged in full-time ODA administration is 24—7 from the embassy; 4 from OECF; and 13 from the government's technical assistance implementing body, the Japan International Cooperation Agency (JICA). Japan's handicap in aid administration is clear if one considers that in 1986, for example, Japan's aid to the Philippines amounted to $530 million, while U.S. assistance totaled $435 million. These figures translate to an ODA volume per staff of $22 million for Japan and $4.5 million for the United States.

In the case of the United States, however, the Philippines incurs costs related to aid administration. The host government bears the costs of office rental, housing, utilities, furniture, and even educational allowance for children of AID mission officials and employees. The Philippine government also pays salaries of local residents hired by the AID mission. In 1987, the cost of aid administration to the Philippine government was about $2.7 million. This may seem a small sum compared with the annual U.S. ODA total. However, the arrangement raises a question of principle, as the cost of maintaining the staffs of other bilateral donors in the Philippines accrue solely to their own accounts.

ODA loan programming is more complex than that for grants, inasmuch as it involves the participation of several government agencies. Project identification and monitoring for loans differ significantly between the United States and Japan.

In project identification, the United States takes the initiative in determining how much and for what purpose AID loans should be allocated. Survey missions assess the economic needs and situation of the Philippines, and their reports serve as the basis for defining medium-term (five-year) objectives and thrusts of assistance for the Philippine government. Subsequently, AID identifies the projects necessary to achieve the goals of the five-year program. It prepares the proposals and feasibility studies, sometimes with the assistance of foreign and local consultants. As a matter of practice, AID consults NEDA before presenting its proposals to Washington for approval. Upon approval by Congress, funds are released to the implementing agencies; NEDA acts as the overall coordinator in the use of funds and in the monitoring of project implementation.

For Japanese ODA loan programming, the Philippine government identifies projects within the framework of its development plans. In some cases, Japan dispatches project-finding missions to determine economic areas that the recipient country needs to tap. Once the projects are identified, the Philippine government prepares feasibility studies, following certain criteria and formats required by the Japanese government. Where it is difficult, for technical or financial reasons, for the Philippines to prepare feasibility studies, OECF offers technical assistance from JICA on a grant basis, and an engineering services loan to finance detailed engineering and the preparation of tender documents.

After identifying and designing the projects, the government of the Philippines submits a proposal to OECF which appraises the projects and issues pledges for those it finds acceptable. Approval of the assistance package is based on a consensus among four Japanese government bodies: the Ministry of Foreign Affairs (MOFA), the Ministry of Finance (MOF), the Ministry of International Trade and Industry (MITI), and the Economic Planning Agency (EPA).

An implementing officer and a secretariat represent the Philippine government in its dealings with various Japanese government agencies. The implementing officer coordinates the implementation of OECF-funded projects.

Procurement

Procurement of goods and services may be either tied or untied. In the case of the United States, procurement is generally tied. Although AID allows procurement from U.S. allies, an inventory of the agency's projects in the Philippines suggests that procurement has come solely from the United States.

In the case of Japan, procurement of goods and services is generally untied, but procurement of consultant services, financed out of OECF proceeds, is limited to Japan and less-developed countries. Because Japan has more advanced technology and greater experience than less-developed countries, Japanese firms invariably corner consultant services contracts.

In the preparation of projects, consulting and engineering services provided by the Japanese use specifications based on the Japanese International Standards, which tend to favor Japanese firms, manufacturers, and general contractors in the bidding for capital goods. Experience shows that virtually all capital goods contracts have gone to Japanese firms. In very rare instances, South Korea, Taiwan, and Singapore have won the international bidding for procurement of goods under OECF loans.

Though it is not only true in the case of the Japanese, critics have observed that Japanese firms are very active in "lobbying" for projects within the recipient country, in a way creating a demand for the goods and services they offer. According to some reports, Japanese firms have gone to the extent of promising grant or loan assistance from their government, provided the Philippine government endorsed their projects. Other reports note that the award of supply contracts for grant assistance does not seem to be subject to competitive bidding among Japanese firms.

Policy Conditionalities

So far, Japan has attached no policy conditionalities to ODA to the Philippines, and this approach is not likely to change in the foreseeable future. The United States imposed no such conditionalities until 1985, when considering a loan to finance rice importation under Title I of P.L. 480; it then specifically required the elimination of the National Food Authority's monopoly in the importation of wheat, and that of the Fertilizer and Pesticide Authority in the importation of various fertilizers.

The question of policy conditionalities is a sensitive political issue in the Philippines. Advocates of these conditionalities view them as a good way of "persuading" the government to adopt needed structural reforms. Others argue that policy conditionalities would not be objectionable if they implemented provisions that the government would have introduced anyway. Yet others resent any policy conditionality, regardless of whether it serves the national interest, for reasons of national sovereignty.

Often, the debate on policy issues becomes muddled, because the cries against foreign intervention cloud the real issue of whether a policy is good or bad for the country. This is particularly true of the discussions involving tariff reform and import liberalization, where pressure from aid donors for more substantive changes can cause a slowing down of the reform process or even a policy reversal, as lobby groups exploit the nationalist sentiments. From the viewpoint of a recipient country, it is therefore highly preferable that ODA have no policy strings attached. Aside from avoiding the kinds of political issues policy conditionalities generate, ODA untied to any such conditionality is more easily negotiated, more readily committed, and more quickly disbursed.

Summary Assessment

Table 4 presents a summary comparison of Japanese and U.S. ODA to the Philippines. A few facts merit attention. The United States has the edge with respect to loan/grant composition and loan interest rate and term structure. On the sectoral allocation of aid, as well as its general orientation, neither country is necessarily better than the other, as the allocation involves some complementarity. In fact, both the United States and Japan have taken initiatives to diversify their ODA: the United States to provide more "hard" assistance, and Japan more "soft" assistance.[3] As for Japan, one study has recommended that "in the future, there should be a significant increase in software-oriented assistance."[4]

With respect to ODA planning and programming, Japan's system is superior in the sense that it permits the recipient country to identify projects for the donor's consideration. In the case of the United States, AID initiates project identification and makes the final selection, though it does consult Philippine government agencies, particularly NEDA. Finally, Japanese ODA is not tied to policy conditionalities, while U.S. ODA is. Certainly, aid that is not subject to such conditionalities is preferable be

TABLE 4. U.S. & JAPANESE ODA TO THE PHILIPPINES: COMPARATIVE
SUMMARY, 1980–1986

Program Characteristic	United States	Japan
SHARE OF TOTAL ODA	14%	23%
SHARE OF GRANTS IN ODA	78%	20%
LOAN TERM STRUCTURE		
Annual interest rate	2% for first 10 years, 3% thereafter	3.0%–3.5% p.a.
Repayment period	40 years	27–30 years
Grace period	10 years	10 years
SECTORAL ALLOCATION	agriculture—58% social services—24% power/energy—11% transportation—7%	energy—35% transport & public works—31% industry—12% water resource—11% agriculture—8% communication—3%
PLANNING & PROGRAMMING		
Aid policy formulation	U.S. Congress, based on reports from survey missions	Consensus among Japanese MOFA, MITI, MOF, & EPA
Project identification	U.S. AID	Philippine government
Preparation of feasibility studies	U.S. AID	Philippine government with Japanese technical assistance
PROCUREMENT		
Loan assistance	Largely untied	Generally untied; technical consultancy is tied to Japan & LDCs
Grant assistance	Tied to the U.S.	Tied to Japan
POLICY CONDITIONALITIES	Yes	No

133

cause, among other reasons, it avoids the sorts of political issues that policy conditionality generates.

CONCLUSION

ODA from the United States and Japan undeniably has contributed positively to Philippine development. It has supplemented domestic savings, making additional resources available for the support of the institutional and physical infrastructure necessary to achieve Philippine development goals.[5]

Nonetheless, this contribution does not detract from the many imperfections in the process of aid giving and receiving. As John White aptly puts it: "In the history of aid, there are numerous cases of aid foolishly given, and even more foolishly accepted, the effect of which has been harmful. Every specialist in this field has his own collection of 'horror stories.'"[6] Among such horror stories, one can cite underutilized training facilities, overdesigned buildings, inappropriate technology, and an incompatible array of equipment. But one can certainly make a list of "success stories"—school buildings, roads, health clinics, water supply systems (particularly in the rural areas), irrigation facilities, power generation plants, major highways and bridges, and ports and airports.

The terms and conditions, as well as procedures, involving Japanese and U.S. ODA to the Philippines can stand improvement. For its part, the United States should adopt procedures allowing the recipient country to play a more substantive part in project identification and development. Moreover, it should find ways to reduce the red tape in the disbursement of ODA.

Japan, meanwhile, should consider the following measures: setting lower interest rates and longer repayment periods for loans; expanding the share of grants from the current 20 percent to at least 50 percent; completely untying consultancy services for OECF loans; expanding the volume of non-project loans; and conducting competitive bidding among Japanese firms in the case of projects involving grant assistance. Furthermore, Japan should pursue other modalities of financing, such as cofinancing with other bilateral agencies and multilateral institutions.

How effective is Japanese and U.S. ODA to the Philippines? This is an important but tricky question and is related to the issue of aid evaluation. The main issue is whether or not the implementation of donor-supported development programs has made any difference at all to the targeted program beneficiaries. In a report on aid evaluation, the Swedish International Development Authority concluded that both donor and recipient countries have placed little emphasis on this question.[7] AID supported a major activity in the Philippines in 1978 along this line, but the Philippine government and AID have not adequately followed up the effort. No such initiative has come from Japan.

At least two (not mutually exclusive) ways are available in which to address this gap in aid planning and policymaking. First, the United States and Japan can consider providing assistance to the Philippine government to strengthen the evaluation capacities of the appropriate government agencies. Second, they can consider integrating evaluation components into programs and projects that they finance.

Notwithstanding what the donors should do, the ultimate impact of development assistance depends on how effectively and efficiently the recipient country uses the assistance. Thus, the ball ends up in the court of the Philippine government, which must continuously strengthen its investment programming, its program implementation, its monitoring and evaluation, and, as a whole, its absorptive capacity for aid utilization.

NOTES

1. Based on commitments as of September 30, 1986.
2. The interest rate on OECF loans actually reached 4.25 percent in 1979; it dropped to 3.0 percent in 1984.
3. Hard assistance is that provided for economic infrastructure and soft assistance is for social services and basic human needs.
4. Akira Takahashi, "Country Study for Development Assistance to the Republic of the Philippines." (Paper prepared for the Country Study Group

for Development Assistance to the Philippines, Japan International Cooperation Agency, JICA, Tokyo, Japan, April 17, 1987), 4.

5. In 1980–1986, Japanese and U.S. ODA accounted for about one-fifth of foreign savings.

6. John White, *The Politics of Foreign Aid* (New York: St. Martin's Press, 1974), 22.

7. L. Johansson and M. Paues, "Aid Evaluation as a Form of Development Cooperation—What Can Donors Do?" report submitted by the Swedish International Development Authority (SIDA) to the Development Assistance Committee/Organization for Economic Cooperation and Development Expert Group on Aid Evaluation (SIDA: Stockholm, 1984).

III

Private-Sector Participation

JAPANESE DIRECT INVESTMENT AND DEVELOPMENT FINANCE

Hiroya Ichikawa

During the 1960s and early 1970s, the low-income developing countries increasingly relied upon official aid, while the middle-income countries financed their development needs with private capital.[1] In the 1980s, the dollar value of overall official development assistance (ODA) increased after reaching a trough in 1983. Private flows and export credits, however, fell off significantly. Between 1981 and 1986, for example, bank loans dropped from $52 billion to $5 billion, and official and private export credits fell from $18.4 billion to $2 billion.

Meanwhile, developing countries—the traditional net recipients of capital—have been transferring net resources to the outside world. As a result, their living standards and levels of income and investment have suffered. The outflows, running at an annual rate of $30 billion in 1985–1986, are likely to continue in the near future, rising to nearly $40 billion in the early 1990s.

Another remarkable imbalance has characterized the 1990s. The United States has become the world's largest capital importing and net debtor nation, while Japan has emerged as the world's largest capital exporter and creditor. In 1987, Japan's net outflow of long-term capital (including private overseas direct investments, portfolio investments, and loans) totaled $137 billion, and its current account surplus reached a peak of $87 billion. However, most of Japan's capital outflow went to advanced countries in 1986; only 12 percent flowed to developing countries.

Against this backdrop, many observers—and most notably, the World Institute for Development Economics Research (WIDER)—have stressed the importance of finding an appropriate mechanism for recycling Japan's current account surplus to developing countries. Assuming these surpluses of Japan and some other developed countries are likely to continue for the next several years, the WIDER report has emphasized that Japan should take the initiative to bring about a restoration of resource transfer to the level of the early 1980s, when net inflows into developing countries were around $30 billion.[2] To achieve this objective, it will be necessary to effect financial transfers of at least $60–$70 billion annually over the next seven or eight years. While the social marginal productivity of these resources would be very high in the developing countries, an appropriate mechanism is lacking for transferring the savings of surplus countries to productive investment in deficit developing countries.

The Japanese government seems to have gone some distance in finding such a mechanism. In 1989, it committed to transfer more than $65 billion to the developing world over the period 1987–1992. This recycling mechanism involves enhanced access for the World Bank to Japan's domestic capital market; contributions to the International Development Association (IDA) and the International Monetary Fund (IMF); cofinancing with the World Bank by Japan's Overseas Economic Cooperation Fund (OECF), the Export-Import Bank of Japan (Exim Bank), and private banks; and direct untied financing by Exim Bank.

While Japan's official policy intention is to facilitate the flow of public and private financial resources to the middle-income debtor countries through the $65 billion Recycling Plan, the plan so far has failed to stimulate heavy private-sector involvement. For example, Exim Bank's cofinancing with the World Bank has induced very limited participation by private banks.

The purpose of this chapter is to argue that foreign direct investment is the most effective vehicle for Japan's private sector to provide development finance. This next section summarizes the distinguishing features of foreign direct investment and host-country conditions for attracting it, along with a regional breakdown of trends in, and the problems and prospects for, Japanese direct investment in the Third World. Following that is an examination of the role of public policy for encouraging private foreign direct investment, including discussion of a recent private-sector initiative in Japan for promoting direct investment in the developing world.

JAPAN'S DIRECT INVESTMENT IN THE THIRD WORLD

In the case of direct investment, capital flows largely to industries in which the investing country has the comparative advantage but in which it is possible for the recipient country to gain. Direct investment, unlike portfolio investment, exerts a degree of control over the management of the business unit. It promotes the dissemination of valuable knowledge and entrepreneurship in the form of research and development, production technology, marketing skills, managerial expertise, and so on. That is, direct investment is a vehicle for the dissemination of these inputs and services, not simply a provider of finance. Thus, direct investment—particularly in manufacturing—is more likely than portfolio investment to promote economic growth.

When private enterprises consider investment possibilities, they examine such issues as political stability, whether or not the recipient government is democratically elected, and the legal framework affecting the nature and scope of foreign investment. Foreign investors look for countries with comparative advantage in terms of the cost of certain inputs, including labor and natural resources. Countries with an open, receptive attitude toward foreigners and foreign capital, as well as strong, sophisticated local partners to do business with, are the most attractive to foreign direct investors. By contrast, investors avoid economies that are overregulated or where excessive government intervention stifles entrepreneurship. Businessmen favor countries that have normal, smooth relations with their trading partners and their creditors around the world. Finally, the size of domestic markets is an important factor, because strong local demand can complement export potential.

Recent Japanese direct investment overseas, particularly after the Plaza Agreement on currency realignment in 1985, appears to have had two primary motivations. The first is to establish manufacturing facilities in Japan's major foreign markets in response to protectionist pressures. The second is the search for low-wage production sites. Japanese companies are shifting their assembly away from the newly industrialized countries (NICs), where labor costs are no longer attractive. The appreciation of the NICs' currencies against the dollar also eroded the competitiveness of their business operations. While much of Japanese investment in the United States and Europe may be a response to trade friction, direct investment in Asia is often aimed at building up offshore export bases. The advantage of low production costs and incentives by host governments in the region influence Japanese investment behavior.

The Association of Southeast Asian Nations

Japan's direct investment in Asia amounted to $32 billion over the period 1951–1988, accounting for 17 percent of its direct investment overseas (Table 1). Following the Plaza Agreement in September 1985, Japanese direct investment to members of the

---

TABLE 1. JAPANESE DIRECT INVESTMENT OVERSEAS, BY REGION
(*in billions of dollars*)

Fiscal year	North America	Europe	Asia	Central & Latin America	Oceania	Africa	Middle East
1984	3.54	1.94	1.63	2.30	.16	.33	.27
1985	5.50	1.93	1.44	2.62	.53	.17	.05
1986	10.44	3.47	2.33	4.74	.99	.31	.04
1987	15.36	6.58	4.87	4.82	1.41	.27	.06
1988	22.33	9.12	5.57	6.43	2.67	.65	.26
1951–1988	*75.09*	*30.16*	*32.23*	*31.62*	*9.32*	*1.30*	*.33*
(% share)	(40.30)	(16.20)	(17.30)	(17.00)	(5.00)	(2.50)	(1.80)

Source: Japan External Trade Organization, "1990 JETRO White Paper on Foreign Direct Investment" (in Japanese), Toyko, January 1990.

Association of Southeast Asian Nations (ASEAN) increased rapidly (Table 2).

Each ASEAN member-country has specified policies on how and where foreign investors may participate. They have drawn up general guidelines and identified specific priority industries. Since these nations consider foreign direct investment, particularly from Japan, as vital to industrialization and balance-of-payments stability, they have been more than willing to attract it by relaxing policies on foreign investment and offering attractive tax incentives.

According to estimates by the Ministry of International Trade and Industry (MITI), in 1988 Japanese companies located overseas produced goods equivalent to 4 percent of Ja-

TABLE 2. JAPANESE DIRECT INVESTMENT IN ASIA
(*in millions of dollars*)

Country	1986	1987	1988	1951–1988	% share 1951–1988
NIEs*					
Korea	436	647	484	3,248	1.7
Taiwan	291	367	372	1,791	1.0
Hong Kong	502	1,072	1,662	6,167	3.3
Singapore	302	494	747	3,812	2.0
ASEAN					
Thailand	124	250	859	1,992	1.1
Malaysia	158	163	387	1,834	1.0
Philippines	21	72	134	1,120	0.6
Indonesia	250	545	586	9,804	5.3
Others	243	1,258	337	2,459	1.3
Total	*2,327*	*4,868*	*5,569*	*32,227*	
(% share)	(10.4)	(14.6)	(11.8)	(17.3)	

Source: Japan External Trade Organization, "1990 JETRO White Paper on Foreign Direct Investment" (in Japanese), January 1990, Tokyo.

*Newly industrializing economies.

pan's gross domestic product (GDP), or roughly $100 billion. By 1993, this figure might rise to 8 percent, or $230 billion. About one-quarter to one-third of this increase—representing a volume of output comparable with that of ASEAN's industrial sector—is likely to originate from Japanese firms located in Asia. Japanese companies in ASEAN countries export an estimated 40–70 percent of their total sales, primarily to third countries and, in the latest wave, back to Japan. Japanese direct investment is likely to play a critical role in raising the capacity of ASEAN economies to industrialize, accelerate the inflow of non–debt-creating resources, boost exports and foreign exchange earnings, and effect real technology transfer.[3]

Most Japanese-affiliated companies overseas have promoted the localization of their parts production, fostering related industries in the host economies. In a move toward export-oriented industrialization from the earlier import-substitution approach, the ASEAN countries have had to acquire higher technologies, technical know-how, managerial skills, and knowledge of international business. In this transition, the ASEAN governments have provided incentives to foreign companies that own higher technologies and have export knowledge, and the Japanese companies have responded to these demands.

Latin America

Reported data show that Japanese direct investment in Latin America increased during the 1980s (Table 3). The 1988 total of $6.4 billion was about eleven times the 1980 figure (not shown). However, most of the recent Japanese investments in the region went to the Cayman Islands and the Bahamas for tax haven-related financial services and insurance, and to Panama for flag-of-convenience shipping. No substantial manufacturing investments were made in Brazil, Mexico, Argentina, or other heavily indebted countries. Certainly, investment in banking and insurance services can bring benefits to the host countries. However, in view of current economic conditions prevailing in Latin American countries, it would seem much more important for these

TABLE 3. JAPANESE DIRECT INVESTMENT IN LATIN AMERICA
(*in millions of dollars*)

Country	1986	1987	1988	1951– 1988	% share 1951– 1988
HEAVILY INDEBTED					
Brazil	270	229	510	5,596	3.0
Mexico	226	28	87	1,671	0.9
Argentina	17	15	24	215	0.1
Chile	2	7	46	235	0.1
Venezuela	4	3	51	189	0.1
OTHER					
Panama	2,401	2,305	1,712	12,858	6.9
Cayman Islanas	930	1,197	2,609	5,085	2.7
Bahamas	792	734	737	2,718	1.5
Antilles	66	199	172	747	0.4
Bermuda	16	36	337	991	0.5
Total	*4,737*	*4,816*	*6,428*	*31,617*	*17.0*

Source: Japan External Trade Organization, "1990 JETRO White Paper on Foreign Direct Investment" (in Japanese), January 1990, Tokyo.

economies to accommodate expanded foreign direct investment in the manufacturing sector.

In particular, foreign direct investment can serve debtor Latin American economies in the following two ways. First, the inflow of investment supplies greatly needed funds without increasing repayment obligations. Second, direct investment transfers technologies and know-how that are essential for private-sector development. Private enterprises usually undertake thorough feasibility studies before implementing capital outlays because they have to directly bear the risks involved. Therefore, they generally use funds from direct investment with maximum effectiveness.

Various obstacles, however, discourage Japanese direct investment in Latin America. In March 1989, the Japan-Venezuela

Economic Committee of Keidanren (Japan's Federation of Economic Organizations) conducted a survey of the 40 Japanese corporations that make up its membership. Regarding Venezuela's investment environment, 50 percent of the respondents said that "some improvement" has occurred but not enough to "substantially encourage" their investment activities in the country. In addition, 25 percent felt that "the environment is getting worse." Table 4 presents a summary of the respondents' assessment of the investment environment of six Latin American countries as compared with that of Venezuela. Chile emerges as the country providing the most favorable environment for direct investment, whereas Peru turns out to be the least attractive.

In February 1989, under the auspices of MITI, a joint government-industry mission visited Brazil and Mexico to study the environment for foreign investment in those countries. According to the mission's report, factors inhibiting direct investment in Brazil included "restrictions on the ratio of foreign equity ownership," "local content requirement," and "progressive taxation and restrictions on the repatriation of dividends and royalties." Regarding Mexico, the report points to the following areas as requiring improvement: "industrial infrastructures such as water supply, telecommunications, electric power supply and harbor facilities"; "the development of supporting industries such as materials and parts and components"; and "the education of technicians and engineers."[4]

The debt problem is also an obstacle to direct investment in Latin America. The foreign exchange scarcity forces an increase in Latin American exports, but this surge in exports is often the consequence of reduced domestic consumption rather than newly installed production capacity. The absence of new flows of resources and the necessity to generate trade surplus prevent attaining desirable levels of income and domestic consumption.

PUBLIC POLICY AND PRIVATE INITIATIVES

Governments, the private sector, and international financial institutions must look for new mechanisms to finance economic

TABLE 4. KEIDANREN SURVEY RESULTS: HOW THE INVESTMENT ENVIRONMENT
IN SIX MAJOR LATIN AMERICAN COUNTRIES COMPARES WITH VENEZUELA

Characteristic	Brazil	Mexico	Peru	Chile	Argentina	Colombia
Macroeconomic environment	worse	unsure/ better	worse	unsure/ better	worse	worse/ unsure
Infrastructure	better	better	worse	unsure	unsure/ better	worse
Efficiency of administration	unsure	unsure	worse	better	unsure/ worse	unsure/ worse
Overall production control	better	better	worse	better	unsure/ better	unsure
Quality control	better	better	worse	better	better	unsure
Delivery term control	better	unsure/ better	worse	better	unsure/ better	unsure
Strict observation of contracts	unsure/ better	unsure/ better	worse	better	unsure/ better	unsure
Overall labor environment	unsure/ better	better	worse	better	unsure/ better	unsure/ worse
Quality of workers	better	unsure	worse	better	better	unsure/ worse
Wage level	unsure	unsure	worse	better	unsure/ better	unsure/ worse
Leave, working regulation, & other aspects of labor law	unsure	unsure	unsure	unsure	unsure/ better	unsure/ worse
Taxation	unsure	unsure	worse	unsure	unsure	unsure
Financial aspect	unsure/ worse	unsure	worse	unsure/ better	unsure/ worse	unsure
Import control	unsure/ worse	unsure/ better	worse	unsure	unsure/ worse	unsure/ worse
Remittance of dividend	unsure/ worse	unsure	worse	unsure	worse	unsure/ worse
Foreign exchange policy	unsure/ worse	unsure	worse	unsure	worse	unsure

Source: "Economic Relations Between Venezuela and Japan," a March 1989 Keidanren survey of
executives of 40 major Japanese corporations operating in Latin America (unpublished),
Toyko, November 1989.

Note: When more than one assessment appears, respondents were equally divided between the two.

147

development and promote growth in debtor developing countries. A number of Latin American nations, including Mexico, are making serious efforts toward economic structural adjustment. These efforts include boosting national savings and allocating them to more efficient investment; promoting import liberalization under realistic exchange rates; improving the trade balance by encouraging export-oriented industries; and promoting privatization of inefficient state-run enterprises.

While the fundamental incentives to accelerate private international direct investment into Latin America will be political and economic stability and an improved investment environment, the response of developed countries is also critical. Fulfillment of a number of vital conditions is necessary for private business enterprises to engage themselves in market-oriented activities that contribute to international social and economic welfare. Among these conditions are concluding intergovernmental investment guarantee treaties, improving the insurance system for deferred export payments and overseas investment, improving the tax system to allow more reserves for losses incurred as a result of overseas investment, and ensuring assistance from the Multilateral Investment Guarantee Agency (MIGA).

Viewed from Japan, for instance, the trade insurance system under the jurisdiction of MITI and the guarantee function of Exim Bank play an extremely important role in the development of overseas direct investment by private companies. Since private banks and other private financial institutions face difficulties in providing new loans to high-risk debtor nations, the reduction of risk is essential to the promotion of overseas direct investment and new lending to developing countries experiencing debt-servicing problems.

Unless creditor governments and multilateral development and financial institutions play an active part in reducing risk, private enterprises are not likely to seek involvement in Third World projects. For example, the rigidity of the deeply interconnected system of Exim Bank's finance, MITI's trade and investment insurance, and MITI's export license of transactions that involve deferred payments over a period in excess of two years hinder Japanese direct investment in developing countries. Under the present system, unless potential investors have the coverage of MITI's trade and investment insurance system, Exim Bank will not finance projects. But the weak finance base of MITI's trade and investment insurance system makes it difficult to provide insurance coverage for trade with and investment in debtor countries. Without appropriate support from the Japanese government, however, private enterprises are not likely to promote overseas investment projects, thus hindering government efforts to recycle Japan's private-sector surplus into developing countries.

A Japanese Private-Sector Initiative

The Japanese business community established the Japan International Development Organization (JAIDO) in April 1989 for the promotion of export industries in developing countries and for the expansion of exports of their products into the Japanese market. JAIDO's philosophy is that the private sector's economic cooperation in the form of overseas private investment, financing, technology transfer, and identification and planning of potential development projects for developing countries has an important role to play.

The organization, which is open to Japanese and foreign firms alike, makes equity investments of a pump-primer nature to encourage private enterprises to participate in development projects. Another important feature of JAIDO is that it seeks various governments' support for projects through close communication and consultation with related government agencies and international organizations. Projects eligible for JAIDO investment are associated with a variety of difficulties and risks, and they require sophisticated considerations related to foreign policy.

The purpose of such experimental activities is to demonstrate that private overseas direct investment in developing countries can successfully take place when governments, the private sector, and international financial institutions are prepared to coordinate with each other. JAIDO's investment projects are strategically confined to those that will improve export earning capacity of the host countries and, whenever possible, produce for imports back into the Japanese market. When these conditions are fulfilled, JAIDO will seek MITI trade insurance coverage, as well as MIGA financing and Exim Bank guarantees to implement the projects. In addition, it will seek ODA resources partially directed toward improving infrastructure for private-sector development projects. JAIDO would also like to see more cooperation between the bilateral aid organizations of different countries.

CONCLUSION

Current trends suggest that Japanese direct investment overseas will increase greatly in the future. Japanese investors are, however, not particularly interested in developing countries outside Southeast Asia. While the developing countries express great interest in attracting foreign investment, many of them have not yet undertaken economic and political reforms sufficient to attract Japanese investors. Unless they do, JAIDO's efforts may turn out to be just a drop in the ocean.

Over the longer haul, however, foreign investment will have a growing importance in financing development. More and more developing countries will seek assistance to build market economies and rely on private-sector initiatives for fostering economic development. While old ideological debates still echo, the new consensus on the importance of private-sector growth is basically a pragmatic response to a search for faster growth and more efficiency in achieving social objectives.

NOTES

1. According to the 1990 World Bank definition, low-income developing countries are those with a 1988 per capita GNP of $545 or less, and middle-income developing countries are those with a 1988 per capita GNP of between $546 and $5,999. World Bank, *World Development Report* (Washington, D.C.: 1990).

2. "Mobilizing International Surplus for World Development—A WIDER Plan for a Japanese Initiative," World Institute for Development Economics Research of the United Nations University, *Study Group Series,* no. 2, Helsinki, Finland, May 1987.

3. Stefen C. M. Wong, "Japan's Contribution to ASEAN Economic Cooperation: Managing Change in a Relationship." (Paper presented at the Second Japan-ASEAN Conference, Bali, Indonesia, March 1989).

4. Japan Overseas Enterprise Association, "Report on the Investment Climate in Brazil and Mexico" (in Japanese), Tokyo, June 1989.

JAPANESE BANKS AND THIRD WORLD DEBT

Shoji Ochi

Nearly a decade has passed since the Mexican government requested a moratorium on its debt repayments in 1982. These years have included periods of hope, such as in 1984, when it appeared that the Third World debt problem might be resolved in the midst of the worldwide economic boom. Since then, however, the debt crisis has intensified, and prospects for a solution again look grim. At first it seemed that resolving the problem would take five to ten years. Today, however, it has become clear that the issues regarding debt must be thought through over a period of a decade or two.

In light of these circumstances, the attitudes of the Japanese commercial banks toward Third World debt have undergone subtle changes. Until 1986, the Japanese banks were relatively passive, owing to their belief that the debt problem was basically a U.S. bank problem and that they would not be badly hit. However, the increasing realization of the prolonged nature of the problem has led the Japanese banks to understand that they need to move more actively and strategically. The objectives these banks are trying to pursue, although still not concrete, come down essentially to two points:

- Evade the extension of new money.

- With voluntary debt reduction as the base, press for reasonable burden-sharing among the parties concerned.

In this chapter, I summarize the evolving response of the Japanese banks to the debt problem by focusing on the above two points.[1]

THE DEBT PROBLEM: THREE STAGES

It is useful to divide the years since 1982 into three stages to understand the policies of Japanese banks regarding Third World debt. The first stage was a three-year period that started in August 1982, when the Mexican government sought a suspension of its debt repayments. During this period, the Japanese banks' first task was to conduct so-called fact-finding. They tried to estimate the total exposure of Japan's commercial banks to developing countries and the total outstanding debt of each debtor country to banks all over the world.

The Japanese banks went along with reschedulings and offered new loans to debtor countries, in the belief that these countries were simply confronted with a liquidity problem. Accordingly, Japanese banks' total claims on developing countries did not decline during this period; rather, in fact, they showed a slight increase.

The second stage began in September 1985, when the Baker Plan (a program that emphasized growth over austerity for the debtor countries) was announced, and continued for almost two years. At first, the Japanese banks reacted favorably toward the Baker Plan. However, they began to feel profound dissatisfaction with it because they realized that the plan requested new loans only from international organizations and commercial banks, and did not demand any commitment from creditor governments.

The Japanese government, as well as the U.S. government, held the notion that the debt problem was a problem of commercial banks and should be resolved by the banks themselves—a notion that engendered a negative attitude toward the Baker Plan among the banks. At the same time, the banks asked that the government give them careful consideration in exchange for their extending new credit to indebted countries; in particular, they requested changes in both the taxation and the accounting systems regarding loan-loss reserves. Under these circumstances, many banks concluded by 1987 that the time had come for them to dispose of their loans voluntarily, either in the secondary market or through debt-equity conversion schemes.

Thus the third stage, which remains in progress, began at the end of 1987. The most significant characteristic of this stage is that the Japanese banks now view the debt problem as a matter of insolvency, or, at least, they regard insolvency as a large part of the problem.

Another characteristic of this stage is that the almost doubling of the value of the yen against the U.S. dollar after the September 1985 Plaza Agreement, to drive the dollar down among the group of five major industrialized countries, substantially reduced the yen value of the dollar-denominated exposure to heavily indebted countries. The outstanding amount of such loans of the 23 largest Japanese commercial banks has remained around $38 billion from 1983 to 1987. However, the yen value has declined from approximately 10 trillion yen at the end of 1983 to 5 trillion yen in 1987. Moreover, the Japanese banks have increased their total assets from approximately 300 trillion yen to 500 trillion yen during this period. Thus, the Japanese banks can write off their outstanding loans and feel little pain, as the heavily indebted countries' loans now represent only 1 percent of their total assets.[2]

THIRD WORLD LOANS: PRIVATE EXPOSURE AND PUBLIC RESPONSE

The Japanese banks are in a much better position than their American and European counterparts in terms of their degree of exposure relative to their financial strength (Table 1). In all, 14 U.S. banks have $59.5 billion in outstanding exposure to developing countries, while the figure for 8 Japanese banks is $20.8 billion; these totals represent 115 percent and 30 percent, respectively, of the banks' primary capital. Furthermore, 13 Japanese banks have combined hidden assets (capital gains on equity holding) of 29.7 trillion yen, or about $240 billion.

The discounted price of debts in the recent secondary market is roughly 30 percent. Therefore, if 70 percent of the out-

TABLE 1. COMMERCIAL BANKS' EXPOSURE TO DEVELOPING COUNTRIES

	United States*	Canada†	England‡	France§	West Germany**	Japan††
	In billions of $					
Exposure to developing countries	59.5	14.1	21.3	23.9	10.7	20.8
Hidden loss (assumed to be 70% of exposure)	41.7	9.8	14.0	16.7	7.5	14.6
Loan-loss provisions for exposure	15.4	6.5	10.1	12.1	5.7	3.1
Primary capital	52.8	20.3	29.0	26.3	14.6	67.0
	In percent					
Provisions/exposure ratio	25.9	46.1	47.4	50.6	53.3	15.0
Exposure/capital ratio	112.7	69.5	73.4	90.9	73.3	30.6
Hidden loss/ provisions ratio	270.8	152.2	147.5	138.0	131.6	471.0
Hidden loss/capital ratio	79.0	48.8	51.3	63.5	51.4	21.5

Source: Compiled by the author from resources at the Japan Center for International Finance, Tokyo, Japan.

* Exposure and loan-loss provisions as of end of 1988. The banks involved are Bank of New York, Bank of Boston, BankAmerica, Bankers Trust, Chase Manhattan, Chemical, Citicorp, First Chicago, First Interstate, J.P. Morgan, Manufacturers Hanover, Republic Bank of New York, Security Pacific, and Wells Fargo.

† Exposure and loan-loss provisions as of July 31, 1989. The banks involved are Bank of Montreal, Canadian Imperial, National Bank, Royal Bank, Scotiabank, and Toronto-Dominion.

‡ Exposure and loan-loss provisions as of June 30, 1989. The banks involved are Barclays, Lloyds Bank, Midland Bank, and National Westminster.

§ Exposure and loan-loss provisions as of end of 1988. The banks involved are Banque Indosuez, Banque Nationale de Paris, Banque Paribas, Crédit Agricole, Crédit Industriel et Commercial, Credit Commercial de France, Crédit Lyonnais, Groupe Paribas, and Société Générale.

** Exposure and loan-loss provisions as of end of 1988. The banks involved are Commerzbank, Deutsche Bank, and Dresdner Bank.

†† Exposure and loan-loss provisions as of March 31, 1989. The banks involved are Bank of Tokyo, Dai-ichi Kangyo, Fuji Bank, Industrial Bank of Japan, Mitsubishi Bank, Mitsui Bank, Sanwa Bank, and Sumitomo Bank.

standing loans represent hidden losses, these losses approach an estimated 80 percent of primary capital in the case of U.S. banks. In the case of Japanese banks, however, they equal only 22 percent of primary capital. Moreover, by taking advantage of their enormous hidden assets, the Japanese banks may not have to set aside profits to absorb the hidden losses. In other words, these banks have the strength to cope with any unfolding circumstance. The conclusion remains valid even if we consider the financial positions of the individual Japanese banks (Table 2).

Japanese banks, however, do have specific criticisms of Japanese government policies. In this regard, two points are crucial.

First, government restrictions limit the banks' loan-loss reserves for outstanding exposure to problem nations to merely 25 percent. The U.S. banks, on the other hand, have accumulated reserves of close to 50 percent, and many European banks have reserved or written off even more aggressively. Accumulation of adequate loan-loss reserves is an iron rule of sound banking. Thus, the Japanese restrictions not only financially weaken the

---

TABLE 2.   DEVELOPING-COUNTRY LOAN EXPOSURE OF MAJOR JAPANESE
BANKS, DECEMBER 31, 1988

Bank	Equity (billions of yen)	Gross exposure (billions of yen)	Equity as % of exposure	Gross exposure (millions of $)
Bank of Tokyo	674	664	98	5,008
Dai-ichi Kangyo	1,321	339	26	2,557
Fuji Bank	1,378	329	24	2,485
Ind. Bk. of Japan	1,149	262	23	1,977
Mitsubishi Bank	1,284	339	26	2,558
Mitsui Bank	720	131	18	988
Sanwa Bank	1,159	300	26	2,264
Sumitomo Bank	1,284	380	30	2,868
Total	8,969	2,743	31	20,705

Source: Salomon Brothers, "Stock Research," November 16, 1989, Figure 1, pp. 2–3.

banks but also significantly limit their flexibility in managing their loan positions.

Second, Japanese policy forbids the sale of developing-country loans except for debt-equity swaps, which are permitted on a case-by-case basis. The declared intent of this rule is to prevent prices from falling in the secondary market. At the same time, another purpose seems to be that of averting a reduction in the tax revenue resulting from the losses caused by such sales. These restrictions, along with the low level of loan-loss reserves, are the major factors barring the Japanese banks from participating in the secondary market.

DEBT REDUCTION: FROM MIYAZAWA TO BRADY

Since the U.S. administration stuck to a rather conservative stance on the debt strategy in 1986 and 1987, the expectation that Japan will play an active role has been growing. In addition to the 1987 announcement of the $30 billion Recycling Plan, in 1988 the Japanese government proposed the Miyazawa Plan, which aimed at alleviating the debt burden of middle-income debtor countries.

The important characteristics of the Miyazawa Plan were as follows:

- Kiichi Miyazawa, finance minister of the Japanese government, proposed the initiative as an additional item to the U.S.–sponsored "menu approach," for relieving the burden of debtor countries.

- The plan preserved the principles of the case-by-case approach and voluntary participation of private banks, as well as the conditionality of International Monetary Fund (IMF) economic reform programs.

- In terms of burden-sharing between the private and official sectors, the plan put an emphasis on the possibility that bilateral funds from the industrialized countries, as well as multilateral funds from the international financial institutions, would support the structural adjustment programs.

- The debtor countries' special reserve accounts, which they funded with their own resources and which the IMF held in trust, were to "enhance" the restructured loans.

The Japanese banks generally welcomed the scheme because the framework was broadly consistent with their strategy. They especially welcomed the case-by-case approach and the burden-sharing principle. Domestic U.S. electoral politics, however, prevented the United States from supporting the plan, effectively nipping it in the bud.

In March 1989, elements of the Miyazawa Plan resurfaced as part of a new debt strategy proposed by U.S. Treasury Secretary Nicholas Brady. Initially, the Japanese banks warmly accepted the Brady Plan, chiefly for two reasons. First, it endorsed debt and debt-service reduction as a necessary measure for dealing with the debt problem, thus opening the way to resolve the impasse of the Baker Plan. Second, the Brady Plan called for an increased role of international financial organizations and the governments of creditor countries, reflecting the recognition that no solution to the debt problem will be possible unless those official institutions assume a more positive role.[3]

However, in the summer of 1989, when the Brady Plan was first employed during Mexico's debt negotiations, a number of problems emerged, owing to inappropriate applications—and not to any defect—of the plan. Among them, Japanese banks considered the following the most important:

- The contradiction between allowing debt reduction and extending new money to the same debtor.

- The apparent shortage of credit enhancement provided by official institutions and creditor countries.

- The lack of a concrete proposal by the Mexican government to prevent capital flight and to promote the repatriation of such capital.

As a result, the basic attitude of the Japanese banks toward the debt problem is once again changing. They have decided to act more positively and strategically. Although it is not easy to say precisely what strategies they will pursue, the banks seem to want to do the following:

- Avoid any increase in their claims on the problem countries.

- Ask for further deregulation on the sales of such claims in the secondary market.

- Achieve an equal burden-sharing among the official institutions and banks.

- Require that debtor countries pursue a strict financial and fiscal discipline.

CONCLUSION

Three points regarding a possible solution to the debt problem deserve emphasis.

First is the relation between the Brady Plan and the Mexican package. During the Mexican debt negotiations, the expectations of the private banks toward the plan turned into despair. The Brady Plan came onstage hastily, without adequate attention given to its implementation; for example, it lacks a concrete mechanism of burden-sharing.

Second, the U.S. government should demonstrate leadership with respect to the debt problem. It is difficult to obtain the cooperation of European countries when the U.S. government does not provide sufficient financial support, and it is impossible for Japan to provide all of the necessary funding.

Third is the issue of consultation with Japanese banks. As pointed out earlier, Japanese banks are rapidly strengthening their strategic response to the debt problem, taking a flexible but somewhat firm stance. In other words, they are prepared to assume a confrontational position if necessary. It has become critical, therefore, for the governments as well as commercial banks in creditor nations to take into account the views of the Japanese banks in dealing with the debt problem of developing countries.

NOTES

1. I have used the comprehensive term "Japanese banks," but among institutions, needless to say, viewpoints differ.
2. This estimate and the data cited in the following two paragraphs refer to the situation prevailing in 1988–1989; the Japanese banks' capital base and hence their capacity to absorb loan losses have deteriorated since then.— *Editor's Note.*
3. Similarly, the Japanese banks had welcomed the July 1988 decision of the Japanese government to offer $12 billion to be utilized for implementing debt reduction. This was included in the $35 billion component added to the Japanese trade surplus Recycling Plan in 1989, bringing the total plan to $65 billion.

COMMENT

Barbara Stallings

People in all parts of the world—from voters in Lima to politicians in Washington—are demanding that Japan take a leading role in the promotion of development in the Third World. The basis for this demand is Japan's enormous trade surplus, juxtaposed with the equally enormous need for capital in most parts of Africa, Asia, and Latin America. The lack of alternative sources of funds—since the United States has become a capital importer and Western Europe has turned its sights toward the needs of its neighbors to the east—buttresses the demand.

The main problem with the expectations about Japan is that the country's surplus is in the hands of the private sector, while the central government is in deficit. Thus, if Japan is to participate in the development process, the private sector must play a crucial role. Because the private sector's goal is not to promote development but to make profits, the question arises as to whether the two objectives can be made compatible. My comments will first review what the private sector has done and then make some proposals for future directions.

The very useful chapters by Hiroya Ichikawa and Shoji Ochi discuss the main features of Japanese foreign direct investment and bank loans, the two principal sources of private capital. Similar trends are evident for both during the 1980s, and they suggest some of the difficulties inherent in relying on private capital for the promotion of development. As Table 1 shows, the focus of foreign direct investment and bank loans has undergone a significant move away from the Third World and toward the advanced industrial countries. Thus, in 1980, some 46 percent of Japanese foreign direct investment went to members of the Organization for Economic Cooperation and Development (OECD), and the remaining 54 percent to the Third World. By 1988, the shares had changed to 62 percent and 38 percent,

161

TABLE 1.   REGIONAL COMPOSITION OF JAPANESE OVERSEAS INVESTMENT
(*in billions of dollars*)

Type of resource & region	1980		1988	
	Amount	% of total	Amount	% of total
FOREIGN DIRECT INVESTMENT (CUMULATIVE)				
OECD	16.8	46.0	114.6	61.5
Third World	19.7	54.0	71.8	38.5
Asia	9.8	26.9	32.2	17.3
Latin America	6.2	16.9	31.6	16.9
Africa	1.4	4.0	4.6	2.5
Middle East	2.3	6.2	3.3	1.8
Total	*36.5*	*100.0*	*186.4*	*100.0*
PRIVATE BANK DEBT (MEDIUM- & LONG-TERM)*				
OECD	12.3	35.7	155.7	62.8
Third World	22.2	64.3	92.3	37.2
Asia	3.8	11.0	38.5	13.6
Latin America	14.2	41.3	45.8	16.1
Africa	3.5	10.1	7.0	2.5
Middle East	0.7	1.9	1.0	0.3
Total	*34.5*	*100.0*	*248.1*	*100.0*

Source: Estimates provided to author by Ministry of Finance, Tokyo, Japan.

* Excludes Eastern Europe and international organizations. Medium- and long-term is
defined as longer than one year.

respectively. Similarly, the OECD share of private bank loans
rose from 36 percent in 1980 to 63 percent in 1988, while the
Third World portion fell correspondingly from 64 percent to 37
percent.

These trends are not surprising; they reflect the belief of
Japanese investors, whether banks or nonfinancial corporations,
that the advanced industrial countries could provide better returns. Many factors contributed to this belief: relative growth
rates generally favored the United States and Western Europe

(the Asian exception is discussed below). So did the need to get inside those markets to prevent exclusion in the future, whether owing to the 1992 processes in Europe or to domestic protectionism in the United States. At the same time, through the 1980s, much of the Third World was mired in the worst economic crisis since the depression of the 1930s, and unstable political environments exacerbated the economic problems.

Within the Third World itself, an analogous process took place. Japanese aid shifted away from those regions most in need of development assistance and toward those that were already doing well. Thus, trends in Japanese capital to the Third World show an increase in the share of bank debt for Asian countries and a decrease for all others—although Latin America remains the region with the largest absolute debt to Japanese banks. The picture for foreign direct investment is more difficult to interpret. Investment in Latin America appears to have grown very rapidly, from $6 billion in 1980 to $32 billion in 1988. Most of that increase, however, has been financial investment in the Caribbean or flag-of-convenience shipping in Panama. Subtracting those activities suggests that "real economy" investment has also shifted toward Asia. Africa and the Middle East account for a minuscule share of both types of Japanese capital.

Like the move toward the advanced industrial countries, the shifts within the Third World are perfectly comprehensible from the viewpoint of Japanese private investors. Not only is Asia the fastest-growing region in the world, it also is more open to foreign capital than others, and more familiar to the Japanese for historical and cultural reasons. Thus, it is quite logical that Japanese firms would have greater interest in investing in Asia than elsewhere. The apparent move toward greater integration of the Asian economies provides an added impetus in this direction.

Apart from the geographic shifts, what can be said about Japanese private capital flows in the 1980s? In terms of foreign direct investment, sectoral changes have also been very important in Third World countries. Investment in the 1970s was concentrated in the productive sectors. In Latin America, for example, 46 percent of Japanese direct investment was in manufacturing (mainly in Brazil and Mexico). Another 30 percent was in agriculture, fishing, mining, and construction. Only 24 percent was in services (including finance and transportation). By the second half of the 1980s, those figures had changed dramatically. The share going to manufacturing was down to 7 percent, that to other productive sectors had dropped to 1 percent, while the proportion going to services (mainly shipping in Panama and financial services in the Caribbean) had ballooned to 92 percent.[1]

While finance and transportation are certainly necessary for development, the particular investments mentioned above are not geared toward the developing countries themselves. The financial investments are probably a base for lending to the United States, unrelated to the economies of the Caribbean islands, while flag-of-convenience shipping in Panama and Liberia serves Japan's worldwide trading network rather than the host countries' development needs. The older style of direct investment—in manufacturing, or even in natural resources—had a bigger spinoff for development purposes, even if those investments were also aimed at supplying the Japanese market. They had a larger potential for generating local employment and for creating linkages with the domestic economies in host countries.

The activities of Japanese banks in the 1980s also raise questions with respect to the development process. In relative terms, Japanese financial institutions have been better "citizens" than their counterparts in the United States and Europe. They have stayed in Third World lending and participated actively in the rescheduling agreements. As a result, they increased their Third World exposure from $38 billion in 1982 (when the debt crisis began) to $92 billion in 1988. Nonetheless, two comments are in order. First, the large increase in the dollar value of the debt represented a much smaller rise in yen terms. At the same time, the increased value of the banks' "hidden assets" in Tokyo real estate and the Japanese stock market meant that Third World loans fell sharply as a share of bank assets. Second, the

Japanese banks—like all others—were lending money basically to protect their previous investments. The so-called new money was going almost exclusively to enable the debtors to keep up with interest payments; the alternative would have been default. The new loans did not provide funds for crucially needed investment projects.

It is important to recognize that the patterns described for foreign direct investment and bank loans are in no way unique to Japanese investors. Their U.S. counterparts have behaved in very similar ways. U.S. financial and nonfinancial firms have also shifted their investments toward the advanced industrial countries and, within the Third World, toward Asia. Likewise, U.S. foreign direct investment has moved toward the Caribbean, and many U.S. banks have pulled out of Third World lending altogether.

An implication of these trends is that public-sector actors are better placed than the private sector to promote development, since doing so means going against the grain in terms of short- and medium-term profit possibilities. Indeed, the Japanese government has taken a more active role than governments of other advanced industrial countries with respect to debt problems. Finance Minister Kiichi Miyazawa took the first step toward providing debt relief in the initiative he introduced in 1988. Although the United States initially rejected the Miyazawa Plan, it later broadened it somewhat and renamed it the Brady Plan. Japan, in turn, has provided most of the bilateral support to back up the Brady Plan through funds to guarantee the discounted bonds that banks purchased. Even more important, the Japanese government has allocated some $65 billion for recycling to heavily indebted countries, both directly, through loans from the Export-Import Bank of Japan (Exim Bank) and the Overseas Economic Cooperation Fund (OECF), and indirectly through support for the international financial institutions.

One alternative, then, would be for the private sector to get out of the development business and leave it to public actors—bilateral and multilateral. This would seem to be the recommendation of the United Nations Economic Commission for Latin

America and the Caribbean (ECLAC), whose executive secretary reportedly has said: "I think the commercial banks should go back to doing what they do well, which is short-term lending for trade and business . . . and that international agencies should do the long-term development lending."[2]

While it is easy to understand the logic of the ECLAC position, some alternatives may nonetheless be worth exploring. This is especially true for Japan, since it would be desirable, if possible, to tap the large volume of funds in the hands of the private sector. Underlying the several proposals is the assumption that the government wants to support Third World development but prefers to do it indirectly, by encouraging the private sector to participate. Implementing any of these measures clearly would entail certain domestic political problems—including problems within the bureaucracy—but the alternative is severely limiting the development potential of private funds.

A first proposal is some kind of government guarantees for both private investment and private lending. These could be bilateral guarantees by the Japanese government, such as an expanded version of the U.S. Overseas Private Investment Corporation (an arm of the U.S. Treasury that facilitates the flow of American direct investment to developing countries), or increased contributions to the World Bank Multilateral Investment Guarantee Agency (MIGA). (A Japanese banker is already director of the latter.) The particular size of the guarantees and the nature of their coverage would have to be negotiated, but as Ichikawa points out, some kind of guarantee is necessary before Japanese business will invest heavily outside of Asia.

An extension of the first proposal would be tax incentives for Third World loans and investment. The Japanese government allows commercial banks to put reserve provisions against only 25 percent of their Third World loans outstanding (up since 1989 from 15 percent); only 1 percent is tax-deductible. Japanese banks have protested strongly and lobbied the Ministry of Finance for greater flexibility, as Ochi points out. Although the establishment of JEI, Inc.—a factoring company in the Cayman Islands to buy Latin American loans at a discount and thus provide tax relief—was an imaginative arrangement, little use has been made of this vehicle. Other avenues could usefully be explored.

Another alternative, which the Japanese private sector has advocated repeatedly, is more cofinancing with public-sector entities. Support of this type could be either bilateral or multilateral, and it already exists to some extent. For example, much of the recycling scheme involves cofinancing, with both Exim Bank and OECF, as well as the World Bank. During the 1970s, the Japanese government frequently became a partner in large-scale resource projects in the Third World. In fact, its participation was usually the sine qua non for the private sector to invest. The structure behind the Japan International Development Organization (JAIDO), another imaginative venture to stimulate capital flows to the Third World (discussed in the Ichikawa chapter), rests on the need for government participation in the organization's projects. Unfortunately, the organization is very small scale, but it can be expanded if it proves successful.

In the longer term, the Japanese government could use other means to encourage its private sector to invest in Third World countries. One of the most frequently heard problems, in both the private and the public sectors in Japan, is the lack of expertise in non-Asian developing countries. The government could put more money into training experts in the universities or other institutions, which would provide greater expertise than government agencies, banks, nonfinancial firms, and trading companies possess. A related goal would be assistance in providing information for potential investors. The formation of the Japan Center of International Finance was a step in this direction, specifically targeted at the banks and the debt problem, but similar organizations would be useful in assisting firms wanting to invest abroad.

These and other proposals for public-private cooperation in the area of development assistance are not a substitute for strong government programs. They are only a complement, but one that could have important ramifications, given the resources in the hands of Japan's private sector. In the short run, an expanded partnership between public and private actors could be very important in renewing growth in many Third World countries. Renewed growth, in turn, would be great incentive to further private investment. In the longer run, the objective would be for private firms to act on their own—assuming, of course, that Latin American and African countries follow policies that make their economies attractive to foreign capital.

NOTES

1. Calculated from data provided by the Japanese Ministry of Finance.
2. Shirley Christian, "Banks Urged to Take Role on Latin Debt," *New York Times,* May 21, 1990, D1.

IV

The Human Dimension

JAPAN'S LEADERSHIP ROLE IN THE MULTILATERAL DEVELOPMENT INSTITUTIONS

Ryokichi Hirono

Japan emerged in the early 1970s as a new major economic power, along with the United States and some European countries, as indicated by its gross national product and levels of international trade, finance, direct investment, and aid. Since that time, expectations abroad have been rising about a possible new role for Japan in an international community seeking to maintain world peace and development through multilateral cooperation.

Belatedly but steadily, the Japanese people have awoken to the need for a more positive response to these rising expectations overseas. When the Takeshita administration announced in 1988 that Japan was ready to "contribute to the international community" through expanded efforts in peacekeeping operations, cultural exchanges, and official development assistance (ODA), the general public readily accepted this new foreign policy initiative. While a number of domestic issues forestalled vigorous implementation of the initiative—specifically political debacles following the Recruit scandals and the consumption tax issues in 1989, and the behind-the-scenes talks within the ruling Liberal Democratic Party preceding the general election in early 1990—Japan's commitment to "expanded contributions to international peace, understanding and development" will persist in the 1990s and encompasses the efforts of both the Japanese government and the private sector.

After briefly sketching the postwar history of Japan's participation in multilateral efforts for world development, this chapter discusses Japan's financial contributions to and leadership role in multilateral financing and development institutions. Second, it analyzes the major issues involving Japanese participation

171

in these institutions. Finally, it makes a few policy recommendations for immediate actions by Japan, by Japan's major partners,
and by the multilateral institutions.

JAPAN'S EMERGENT PARTICIPATION IN
MULTILATERAL INSTITUTIONS

Upon regaining political independence in 1952, Japan immediately became a member of the International Monetary Fund
(IMF) and the World Bank; it joined the General Agreement on
Tariffs and Trade (GATT) in 1955 and the United Nations (UN)
the following year.

During this period two major objectives motivated Japanese
participation in the multilateral institutions. The first was to gain
access to financial resources the World Bank and other major
international donors could provide to assist Japan in reconstruc-
ting its economy, devastated by World War II. The second was
for Japan to regain political recognition and respect in the international community after its defeat in the war. As history has
shown, both the Bretton Woods institutions and the UN, with its
specialized agencies, have been an enormous help to Japan in
attaining those objectives. These institutions have provided an
excellent opportunity for Japan to learn the intricate inner work-
ings of international economic and political negotiations and
decision-making processes; they have also represented an appropriate forum for Japan to express its views on the goals,
instruments, and financial resources of the international community in the effort to promote world peace and development.
Gaining both the economic and political benefits associated with
such multilateral institutions thus was vital to Japan, as the country was struggling with postwar economic reconstruction and
political reentry into the international community.

The Japanese government was aware of the need to develop
a positive identity and role in Asia, and to this end it announced
its Plan for Economic Cooperation for Southeast Asia and joined
the UN Economic Commission for Asia and the Far East
(ECAFE) in 1953. The next year, Japan initiated its technical

assistance to developing Asian neighbors through the British-led Colombo Plan and, in 1958, it set up the Southeast Asia Development Cooperation Fund in the Export-Import Bank of Japan.

Japan likewise recognized the importance of becoming a full-fledged partner in international development cooperation, and began taking steps to meet this objective in 1960. That year, Japan joined the International Development Association (IDA), and the following year, it joined the Development Assistance Group (DAG, now called DAC), a group of eighteen nations within the Organization for Economic Cooperation and Development (OECD). In 1961 and 1962, respectively, Japan established the Overseas Economic Cooperation Fund (OECF), the capital assistance arm of the government, and the Overseas Technical Cooperation Agency (the forerunner of the Japan International Cooperation Agency, or JICA), the technical assistance arm. Japan became a member of the OECD in 1964 and became a party to the Generalized System of Preferences for Developing Countries, under the auspices of the UN Conference on Trade and Development (UNCTAD) in 1967.

Japan has actively supported various regional cooperation activities under ECAFE auspices since the early 1960s, including the setting up and funding of the Asian Development Bank (ADB) in 1965–1966. In consultation with its Asian neighbors, Japan initiated the Ministerial Conference for the Economic Development of Southeast Asian Countries in 1966 and, three years later, it announced a plan to double its ODA to the Asia and Pacific region.

After the collapse of the Bretton Woods regime in 1971, Japan recognized the need for joint leadership to better manage the global economy. As a result, it established the Ministerial Consultative Group for External Economic Cooperation and responded positively to French President Giscard d'Éstaing's 1975 call that led to the Summit of the heads of the major seven nations.

With a view to further strengthening global efforts to accelerate Third World economic and social development, the Japanese government announced a series of ODA doubling plans, beginning in 1978, effective through 1992. Meanwhile, in 1983 and 1986, respectively, Japan joined the African Development Bank (AFDB) and established the Japan Fund in the World Bank. Tokyo also initiated a special $500 million 1987–1989 program of untied, nonproject grant assistance mainly for Sub-Saharan African countries. At the Toronto Summit in 1988, Japan expressed its readiness to join other major donors in canceling the outstanding official debts of the least-developed countries. It also pledged to provide substantial financial and in-kind contributions to the UN programs for relief and resettle-ment of Afghan refugees and reconstruction of Afghanistan's economy after the Soviet military withdrawal, and for the Iran-Iraq postwar relief and reconstruction.

JAPAN'S ROLE IN MULTILATERAL INSTITUTIONS

Ever since joining the Bretton Woods institutions and the UN in the early 1950s, the Japanese government, with overwhelming public support, has consistently backed the multilateral financ-ing and development institutions' efforts to assist Third World economic and social development and to strengthen the interna-tional development cooperation regime. One prime minister after another has emphasized in his inaugural policy speech his strong commitment to the spirit and the charter of the UN in Japan's foreign policy conduct.

The Japanese government, a borrower from the World Bank through the early 1960s, has steadily increased its annual subscriptions and financial contributions to the UN and its agen-cies, the Bretton Woods institutions, and other international organizations. These contributions reached $2.7 billion in 1988, on a net disbursement basis. Rising from 9 percent during 1975–1976, Japan's financial contributions constituted 22 per-cent of total DAC contributions to the multilateral institutions in 1986–1987, slightly surpassing the U.S. share (21 percent). Japan's $2.7 billion contribution in 1988 accounted for 30 per-cent of its overall ODA. Some $2.3 billion of that total went as capital subscriptions and contributions to the multilateral financing institutions at the global and regional levels. As a share of its total ODA, Japan's $420 million grant to the UN and other multilateral institutions was slightly less than the DAC average. It is notable, however, that Japanese financial contributions to the UN and its specialized agencies in 1986 were second only to those of the United States. Amounting to $470 million, the Japanese contributions represented 18 percent of all DAC contributions ($2.7 billion) and 11 percent of the world's total ($4.2 billion).[1]

Against the rapid expansion of Japan's financial contributions to the multilateral institutions during the last 30 years, increases in the number of Japanese nationals on the staffs of these institutions, with the exception of ADB, have been rather modest, if not negligible. By the end of 1988, all multilateral institutions combined had only 952 Japanese staff members, including 43 JICA experts and 122 junior professional officers, all paid by the Japanese government. This represents roughly 1.2 percent of the total number of staff on the payroll of the multilateral institutions. The number of Japanese staff in the UN has in fact declined since 1985; it now stands at around 90, far below the quota of 145–197 allocated to Japan, and constitutes about 1 percent of the total. The financing institutions—including the World Bank, IDA, the International Finance Corporation (IFC), ADB, and the Inter-American Development Bank (IDB)—had 195 Japanese nationals on their professional and general service payrolls, constituting approximately 2 percent of the total.

Participation by Japanese in the leadership and management of the multilateral institutions, again excepting ADB, also has lagged. Japanese nationals occupy fewer senior management positions in the UN than do representatives of the traditional major five countries (the United States, the United Kingdom, France, the Soviet Union, and China), and fewer such positions within the IMF and World Bank than representatives of the major four (the United States, the United Kingdom, France, and West Germany). Up to the mid-1980s, only three Japanese were among the senior management of these institutions. Since then, three Japanese men with the rank of assistant secretary-general or above have been added to the UN and its specialized agencies, and one has been added to the World Bank. The imbalance in senior management staffing between Japan and the rest of the major powers becomes even sharper when one considers the relative weight of these countries in terms of financial contributions.

Since the mid-1980s, however, Japan has taken a more aggressive approach for strengthening its leadership role in the multilateral financing institutions, specifically with regard to addressing the economic crisis of the highly indebted developing countries. Tokyo has repeatedly requested that the World Bank, ADB, AFDB, and IDB act as cofinancing, joint financing, or parallel financing institutions, together with Japan's public- and private-sector partners, to both share the risk associated with such project financing and contribute more effectively and efficiently in the global efforts for short-term debt relief and long-term development of the debtor countries. The Miyazawa Plan—for easing the burden of servicing bank debts of middle-income countries—announced at the joint IMF/World Bank annual meeting in West Berlin in 1987 was a salient example of this.

Likewise, Japan has been taking a more aggressive approach in the UN and other international development institutions. It has been increasingly involved in the working groups of the UN and its specialized agencies at which the international community makes decisions on policies, mechanisms, rules, and procedures governing international economic and political relations among nations. In addition, Tokyo has initiated efforts to streamline and strengthen the existing agreements and rules of international relations, as in the GATT's Uruguay Round negotiation.

As Japan expands its ODA, it faces an ever sharper need to work together with multilateral institutions to develop viable development projects and programs in developing countries requiring external financing or technical assistance. Japan has also been seeking help from multilateral development institutions—the UN Development Programme (UNDP) and others—to provide both technical and management services for its bilateral aid programs, with a view to enhancing the overall efficiency and effectiveness of its international development cooperation.

In contrast to these sustained imbalances between Japanese financing, staffing, and management contributions to multilateral institutions at the global level, Japan has maintained consistently high visibility in all respects at the regional level, though strictly in the Asia and Pacific region. Japan has been not only the largest financier of the UN Center for Regional Development, the UN Statistical Institute for Asia and the Pacific, the UN University, and the Asian Productivity Organization, but also a host to these multilateral development institutions. Interestingly, these organizations have significant numbers of Japanese nationals on staff in both professional and general service categories, and their heads or deputy heads are often Japanese nationals. Still, in other multilateral development institutions—for example, the UN Economic and Social Commission for Asia and the Pacific (formerly ECAFE), headquartered in Bangkok; the Asian and Pacific Development Center in Kuala Lumpur; and the Regional Center for Mineral Explorations and Research in Bandung—Japan has been both the largest financier and an active participant in management.

Japan's interest in regional development institutions outside the Asia and Pacific region, however, remains modest, as evident by the size of its financial, staffing, and managerial contributions. Only since 1988 has Japan expanded its involvement in the activities of IDB and AFDB, increasing its financial contributions to those organizations. By having its own representatives sitting on the Executive Board, the Japanese government intends to enhance its supervisory and managerial role in these regional development banks.

JAPANESE PARTICIPATION IN MULTILATERAL INSTITUTIONS: THE MAJOR ISSUES

To gain political recognition in specific multilateral financing and development institutions and in the international community in general, Japan has continually focused on increasing its financial contributions. However, Tokyo has been largely unsuccessful in getting Japanese nationals placed in senior management and leadership positions in the multilateral institutions, and Japanese intellectual participation has been limited. Thus, the international community sees Japan only as a major financial power—not as a political power expected to provide a leadership role, together with other major donors, in multilateral institutions and in the international community.

Japan must recognize that a financial contribution, however large it may be, cannot by itself win political recognition from the international community, but that an intellectual contribution can. Furthermore, to be viable, Japanese intellectual leadership must have the full acceptance and greatest possible support of the international community. This is most important in the UN and its specialized agencies, where decisions are based largely on the persuasiveness of intellectual arguments presented in working groups and of political leadership on the general debate floor, rather than on the amount of financial contributions, as in the Bretton Woods institutions.

Major donors in the multilateral institutions have displayed a persistent reluctance, if not resistance, to giving Japan a prominent leadership role or sharing leadership with Japan. Debate in the IMF's executive board during the years 1987–1989 on the question of increasing Japan's subscription quota in the institution clearly illustrates this point. It was only at the 1990 session of the executive board that, in spite of a decline in their relative weight of voting power, British and French representatives finally agreed to Japan's persistent four-year request to increase its subscription quota. Such reluctance stems partly from the sense of uncertainty among major donors on the readiness of Japan to cooperate with them on international development and cooperation issues in general and on IMF/World Bank financing in particular. Also, such resistance, if any, comes from those member-states facing the reduction in voting power that inevitably results from a reduced quota.

The underrepresentation of Japanese professional and management staff in multilateral institutions, however, has resulted not from discriminatory recruitment policies and practices in these institutions, but from Japan's continued inability to provide capable personnel with international-mindedness and bilingual or multilingual proficiency. In fact, these institutions have always been on the lookout for appropriate Japanese applicants and have often sent their recruitment missions to Japan to seek qualified candidates, but in vain.

It may, in fact, be far less difficult for the multilateral institutions to find qualified Japanese applicants among those attending graduate schools or working with Japanese or foreign corporations overseas than to do so in Japan. Also, the keenly competitive, lifetime employment system of the Japanese organizations, with its emphasis on human relations, has worked against the secondment of the few eligible Japanese to these multilateral institutions, though the system has been slowly breaking down for some time, particularly among younger Japanese with higher education. Even when seconded, because of home institution personnel policies and practices, Japanese staff members usually associate themselves for only a relatively short period of time with multilateral institutions, which makes it quite difficult for them to provide leadership and for their non-Japanese colleagues to accept it.

Furthermore, the rise of pay scales in Japan, along with the yen's appreciation, the country's rather advanced social amenities, the degree of personal safety and security it offers, and the large variety of cultural activities now available in metropolitan areas, explain why many Japanese professionals do not find it attractive to work in multilateral institutions overseas. Also, many Japanese accustomed to working under the group orientation and paternalistic protection in Japanese organizations, public and private, find it difficult and frustrating to work with, and manage, non-Japanese personnel with individualistic orientations. Under these circumstances, Japanese nationals obviously lack the self-confidence to take a leadership role.

POLICY RECOMMENDATIONS

As the number-two economic power and as the number-one creditor nation, Japan will have to continue increasing its financial contributions to multilateral financing and development institutions. This will be particularly true with regard to those effectively and efficiently run multilateral technical cooperation agencies, such as UNDP, where despite the steady increase in dollar terms of Japan's contributions, its donor position has declined significantly.

Tokyo should intensify its efforts to provide incentives for qualified nationals to work with multilateral financing and development institutions, and to spend longer periods of time in those jobs. Such incentives will have to go beyond merely pecuniary ones and include both job security and guarantees against loss of seniority and associated opportunities for nationals returning home after service overseas. Furthermore, Japan will require increasing assistance from multilateral institutions in planning, implementing, and evaluating ODA projects and programs on the basis of agreed formulas such as cost sharing, cofinancing, parallel or joint financing, and programming, as well as management service agreements. By the same token, efforts must be mobilized to solicit the cooperation of national (whether Japanese or recipient country) and international nongovernmental organizations in all phases of project cycles.

For their part, multilateral financing and development institutions must invite Japanese officials and private experts to participate in all the important meetings where the agenda for international action on macroeconomic, trade, finance, investment, and ODA issues are to be determined. It would be advisable for these institutions to solicit from Japan a set of concrete policy proposals for actions at the national, regional, and international levels, with a certain amount of flexibility to accommodate proposals made by other member-states.

Multilateral institutions should make concerted efforts to enlist Japan's cooperation in encouraging qualified Japanese nationals' long-term involvement, particularly as senior managers. They could also focus on stimulating Japanese consulting firms' or individual consultants' participation in feasibility study and other project-related missions. Above all, multilateral financing and development institutions should organize annual meetings, seminars, workshops, and symposia in various parts of Japan and involve Japanese mass media organizations in such undertakings, with a view to enhancing interest in and understanding of the work of international organizations among Japanese government ministries, semigovernmental agencies, local governments, research institutes, universities, nongovernmental organizations, and, in particular, the general public. This type of initiative is vital, in view of the Japanese public's increasing concern and criticism of how its tax money is being used on both bilateral and multilateral development cooperation.

NOTE

1. Ministry of Foreign Affairs, *Japan's Official Development Assistance: 1989 Annual Report* (Tokyo: 1990), 260–261.

COMMENT

Ernest Stern

In the preceding chapter, Ryokichi Hirono offers a clear description of the growth of Japan's role in providing bilateral and multilateral assistance to the developing countries, and examines an area that continues to be a major point of frustration—namely, Japan's inadequate representation in the management and staff of some of the important international and regional organizations. Hirono rightly considers this a basic issue, since the problem is very important to Japan's view of its future development assistance strategy and its role in international organizations.

Two aspects of this problem should be of particular concern to the international institutions. First, equity suggests that there be a reasonable relationship between financial participation and participation in management and operations of the international institutions. If this expectation remains unfulfilled over a protracted period, a likely result is disenchantment with these organizations as effective channels of international collaboration. Second, Japan is one of the most effectively managed economies in the world. Its limited involvement in the staffing of the international institutions means that little of that experience influences their operation. This is difficult to understand in Japan and deprives developing countries of valid choices of strategies.

Hirono's overall context is a discussion on Japan's role in development cooperation, and his points have general applicability. My comments, inevitably, are heavily influenced by my experience in the World Bank, but are of more general relevance. To help understand the current situation and establish realistic expectations for change, I will seek to place three aspects of the issue in perspective.

The growth of Japanese official development assistance (ODA) has been rapid and fairly recent, as has been the broadening of Japan's interest in developing countries outside East Asia. As Japan's aid efforts have grown and its geographic involvement has expanded, so has domestic interest in defining Japan's objectives and its role more explicitly. The focus has shifted from a simple willingness to provide aid funds, often linked to commercial objectives, to trying to link the ever increasing volume of such funds, much now untied, to broader views of Japan's interest in the development process. In addition to direct contributions, Japan has, since the mid-1980s, expanded its cofinancing with the Bretton Woods institutions and other multilateral development banks, especially in the highly indebted countries. This is the main part of Japan's Recycling Plan, which has helped to offset the decline of commercial bank lending. Japan has thus played an important role in facilitating the debt restructuring of these countries. Given this broader and more active involvement, Japan's role as shareholder in the Bretton Woods institutions, its representation in the staff and management of these institutions, and its general influence on development policies and strategies have received growing attention.

Changes in ownership of the Bretton Woods institutions come about gradually. The reason is simple. Increasing the shares of one country necessarily requires reducing the shares of others. These changes reflect shifts in relative economic position but, as is usually the case with changes in relative power, current holders are reluctant to relinquish their positions. Consequently, changes in share holdings tend to be the result of negotiations rather than of strictly objective criteria automatically calculated. A capital increase in the World Bank, or a quota increase in the International Monetary Fund, permits some flexibility in altering relative share holdings, but these occasions are infrequent. Even then, negotiations can be protracted. For instance, the articles of agreement of the World Bank provide that in any capital increase, members have an option of exercising preemptive rights, if the new shares are allocated disproportionately. Obviously, if all members exercised preemptive rights, any capital increase could only be strictly proportional. The negotiation process involves many countries with divergent views about their role, actual or potential, in the world economy. Nonetheless, progress is possible, and Japan has become the second-largest shareholder in the World Bank, after the United States.

While the share of ownership is important, it is not a good proxy of influence in the World Bank. Most issues are resolved by discussion and consensus, and voting is rare. Moreover, while the board is the policymaking body, in an institution as large as the World Bank, with so diverse a set of operations, the management and staff play a central role. For that reason, many countries also look to a relationship between their share of capital and their participation in management and staff. In this regard, Japan is no exception.

The senior management level (vice presidents and senior vice presidents) comprises sixteen positions against a total of 152 member-countries. Virtually all of these positions are filled by appointment from within as the World Bank has always been a career-oriented institution. The composition of this group by nationality has varied considerably over time. At present, the senior management represents developing and industrialized countries about equally. The group includes one Japanese national, but no French or British, although they have held top-level positions in the past. Most are career staff members, who were appointed without regard to their nationality.

Representation in the senior management and, indeed, at other management levels is, in a career-oriented institution, a function of representation in the staff. And here the World Bank clearly suffers from a shortage of Japanese nationals. It is a long-standing problem, and the institution has made a major effort, in collaboration with the government, to increase Japanese recruitment. Results have been less than satisfactory to both sides. Several factors have prevented more rapid progress.

One is the strong career commitment in Japan, in both the public and the private sectors. The average age at recruitment in the World Bank is 42, which means that the bulk of the Bank's intake is of technical and professional staff who already have a significant career in another organization. In many member-countries, it is possible for staff to leave their current employer and come to the World Bank. In Japan highly qualified mid-career managers and professionals often are reluctant to leave their current employers, except for short periods.

Another hindrance to Japanese recruitment is the inability of the compensation package to completely offset a number of potential disadvantages for foreign staff working in Washington. While in the United States salaries at the World Bank may seem ample, this perception ignores two important elements: exchange rates and employment practices elsewhere—which are relevant to recruiting and retaining staff from other countries. The Bank's ability to attract non–U.S. nationals to work in Washington is not a function only of its compensation, but it is important. While prospective staff generally assess the working environment at the Bank as intellectually stimulating and highly interesting, they have more alternatives today than they did in the past. Candidates weigh many personal aspects, including relocation; drying up of contacts in the home country; the inability of staff spouses to work in the United States; and the education of children, who, even though they may attend special international schools, can be cut off from the educational structure of their home country and thus fail to become employable at levels and in the areas they might have preferred. In the past, compensation may have been sufficient to offset some of these drawbacks. Today, while perhaps competitive in a narrow sense, it is less likely to do so, particularly for staff members from countries with strong currencies and where rapid growth offers exciting opportunities at home. The Bank, therefore, finds itself with an inadequate supply of qualified staff from a number of important member-countries in Europe and, particularly, from Japan.

Beyond the number of staff members and managers, a member's ownership and its intellectual contribution to development determine its influence in the international development and financial institutions. The intellectual contribution draws on the base of national knowledge of development—embodied in universities, research institutions, foundations, and non-governmental organizations. These groups help shape a country's public views on international financial and development issues, and their interaction with the international organizations influences the evolution of practices, procedures, and technical knowledge. Furthermore, these organizations provide a pool of individuals from which staff and consultants are drawn. Since the Bank can recruit most effectively among those interested in development and in living overseas for extended periods, the richer this base, the deeper its operating experience in developing countries, and the more likely that a country will be influential on development questions and in international organizations.

It is not my objective here to specify steps that any one organization might take to reflect better Japan's experience in economic development and management and its greatly increased financial role. However, the discussion of the underlying issues suggests some general directions for addressing the problem.

If influence, broadly construed, is anchored in the knowledge of development and the practical understanding of the policy and operational problems of developing countries, one important aspect of a larger role for Japan will involve continued investment in this knowledge base. This investment takes many forms, ranging from the support of research at universities to supplying technical assistance staff to work in developing countries. It means continued and expanded involvement of researchers in technical work in developing countries. It means broad opportunities for those interested in development issues for operational field experience. It means consultant firms interested in institution building and technical advisory services.

Much of this, of course, exists in Japan, but deepening this process would facilitate a greater role for Japan in development strategy and policy. A message, by private or public organizations, that such work has national importance would, no doubt, be helpful. International organizations, in the interest of their members and themselves, can play an important role on the demand side. Ongoing research programs offer great scope for effective collaboration with Japanese researchers and research institutions. Seminars, workshops, and other forms of intellectual exchanges are too heavily oriented toward the United States and Europe. A wide range of issues, from poverty alleviation to environmental problems, would benefit from the involvement of Japanese experts, private and public. Similarly, Japanese consultants can participate in a broad spectrum of activities. And this increased involvement of Japanese staff will make an important substantive contribution to the developing countries. Given the large supply of persons with policy formulation and private management experience in a rapidly growing economy like Japan, the multilateral institutions would draw in management and entrepreneurial skills that could be of great relevance to developing countries. Many are potentially suitable candidates and the barriers—of language, work habits, management style— are surmountable if the institutions and Japan are prepared to make the effort.

The government of Japan has made a major contribution in this area by providing the World Bank with substantial trust funds for a variety of technical assistance activities. Its initiative to augment these funds to emphasize human resource development is a particularly important step. The trust funds will increase substantially the pool of Japanese experts acquainted with developing country problems and with the work of the Bank. But, of course, the availability of grant funds should encourage, not determine, the greater involvement of Japanese personnel in these types of Bank activities.

Beyond these long-term measures, possibilities exist for more direct and immediate action. Observers often suggest that the management styles and the corporate culture of multilateral institutions differ from those in Japan; in fact, however, such differences are not major and would be easy to overcome.

A broader appreciation that a career in international organizations is a desirable and important vocation and is in the interest of Japan will facilitate recruitment in Japan. Staff intake from Japan must increase substantially if the multilateral institutions are to have a qualified pool of people to draw on for promotion into the managerial grades. This requires creative and active recruitment by the international organizations; it also requires support from the government, universities, and corporate leaders. Clearly, the approach must be systemic—achieving broader representation in the staff will not be possible by concentrating on individual vacancies as they arise.

In addition, for an interim period, more flexible hiring practices may be necessary—for example, emphasizing fixed-term contracts in addition to career employment. Such measures, too, can be more effective if private organizations, as well as government agencies, recognize these assignments as valuable career investments, so that individuals will feel free to seek them without fear that doing so will damage their career prospects.

Finally, management must support the objective of increasing Japanese participation of all kinds. Managers have a tendency to recruit the type of individual they are comfortable with. This is not a problem facing Japan exclusively, nor is it limited to nationalities: it manifests itself in gender distribution, in concentration on graduates of certain universities, and in preferences for specific professional groups or degrees (e.g., MBAs). The problem decreases once a critical mass is reached that supports this type of networking. Management in international organizations thus must make conscious efforts to help establish this base.

Hirono has drawn our attention to an important and basic issue. It is complex and requires adjustment and flexibility among all involved. However, the issue needs to be dealt with not only because of Japan's interest, although that is important, but because the supply of qualified personnel is limited, and all institutions would benefit from greater Japanese involvement. Japan's development process differed in many ways from that of some other members of the Organization for Economic Cooperation and Development (OECD). Japan has a large pool of well-trained professionals, scientists, and managers. Its experience and the current management practices and technological developments in its economy hold important lessons. Without broader participation of Japanese staff, this significant intellectual component will continue to elude the international organizations, to the detriment of their member-countries.

V

Yen Diplomacy & U.S. Foreign Policy

BEYOND BURDEN-SHARING: ECONOMICS AND POLITICS OF JAPANESE FOREIGN AID

Shafiqul Islam

Strange things are happening in the world. In August 1990, President George Bush began sending troops to the Persian Gulf to protect oil and freedom from Saddam Hussein, and then dispatched his secretaries of state and the treasury around the world to collect fees. Japan, flush with cash, hesitated to write the check; and America, burdened with deficits and debts, got upset. Although Japan eventually came up with the money, the initial hesitancy once again confirmed the American view that Japan is a selfish superpower that has taken a free ride to economic supremacy, leaving America "imperially overstretched." Meanwhile, the Japanese began a heated debate on whether, as an economic superpower, Japan should share the burden with cash alone, or spill some blood and sweat on the hot desert sands. More fundamentally, however, the debate was not about Japan's role in the Gulf, but about whether it should become a military superpower or not.

Saddam Hussein thus unwittingly set in motion the adjustment of a global imbalance that the end of the Cold War had already made unsustainable—the imbalance between monetary might and military muscle of the world's top two economic superpowers. It is in the context of this imbalance that the economics and politics of Japan's role in Third World development have to be understood. By definition, Japan's development assistance program is a matter of concern to Japan and the Third World; but the two superpowers' monetary-military gaps have made Japan's foreign aid an issue of America's foreign policy as well. Further, the inability of the American business community to compete with Japan even on a level playing field has helped make Tokyo's aid America's business.

191

The purpose of this chapter is to distinguish the bilateral politics of Japanese foreign aid from the development economics of foreign aid, draw implications for U.S. and Japanese foreign policy, and identify criteria for fruitful aid cooperation. A central message of this analysis is that sensible foreign policymaking in both nations and meaningful aid cooperation among the two require replacing the concept of burden-sharing by the concept of global partnership; the former is by definition a unilateralist and contentious anachronism whereas the latter is a multilateralist and cooperative one, suitable for guiding the foreign policies of all major powers in today's multipolar world.

NON-JAPANESE CONCEPTS OF JAPANESE FOREIGN AID

When foreigners, especially Americans, ask Japan to increase its development assistance, they sum up the rationales in catchy phrases. I discuss three of these: burden-sharing, a Japanese Marshall Plan, and recycling the Japanese surplus.

Burden-Sharing

The United States coined the term "burden-sharing" in arguing that it contributes a disproportionate share of the burden of the common defense of its European North Atlantic Treaty Organization (NATO) allies. Burden-sharing, the United States demanded, should be more equitable, with Europe shouldering a greater share of the cost of its own defense. The burden of defense is usually measured in terms of the share of a country's gross national product (GNP) that goes to its military budget. For example, in 1986 America's military budget took 6.7 percent of its GNP, whereas the NATO members spent, on average, 3.3 percent of GNP. This "burden surplus" (of 3.4 percent) led to the U.S. complaint that the allies were not bearing an equitable share of the burden of common defense.

By the late 1960s, Japan had joined the list of America's allies engaging in "unfair burden-share practices" as it became a major source of increasing competitive challenge to American manufacturing prowess and growing deficit in U.S. trade. During the 1980s, Japan emerged as the top "unfair burden-sharer" as it transformed into an economic, financial, and technological superpower and threatened America's supremacy in high finance and high technology. Meanwhile, the United States maintained economic expansion and rising living standards by borrowing huge sums from overseas—a large chunk of them from Japan—and turned almost overnight into the world's largest debtor nation. Consequently, the perception heightened that Japan took a "free ride" to economic supremacy at the expense of America, which is now lying flat on its back under the burden of defending the free world.

With Japan displacing Europe from center stage, the concept of burden has been redefined: Whereas the old concept focused on the cost of military spending alone, the new one refers to the cost of "providing international public goods for maintaining global peace and prosperity." The principal driving force behind this redefinition is Japan's "Made in the U.S.A." Peace Constitution, which prevents Japan from becoming a global military power. The other factor is a growing recognition that even if the United States could once again rewrite Japan's constitution against the will of the Japanese people and their Asian neighbors, forcing Japan to achieve even the "unfairly low" NATO average burden of 3 percent of GNP by allocating an additional 2 percent of its massive and rapidly growing GNP to rearmament, it would serve neither U.S. interests nor the cause of global peace and prosperity.

The attempt to resolve the conflict between the goal of *burden-bearing* and that of *burden-sharing* has thus led to an innovative broadening of the concept of burden. When all is said and done, international public goods consist of one extra item in addition to defense—foreign aid. The underlying assumption is that having Japan spend several percentage points of its GNP on foreign aid can help allay fears that a Japan shouldering its "fair share" of the burden of defending freedom may itself become a threat to peace and stability.

Before turning to the issue of whether foreign aid resolves this conundrum, it is useful to point out that the American concept of "the burden of defending freedom" ignores two basic facts regarding the interest and power of a hegemonic nation as it interacts with its friends and foes around the globe. First, a large and powerful country's international obligations cannot be neatly separated from its national interest. The burden—at least the financial component of it—that the United States seems increasingly unwilling, and apparently unable, to bear is the burden of the powerful; it is the burden of the leader. This burden forms the basis of America's global power, prestige, and privilege. Is the United States spending more than 5 percent of GNP on the military to help out its allies at the expense of its national interest, or is it doing so to pursue its national interest as a global power? Is American foreign aid simply a burden, or is it an important instrument of U.S. foreign policy? Did President Reagan increase defense spending in the 1980s from 5 percent of GNP to over 6 percent to better defend Europe and Japan, or did he do so to strengthen America's own perceived global power and position? The answer to these questions is clear: While U.S. spending on defense and foreign aid benefits other countries, it ultimately promotes U.S. foreign policy and security objectives.

Second, while it is not clear what constitutes a "fair share" of the burden for America's allies and how to measure it, there can be little doubt that increased "burden-sharing" leads to increased "power-sharing." The political arithmetic is simple: If Japan shares more of the burden, America has to share more of its power and leadership. This is as true in military spending as it is in foreign aid. For example, if Tokyo agrees to pay a much larger share of the cost of maintaining U.S. military forces in Japan, it may demand a much greater voice in—even a veto right over—the use of those forces. One question that America must face, therefore, is how much power-sharing it is willing to accept. The naive notion that Japan will bear more of the burden and America will share no more of its power and privilege is simply irresponsible and ultimately unsustainable.

The difficulties in defining the concept of burden are surpassed by the difficulties of measuring it. Using a country's military budget to measure its burden of maintaining peace and stability is questionable, as it requires a great leap of faith regarding the country's overall motives and character on which a global consensus would be impossible to reach. With no military spending, is Costa Rica a free rider? With 20 percent of its GNP allegedly devoted to defense, was the Soviet Union carrying the greatest burden of maintaining global peace against "capitalist imperialism"? Many people from the Third World, and certainly many Soviet communists, thought so.

Making no distinction between one country's military spending and another's foreign aid spending, and then using combined spending on military and foreign aid as the measure of the burden, however, appears worse than adding apples and oranges.[1] This perspective leads, for example, to the presumption that if America decides to spend 1 percent of its GNP on "Star Wars," then Japan is being a selfish free rider if it does not follow by allocating 1 percent of its GNP to development assistance. Such muddled thinking fosters neither global peace and prosperity nor a better U.S.–Japan relationship.

Japan's share of the combined burden (1.3 percent of GNP: 1 percent on defense and 0.3 percent on aid) in 1989 was about 4.5 percent of GNP lower than that of the United States (5.9 percent of GNP: 5.8 percent on defense and 0.1 percent on aid). Critics continually call on Japan to reduce this "bilateral burden deficit" by allocating at least 3 percent of its GNP between defense and foreign aid.[2] The problem with this demand is that Japan simply cannot meet the 3 percent target without either spending massive amounts of resources on rearmament or handing out large sums of money to developing country governments. Japan is the world's third-largest military spender; by spending an additional 1 or 2 percent of GNP on defense, Japan would upset its neighbors and the existing military balance in Asia, and would thus more likely undermine than enhance global security.

While American "Japan defense hawks" increasingly recognize that Japanese rearmament would not promote world peace, awareness that a Japanese plan to pour money into the Third World would not promote development remains low. By spending only 0.3 percent of GNP on foreign aid, Japan has already displaced the United States as the world's top donor. Development assistance of 1 percent—let alone 2 or 3 percent—of Japan's GNP would be about $30 billion in 1990; not only does Japan lack the "administrative capacity" to effectively distribute this volume of assistance, the developing countries lack the "absorptive capacity" to effectively utilize it.

These simple facts, however, are usually obscured by what appears to be a fear of Japanese economic expansion. For some Americans, the ultimate motive behind pressing Japan to take up more of the burden seems to be to "burden" Japan as much as possible. Bluntly put, the goal is no longer to have Japan bear a fair share of the burden of "containing communism," but to use the foreign policy instrument of burden-sharing to "contain Japan."

Apparently, a secondary goal is to pursue a policy of "affirmative action" by using reverse discrimination. Since Japan achieved economic supremacy by free riding on the back of a naive, do-gooder America when it was strong, the argument goes, today's rich and strong Japan should pay back part of its debt by giving America, the weakened global leader, a "reverse free ride." This type of thinking perhaps explains why the U.S. Congress focuses exclusively on burden-sharing and ignores the issue of power-sharing, or why Washington's foreign policy seems increasingly based on the principle of "take the yen and run the world."

A Japanese Marshall Plan

Some have called for a grand Japanese initiative in the spirit of the Marshall Plan to aid developing countries over a number of years with substantial financial assistance. Yet the notion of a "Japanese Marshall Plan" evokes a historical parallel that may be misleading, and if implemented such a plan may not achieve intended objectives.[3] The simple fact is that whereas America demonstrated great global leadership by launching the four-year Marshall Plan to aid postwar Europe in 1948, Japan may not be able to do the same for the developing world today even if it wanted to. At least two reasons explain why.

First is the question of leadership. The United States emerged from World War II as an unquestioned military and economic leader of the noncommunist world, with a huge balance-of-payments surplus and a large federal budget surplus. America had both the money and the mandate to transfer resources, mostly in the form of grants, to war-ravaged Europe, which was suffering from budgetary and external deficits. The idea of the Marshall Plan made sense and worked not only because Western Europe could effectively use America's money; more important, Western Europe largely accepted and welcomed the American leadership and dominance that came with the money.

In the case of today's Japan and the developing countries, such favorable conditions and complementarity are lacking. Japan, having spent decades preoccupied with catching up with the West and mostly uninvolved in global political affairs, does not have yesterday's America's capacity to lead. Nor has it yet earned the political mandate and goodwill for exercising unchallenged—or even shared—leadership over the developing world. The Asian experience with Japanese militarism in World War II and Japan's failure to conduct an open national debate on its role in that war, as well as its postwar political and security dependence on the United States, make it difficult for Japan to exercise leadership over developing countries—even in economic affairs—and for those countries to accept that leadership.

The second reason involves the fundamental difference between reconstruction and development. Europe had the political ability and human resources to use foreign savings for reconstruction and recovery. The political and military threat of communism, as well as the economic threat of the dollar shortage, also strengthened the rationale for the Marshall Plan. Furthermore, the aid efforts were concentrated on a small part of the world that was already industrialized and developed, and culturally close to the donor country. In sum, the Marshall Plan was a great success because Europe had an effective demand for it, and America had a matching effective supply for it.

By contrast, the crisis-ridden developing countries of today do not have postwar Europe's capacity to absorb. The developing countries that can potentially benefit from a massive inflow of resources are not where Europe was 40 years ago—economically, politically, and culturally. While the task of the Marshall Plan was to "reconstruct" Europe, the task now is a much more complex one—to put the highly diverse Third World on a path of "self-sustaining development." That is, while money was the binding constraint limiting Europe's recovery, it is only one of the many key constraints hampering development in the Third World. In low-income Third World countries, the key binding constraint often is not financial resources, but political, social, and human resources. Having lived long under colonialism, these countries are at a very early stage of development. Poverty, political corruption, and social injustice are endemic; a sudden influx of foreign aid without appropriate administration and management is likely to promote aid-dependent growth in these parts of the developing world rather than self-sustaining development.

Many middle-income developing countries—particularly in Latin America—are in the midst of a debt crisis, exacerbated by a vicious cycle of poor macroeconomic policy and political instability. They do not need more loans from Japan to pay interest to their bank creditors or reduce their arrears by adding to their debt overhang. They need a bold approach to resolving their debt problem, and to implementing policy reform that creates conditions for restoring confidence, creditworthiness, investment, and growth. To be sure, the savings-poor developing countries need more foreign financial support, but the money will yield little development if used to service their foreign debts that have long gone sour.

The key problems of much of the Third World are not financial, but political, social, and institutional—dimensions where people are more important than money. A recent study of

the linkage between external finance and economic development in eleven countries reconfirms this view:

> Small amounts of aid—given in the context of a sound policy
> environment for the development of physical, human, and institu-
> tional structure—are far more effective than large levels given
> without attention to issues of development policy.[4]

Thus what today's developing countries need from Japan,
and other rich nations, is not a massive transfer of resources over
a short period of time, but a long, steady, major commitment to
support them on to the path of self-sustaining development.

Recycling the Japanese Surplus

Many foreigners urge Japan to "recycle" its huge current account surplus to developing countries.[5] This idea has its roots in
an earlier experience: Advocates of recycling believe Japan could
do in the 1980s what the members of the Organization of Petro-
leum Exporting Countries (OPEC) did with their oil surpluses
during the 1970s. The assumption seems to be that the Japanese
government should somehow be able to channel the bulk of its
massive pool of surplus savings, most of which goes to financing
America's twin deficits, to the resource-constrained less-developed countries (LDCs). Japan itself has embraced the concept of
recycling and uses it to refer to all financial flows to the developing countries—official grants and loans, as well as all types of
private flows. The use of "recycling" as a catchall word, however,
has created a great deal of confusion as to what the Japanese
government can and cannot do, what it is and is not doing, and
what all this has to do with the Japanese current account surplus.

A comparison of the OPEC experience with the current
situation can shed some light on what it means to recycle a
country's current account surplus. Two key differences are
worth noting. First, the oil shock produced current account
surpluses in the OPEC countries, as well as current account
deficits in the oil-importing developing countries. So recycling
the OPEC surplus to developing countries meant maintaining
more or less the same global pattern of current account imbalances that emerged in the wake of the oil shocks. Since the oil-

importing countries already had major current account deficits, the goal was to finance them with the surplus savings of the OPEC countries. In other words, recycling the OPEC surplus was relatively straightforward because the oil shock created counterpart deficits in many developing countries. Hence, major international banks were only too happy to recycle the oil money from the surplus OPEC countries to the deficit developing countries.

By contrast, the Japanese current account surplus has developed largely as a counterpart of U.S. and OPEC current account deficits. (With the sharp rise of the yen since 1985 and the oil price hike of 1990, this pattern of global current account balances is, however, already changing.) This time the LDC debt problem actually has forced many finance-constrained developing countries to sharply reduce their current account deficits. Consequently, the Japanese current account surplus is being recycled to those deficit countries that have access to the international capital and money markets, most notably to the United States.

Recycling the Japanese surplus to the finance-constrained and debt-distressed developing countries, therefore, requires not recycling but *redirecting* the surplus. In fact, it requires somehow inducing Japanese private investors to lend to and invest in countries from which others are divesting. This redirecting of the Japanese surplus thus means creating a new global pattern of current account balances where the heavily indebted developing countries increase their current account deficits, as they borrow more and add to their debt overhang. In other words, efforts to redirect the Japanese surplus to finance-constrained developing countries without taking bold steps to alleviate their debt problems is not feasible on a large scale; and it does not represent the best use of capital—either for Japan, or for the developing countries.

The second key difference between the Japanese surplus and the OPEC surplus is that the oil price hike created not only *external surpluses* for the OPEC *countries*, but also *budget surpluses* for the OPEC *governments,* which own most of the oil fields.

Consequently, those governments had direct control over the surpluses—they could use some of the money to promote domestic development and imports, some to provide official development assistance (ODA), and the rest to lend to the international money and capital markets.

By contrast, the Japanese external surplus is a private-sector surplus—the central government budget is in deficit. The government therefore has limited flexibility in budgeting a major expansion of ODA. Moreover, the government cannot redirect the private surplus directly to countries with little creditworthiness; it must do so indirectly, either by acting as a financial intermediary or by giving the private sector inducements— heavy subsidies, guarantees, and insurance—to supply the funds. But all this requires the government to come up with more funds even when it is suffering from a shortage of savings itself. The fact that Japan has a massive external surplus does not help very much: The government has to either tax more or borrow more, even if it tries to redirect the Japanese surplus.

Two other related points are worth making. First, as mentioned earlier, commentators are increasingly labeling any type of transfer of resources from Japan for the purposes of development finance a "recycling measure." One example is the Nakasone $30 billion Recycling Plan. No distinction is made between grants, capital subscriptions to the multilateral organizations, concessional official loans, nonconcessional official loans, and various types of private-sector flows. The current account and fiscal implications of these various types of transfer vary greatly. For example, while both official grants and nonconcessional loans represent resource transfer, grants do *not* recycle the Japanese current account surplus; they actually *reduce* it while increasing the government deficit. By contrast, nonconcessional loans, even if official, in effect recycle or redirect the external surplus and do not add to the government budget deficit.

The other point involves the view—expressed by some Americans—that recycling the Japanese surplus to LDCs is yet another mercantilist ploy by Japan to maintain its huge external surplus.[6] This interpretation rests on three implicit assumptions: successful recycling (redirecting) will mean little or no reduction of Japan's external surplus; it will hamper the task of correcting the U.S. external deficit; and even if the U.S. deficit comes down, a persistently large Japanese current account surplus represents a macroeconomic disequilibrium, and prima facie evidence of Japan's mercantilist attitude and behavior.

All three assumptions are incorrect. First, a country's current account balance is the product of complex and dynamic interactions among consumers, producers, governments, and financial markets at home and abroad. What happens to Japan's external surplus depends not only on what the Japanese do, but also on what the United States and Japan's other major trading partners in Europe, Asia, and the Middle East do. For example, the Japanese surplus is likely to be more affected by what the United States does with its budget deficit than by what the Japanese redirect to the finance-constrained LDCs of Asia, Africa, or Latin America. Whether or not Japan succeeds in redirecting a substantial part of its capital to the resource-constrained developing countries, American success in eliminating its savings-investment deficit will translate into a major reduction of the Japanese surplus.

Second, if more Japanese private capital and official untied aid flow to the developing countries and boost investment, growth, and imports, the impact on the U.S. trade deficit can only be positive.[7] This will be especially true in Latin American countries, as they are likely to remain much bigger trading partners of the United States than of Japan in the foreseeable future.

Finally, there is nothing wrong with a future scenario in which the United States succeeds in eliminating its current account deficit and Japan continues to run a reduced but persistently large surplus. In fact, this represents a desirable state of affairs. If most developing countries can overcome their debt and macroeconomic problems, they together will once again emerge as the major demander of the world's surplus savings. The United States is not likely to meet the LDC demand for foreign savings, since it is likely to remain a low-savings country even if the recent drop in its savings rate is partially reversed. Japan, Germany, and a few Asian newly industrializing economies (NIEs) are likely to become the world's source of surplus savings.

In a world where savings are a scarce commodity, we should feel fortunate that a few countries can still afford to supply savings to others that desperately need them to grow and develop. The problem right now is not that Japan has too large an external surplus, but that, thanks to the U.S. current account deficits, the world's two leading economies *together* are running a current account deficit of $40–$50 billion and absorbing scarce savings from the rest of the world. With the U.S. external deficit eliminated and the Japanese surplus reduced, normalcy will return to the international flow of funds: The top two economies of the world will once again supply funds to—rather than absorb funds from—the resource-constrained developing countries.

AID MERCANTILISM AND UNFAIR AID PRACTICES: MYTHS AND MISGIVINGS

While conceptual confusions cloud why, how, and how much Japan should give, myths and misgivings are recycled as definitive answers to what makes Japan give. Japan is routinely accused of engaging in "aid mercantilism" and "unfair aid practices." The following specific criticisms fall under the category of aid mercantilism: Japan makes extensive use of *tied aid* (it restricts aid money to procurement from Japan) and *mixed credits* (it subsidizes sales of Japanese goods by spicing up export credits with concessional development loans); it gains market shares in key sectors and high-technology products by excessive use of aid money on capital projects and large economic infrastructure; the bulk of its aid goes to Asia, where it has close trade and investment links, and the Middle East, the source of much of its oil; and the Japanese aid program is in effect the external finance department of "Japan Inc."—the government works closely with the private sector to design, implement, monitor, and evaluate the aid program.

The accusation of unfair aid practices overlaps with that of aid mercantilism, and contains, among others, the following criticisms: the share of grants in total assistance is too low; too little aid goes to support "basic human needs" of the poorest of the poor; and Japan pays too little attention to the environmental problems of the Third World.

These criticisms are misguided, and they reflect a degree of self-righteousness. First, they ignore the fact that the United States (and all major donors) are no less—and indeed, may be more—guilty of practicing aid mercantilism. Second, many of the "facts" supporting these criticisms are either outdated or simply not true. Finally, by and large, these criticisms are themselves mercantilist in nature reflecting anxieties over the donors' relative performance in the battleground of global economic competition and have little to do with economic development of the recipient countries. Some also reflect a fundamental misunderstanding of the dynamics of self-sustaining economic development and the role of aid in it, as well as the issue of maintaining taxpayer support for foreign aid and developing a domestic aid constituency. I elaborate the first two points.

Susan Pharr, a Harvard expert on Japanese aid, aptly sums up the typical American perception in the following statement:

> Many of the criticisms of Japan's aid program, especially from American development professionals, arise from a firm American belief that a country's aid program, on the one hand, and the commercial interests of the donor country, on the other, should be kept as far apart as possible. Such a view is the logical projection of the premise, going back to Adam Smith, that government and business essentially have an adversarial relationship.[8]

The reality, however, is better captured in two quotations from official U.S. sources. A 1989 report by the administrator of the U.S. Agency for International Development (AID) contained these statements:

> Economic self-interest has become an increasingly prominent rationale for U.S. development assistance efforts, though the great bulk of existing program resources are oriented toward essentially

political and humanitarian objectives. However, since the 1950s, U.S. policy statements about LDC development have emphasized the need to support private sector trade, investment and technology transfer. The Kennedy Administration's overhaul of the development assistance agency and legislative mandate included an emphasis on investment promotion and trade, as did the 1970s overhaul of the Foreign Assistance Act. . . . During the 1950s and the 1960s, U.S. foreign aid and government financial exports were larger than private trade with LDCs.[9]

The other official statement is from U.S. Treasury Secretary Nicholas Brady: "For every dollar provided to these [multilateral] banks, the U.S. economy gets back $9 in U.S. procurements."[10]

It appears that American politicians from President Kennedy on down to the current treasury secretary either are more commercially oriented than Pharr believes they are, or at least choose to sweep Adam Smith under the rug when it comes to development assistance to the Third World. Lest there be a "firm American belief" that politicians do not know what they are talking about, it may be useful to quote a few findings regarding U.S. aid to multilateral development banks (MDBs) from a respectable representative of the American private sector—the U.S. Chamber of Commerce:

While sales of many U.S. exports have dwindled in recent years, some alert U.S. exporters have clinched more than $7 billion in new business in the Third World. . . . Such sales to Third World governments are a bright spot in the U.S. export picture. While exports of many U.S. goods have fallen, hurt by the rising dollar and foreign competition, purchases by Third World governments for MDB-funded projects have steadily increased. During the last five years, U.S. firms sold about $7 billion worth of know-how and gear to developing nations through MDB procurement programs. During the next five years, U.S. sales could top $15 billion—an amount equal to current U.S. exports to Japan. . . . U.S. firms should mine the wealth of information that is easily available to them in Washington, where two MDBs—the World Bank and the Inter-American Development Bank—are headquartered. Foreign rivals cannot readily match such success.[11]

A few additional facts and figures may help to illustrate that as far as the commercial dimension of U.S. aid is concerned, American officials and the business community are much better informed of this reality than are Pharr and the development professionals she refers to. The United States provides two types of aid, economic and military. But a major part of economic aid goes to promoting the nation's military and security objectives, and a large share of both types of aid subsidizes sales of U.S. goods and services.

In fiscal 1989, total U.S. aid was about $15 billion. According to the definition offered by U.S. foreign assistance laws, only $2.4 billion, or 16 percent of the total, was allocated to development assistance. Another $1.5 billion, or 10 percent, however, can also be defined as development assistance, as it consisted of contributions to MDBs and other international organizations. In all, then, less than $4 billion, or about a quarter of total aid, went to promote Third World development.

The Development Assistance Committee (DAC), however, counts the bulk of two other types of U.S. economic aid as development assistance—food aid, under Public Law (P.L.) 480, and the Economic Support Fund (ESF). In 1989, they accounted for almost 45 percent of economic aid. These two programs essentially support American farm and arms sales. In other words, these two types of aid have a very high U.S. commercial (and security) content and very low Third World development content. Under P.L. 480, food aid is provided in close cooperation with the Department of Agriculture to support U.S. farmers, and is almost fully tied.

The ESF is the largest component of economic aid (37 percent of the total in 1989) designed to give money to countries where the United States has special military and security interests. The top recipient of this fund ($1.2 billion in 1989) is not a low-income country, but an upper-middle-income country with a per capita income of over $10,000—Israel. Egypt is the number-two recipient of ESF money. That is, two countries accounted for more than half the ESF money in 1989—the price the U.S. taxpayers paid for America's failure to play a leadership role in resolving the Palestinian problem. The only consolation is that most of this money returned to support U.S. business.[12]

Evidence also does not support Pharr's firm American belief that U.S. aid does not serve the national economic interest but Japanese aid does. According to estimates available from the

U.S. General Accounting Office (GAO), the United States ties its aid far more tightly than Japan does: In 1987, the share of fully and partially tied aid in total *bilateral* ODA was 48 percent for Japan, compared with over 90 percent for the United States.[13] And 1987 was not an exceptional year: As early as 1982–1983, tied aid accounted for 33 percent of total aid in Japan and 44 percent in the United States.

In her testimony, Pharr questioned the validity of these figures and informed the Congress that, by the time an aid project has been requested by the recipient-country government and approved by Japanese aid officials, "the nature and specifications of the project are such that it is exceedingly difficult for a non-Japanese firm to bid for it successfully, even if the bidding process is officially open."[14] She cited the same reason other critics do: Japanese aid is tied to local engineering and consulting services. Data on actual procurement from donor countries clarifies the issue. According to the GAO, in 1987, about 60 percent of Japanese bilateral economic assistance went to procuring Japanese goods and services; in the same year, 70 percent of U.S. bilateral aid financed U.S. procurement.[15] As Japan continues to untie its aid, the rate of home procurement in bilateral ODA *loans* has declined to about 45 percent by 1989; thus, perhaps about half of Tokyo's *bilateral aid* (grants and loans) has returned to the Japanese economy.

Critics also allege that Japanese companies are winning contracts through the back door by setting up "LDC firms" as their fronts in Thailand and elsewhere. This may be true—many such abuses do occur in the aid business—but these firms' contribution in oiling the massive Japanese export machine is likely to be trivial. For example, in 1988, Japan's total merchandise exports was $320 *billion*; its total aid to Thailand was $360 *million*. Also, Japanese market share in exports has shown little evidence of a rising trend in the countries that have been receiving the bulk of Japanese aid money.[16]

Those who believe that the Japanese "aid market" is closed to foreigners may note that only 28 percent of *untied* bilateral ODA loans financed procurement of Japanese goods in 1988;

the share of procurement from countries belonging to the Organization for Economic Cooperation and Development (OECD), excluding the United States, rose from 7 percent in 1982 to 17 percent in 1988; interestingly, the U.S. share fell from 8 percent to 5 percent.[17] Critics may also note that the British firms have cracked open the Japanese aid market: In January 1989, the British General Electric Company beat Mitsui Company to win a $64.8 million contract from the Thai National Railway. Also, Japan has chosen the British Crown Agents (not a Japanese front company) to implement much of the $600 million untied non-project grant to Sub-Saharan Africa.

The U.S. government is also trying its best to help U.S. business get a share of the Japanese aid pie: AID held two conferences in May 1989 and brought in 30 Japanese private-sector and government participants to tell 250 American business representatives how to gain a foothold in the Japanese aid business; the Commerce Department followed up in July with seven commandments to U.S. business on how to do it right, stressing that it is "essential to plug in to key officials in both Tokyo and the aid recipient country."[18]

Finally, the issue of mixed credits warrants mention. In May 1990, the U.S. Export-Import Bank and AID jointly announced a new $500 million program of mixed credits; aid money and export credits will be used together to promote export of American power plants, telecommunications gear, construction equipment, and other capital goods to four countries where Japan is the top donor—Indonesia, Pakistan, the Philippines, and Thailand. This initiative follows a May 1989 study by the U.S. Export-Import Bank showing that American companies are losing $400–$800 million in potential exports each year to foreign competitors benefiting from mixed credits from their governments.[19]

It strains credulity that so much fuss is being made about mixed credits—a foreign aid practice that results in loss of exports of less than $1 billion annually; but even if the loss were five times as much, it would represent only 1.5 percent of 1989 American merchandise exports of $360 billion. Just in 1989,

U.S. exports rose by over $40 billion. It is also noteworthy that according to DAC data, Japan used 0.1 percent of its ODA for mixed credits and such "associated financing" in 1987. The figures for the French and British were 2.1 percent and 3.9 percent, respectively.

Another area of concern for many Americans is Japan's alleged lack of attention to the environment in the Third World. For example, critics accuse Japan of destroying rain forests because it imports timber from Malaysia, and because the Japan International Cooperation Agency (JICA), the government office that oversees technical assistance, financed a logging road in Sarawak. Such criticisms of Japan's environmental abuses in the developing world, however, border on self-righteous cynicism. The concept of ecologically sustainable development entered the thinking of the American development professionals only at the end of the 1980s. And, critics ignore that the U.S. government, which has done so little to protect the environment within its own borders from nuclear waste, chemical pollution, and the timber industry, has done no better in protecting the environment in the Third World.

Whatever its past sins, Japan is putting a high priority on environmental issues in its aid allocation. In 1988, Tokyo spent almost one-fifth of its grant aid and nearly one-tenth of its project loans on such environmental goals as improvement of urban living conditions (water supply, waste disposal, etc.), forest conservation and aforestation, pollution control, disaster prevention, and conservation of the natural environment. With the $2 billion fund for protecting the environment in the Third World it launched at the 1989 Paris Summit, Tokyo is perhaps now the world's "environment donor." Japan is also trying to catch up in one area where it lagged behind—environmental impact study for projects. JICA and the Overseas Economic Cooperation Fund (OECF), the official loan implementing agency, have established guidelines for environmental assessments and are working toward implementing them.

The remaining three criticisms of Japanese aid mercantilism (too much involvement in Asia, too many capital projects, and too close to the private sector) and the two criticisms of unfair aid practices (too few grants and too little allocation to basic human needs) are essentially five dimensions of the same phenomenon: the unique way Japan and the Japanese aid program have evolved, as the chapters by Asanuma and Hanabusa in this volume explain.

It is not so much the case that the government of Japan has been using foreign aid to promote exports; rather, the private sector has been the key factor in developing economic relationships with neighboring countries, by first establishing trade with them and then moving on to finance and direct investment. Foreign aid has often served as a "harmonizer" of these overall bilateral relationships. Shinji Asanuma puts it this way: " . . . imbalances in the economic relationship would emerge, and the country would demand Japanese government aid in maintaining a good and harmonious economic relationship. Invariably, this was the stage at which Japan would introduce foreign aid."

As Asanuma explains further, the three alleged mercantilist features of Japanese aid mentioned above are therefore different facets of this evolutionary process. The deep involvement of the private sector in foreign aid is a natural outcome of its deep involvement in economic development in recipient countries; aid goes mostly to Asia because that is where the private sector has long been doing business, and aid finances largely capital projects because that is what the private sector wishes to do in countries that have already reached a stage of development where capital projects rather than basic human needs projects are the higher national priority. Moreover, as Hanabusa points out, Japan's own development experience likewise favors this choice. Japan's low share of grants in total aid also reflects the nation's experience of relying on development loans and the fact that the bulk of Tokyo's aid finances profitable economic infrastructure projects in middle-income NIEs and neo-NIEs.

The relative roles of the Japanese government and private sector, however, are shifting. As foreign aid increasingly becomes an avenue to assuming global responsibility and an instrument of foreign policy, the government is becoming a more active player, shaping and pushing a conscious policy of internationalizing and diversifying development assistance in a number of directions. Consequently the evolutionary features of Japanese aid are gradually diminishing toward convergence with international norms. For example, the grant element of Japanese ODA rose to 75 percent by 1987; in 1988, Tokyo allocated a quarter of its ODA to meeting basic human needs, and one-third went to the least-developed countries; Japan now gives more aid to Sub-Saharan Africa than the United States does.

The fundamental problem with most American criticisms of Japanese aid, however, is that they reflect the mercantilistic tendencies and economic interests of the donors, and have little to do with the effectiveness of aid in promoting the economic development of the recipients.

AID AND DEVELOPMENT: ECONOMICS, PHILOSOPHY, AND POLITICS

Masamichi Hanabusa, elsewhere in this volume, makes a persuasive case for why many criticisms of Japanese aid have little to do with the key issue of aid's effectiveness in promoting self-sustaining development. Tied aid and mixed credits may adversely affect the efficiency of aid and trade, but on the whole, I share his view: The complaints about quantity of aid, its quality (too few grants, too high interest rates on loans, etc.), regional concentration, and close involvement of the private sector are misplaced because the primary goal of development assistance is economic development.

Economic development is a long-term and complex process, and development aid is not charity. External resources, however, can play a catalytic role in helping developing countries help themselves. No one type of aid is superior to others: The effectiveness of aid depends on many factors, including the recipient country's stage of development, the state of human resources, and, above all, the nature of local leadership and social and political institutions.

Hanabusa believes, however, that the above is a unique Japanese perspective on economic development. Indeed, the perception that the Japanese philosophy of the role of aid in development is different from the American philosophy is widespread among Japanese and Americans alike. For example, in this volume, Bloch, Preeg, and Asanuma all seem to subscribe to this view, although Asanuma is careful to point out, and correctly so, that the philosophy of U.S. aid is not static, but follows the ideological fashion of the time.

I question this conventional wisdom. A careful examination reveals that the difference between Japan and the United States is not so much that they subscribe to a different *philosophy* of the process of economic development, and the role of foreign economic assistance in it, but that they differ in what they *practice*. While Japan consistently practices what it preaches, the United States preaches what it happens to practice at the time, vacillating as the balance between development, security, and humanitarian motives shifts. Despite the volatility of policy, the underlying model of economic development and its link with development aid is little different in the United States than in Japan.

Without an elaborate demonstration, this point can be made by the following three quotations—one expresses the Japanese philosophy and the other two the American philosophy. The first comes from Hanabusa's chapter in this volume:

> An emphasis on "self-help" runs through Japan's aid planning and implementation. . . . In the Japanese view, developing countries should manage or regulate their economies with the objective of achieving self-reliance as soon as possible.
>
> While Japan recognizes that external economic assistance is clearly necessary for developing countries as they start on the road to prosperity, it does not want to see recipient nations develop a mentality or an economic structure that takes the aid for granted.

The next quotation comes from a speech delivered 27 years ago; it stressed that a primary goal of aid should be to:

> . . . achieve a reduction and ultimate elimination of United States assistance by enabling nations to stand on their own as rapidly as possible. Both this nation and the countries we help have a stake in their reaching the point of self-sustaining growth—the point where they no longer require external aid to maintain their inde-

pendence. Our goal is not an arbitrary cutoff date but the earliest possible "takeoff" date—the date when their economies will have been launched with sufficient momentum to enable them to become self-supporting, requiring only the same normal sources of external financing to meet expanding capital needs that this country required for many decades.[20]

The speaker was President John F. Kennedy; he offered this "Japanese" philosophy of development aid in his 1963 Foreign Aid Message.

The final quotation is from an official report on development assistance published in 1989:

Somewhere between 1949 and the present, the original concept of development assistance as a transitional means of helping developing countries meet their own needs has been lost. This has happened despite the fact that most of the major shapers of modern American development assistance have always stressed that it should be a temporary course of instruction. . . . Has America applied the dynamism and realism to its official development programs that have been the keys to development success for ourselves and other individual nations? Is today's U.S. foreign aid fostering healthy development towards independent prosperity—or simply postponing the day of reckoning for governments unwilling or unable to take the politically painful steps needed for their own development?[21]

This "Japanese" criticism of U.S. aid was offered not by someone from Tokyo, but by the then AID administrator.

These three statements embrace the same model of the role of aid in economic development. The only difference has been in the application of this model: On balance, Japanese aid has been effective in fostering development, as Tokyo has consistently applied this model of development aid; America's aid, by contrast, has largely created a host of aid dependencies, as Washington has failed to apply this model with vigor and consistency.

The problem with Japanese aid therefore is not necessarily that its volume is too small, or that the money is being used to promote economic development in Japan rather than in the Third World: Most development experts agree that Japanese development assistance has been more effective than aid from the United States and other major donors. The problem is that Japan's global position and role have changed, and the aid policy that worked so well in the past is not likely to work as well in the future. The basic theory of development aid does not need revision, but the scope and the manner of giving will have to change.

With Japan's growing global responsibility as an economic superpower, the purity of its development assistance will inevitably be lost. Under increasing pressure to use aid for purposes other than development—peacekeeping; managing economic and security relationships with allies and old adversaries; fighting global problems, such as environmental degradation, drug abuse, and terrorism; and so on—Japan will, to some extent, catch the American disease. Japan will have to constantly review and revise its *nondevelopment* aid philosophy; and the combination of more demand for development aid and new demands for nondevelopment aid will likely strain Japan where it still suffers from a shortage—human capital endowed with communications, diplomatic, and leadership skills.

Even in the area of Third World development, Japan cannot become a major player with money alone: Money must be managed with an open mouth not fearful of speaking the mind. Japan has to learn to give political and policy leadership, and others have to learn to share. Japan needs to clearly communicate its development aid philosophy, the development theory to which it subscribes, and its views on the design and implementation of stabilization and structural adjustment policy. And its people need to engage in constructive dialogue with donor and recipient nations bilaterally, and with increased active participation in multilateral development organizations and various international forums and conferences.

All this will not happen overnight, but will take persistent efforts over a long period of time. Japan will have to undergo a fundamental psychological and attitudinal restructuring, and make a major and long-term commitment of its human resources to the process of Third World development. The top priority should be the commitment of Japanese human capital to Third World development, an area where Japan is still underdeveloped. Without this commitment, Japan will have difficulty in assuming greater global responsibility, and developing countries will have difficulty in making the best use of Japan's financial resources. The real question facing Japan as it learns to adapt to its newfound power is not how much to give and where, but how to lead and toward what end.

FROM BURDEN-SHARING TO GLOBAL PARTNERSHIP

Foreign aid is an important instrument of foreign policy for all major donor countries. Even as the United States took the back seat to Japan in ODA in 1989, a congressional task force concluded, "The U.S. foreign assistance program is an important element of U.S. foreign policy. It serves U.S. foreign policy objectives by promoting the political and economic stability of nations important to U.S. interests. It supports U.S. national security by helping allies maintain adequate defense capabilities and stable economies."[22]

Critics routinely accuse Japan of giving "mercantilist aid without any political philosophy or principles," but nine years before Japan became the world's top donor nation, a Japanese study group created by Prime Minister Masayoshi Ohira identified foreign aid as a major pillar of Japan's Comprehensive National Security—a recommendation that Ohira's successor, Prime Minister Zenko Suzuki, enthusiastically embraced. The group's report stressed, "Japan cannot exert influence on the other nations with military power or build friendly relations by contributing to other nations' military security," but "Japan's world historical mission is to play a leading role in creating an order between the North and the South."[23] While this report urged limiting foreign aid to nonmilitary support, it also insisted that "application of Japan's economic cooperation must rest on comprehensive judgments that take into account political as well as economic considerations."[24]

Since foreign aid is a tool of foreign policy, suggestions for reform of donors' aid policies or for aid cooperation must be set in the overall context of foreign policy. The first step, therefore, is to draw implications from the preceding analysis for U.S. and Japanese foreign policy, and then identify a set of preconditions for fruitful cooperation by the world's top two foreign aid donors.

U.S. Foreign Policy

The United States should abandon the concept of burden-sharing as a guiding principle for policy toward its allies, and embrace the concept of "global partnership," or of "sharing collective responsibility." Burden-sharing was not a sensible guide to policy of common defense against Soviet communism even in the bipolar era of the Cold War; now, in the multipolar post–Cold War era, it is a counterproductive anachronism. The reason is simple: A credible exercise of hegemonic leadership requires both monetary might and military muscle. As the 1990 Gulf crisis has demonstrated, if a superpower assumes the burden of flexing its military muscle but lacks the monetary means, it runs the risk of becoming the world's policeman-for-hire; similarly, if an economic and financial superpower unburdened with military prowess tries to help with money alone, it risks becoming a push-button cash dispenser.

The principle of global partnership reduces these risks arising from monetary-military imbalances and seems to offer the most effective guide for the foreign policy of the United States and its allies. While burden-sharing assumes that America is selflessly carrying the burden of defending freedom and peace, and that it is only fair that her allies share it (through military and monetary means), global partnership rests on the premise that promoting global peace and prosperity is the collective responsibility of the leading nations, and that they should exercise joint leadership within a multilateral framework and contribute jointly according to their respective national advantages.

The underlying assumption here is that promoting global peace and prosperity is a responsibility—it is a burden as well as a source of power and influence—and that since the world no longer has one hegemonic superpower, but a group of major powers, this responsibility has to be shared, although not necessarily equally. Nations with greater economic, military, and leadership capacity may shoulder more of the responsibility, and consequently may project more power and influence. For example, the United States is no longer the supreme superpower it was in the 1950s, and it has been suffering from a chronic shortage of financial resources; but it is still the only nation on earth that is both an economic and a military superpower. In other words, America is the first among equals, and thus is still the only power capable of being the leading, or senior, partner of a global partnership—or the largest "shareholder" of collective responsibility.

Global partnership has a number of implications for U.S. foreign policy, three of which merit attention. First, the United States should give up the role of being the world's lone policeman, because it can no longer—politically and economically— afford it: America does not have the will to use its wallet in retaining that role. It should reduce its military commitments to match its financial capacity rather than finance them with aid from allies and with "defense taxes" from nations whose freedom it protects.

As the superpower Cold War gives way to regional hot wars, peace will remain a goal to be protected and maintained; an effective way to reach that goal is to wage a war against the arms race. And no nation can wage this war with more vigor and impact than the world's number-one military power: the United States. If this war on the arms race results in victory, the United States can make substantial cuts in defense spending and yet remain a military power with unmatched global reach.

Furthermore, under the regime of global partnership, the United States can take the lead in developing and managing a United Nations (UN) military apparatus—endowed with a permanent armed force and with the mandate to mobilize national reserves that can collectively deter aggression and maintain peace. The UN already possesses many of the building blocks of such a multilateral security arrangement—the Security Council, the military staff committee, the peacekeeping force, and so on. The real issue is whether America can break out of its history of swinging between isolationism and unilateralism, and embrace multilateralism in an area that even the most ardent "multipolar internationalists" consider off-limits for multilateralization. If it cannot do so, two unpleasant prospects await us. Either demands for burden-sharing by savings-short America will sabotage the emergence of a true global partnership or an isolationist America will breed adventurism elsewhere. In both cases, we will live in a "global village" where tribal leaders with personal armies and wealth will put freedom, peace, and harmony at constant risk.

The second implication of global partnership is that Washington, notably Congress, should stop treating Japan like a selfish little money-lending island prospering under U.S. military and nuclear protection. Two examples illustrate the political irrationality and the risk to global peace and stability of such behavior. One is the 1990–1991 National Defense Authorization Act, containing a section on burden-sharing targeted at Japan. President Bush signed the act into law in November 1989—four months after Japan announced two unprecedented steps to shoulder the burden of aiding the Third World: picking up the major share of the mini–Marshall Plan for the Philippines, and adding $35 billion to its earlier $30 billion Recycling Plan.

The legislation calls on the Japanese government to boost its budget on foreign aid and military spending so that Japan's burden as a share of GNP equals the NATO average by 1992; channel aid to areas of the Third World where Washington has strategic and foreign policy interests; and provide 100 percent—as opposed to the current 40 percent—of the direct costs of maintaining U.S. military bases in Japan.

The other example is the 370–53 vote in the U.S. House of Representatives in September 1990 for an amendment to the 1991 defense appropriations bill in reaction to Japan's failure to quickly respond to the Gulf crisis with an adequate assistance package including mostly money, but also material, machinery, and manpower. The amendment proposed the withdrawal of 5,000 U.S. military personnel a year from Japan unless it pays the full non-salary cost ($7.5 billion) of maintaining 500,000 Americans there. With the Appropriations Committee approving the amendment in October, the message came out loud and clear that America has yet to learn how to behave with respect to the world's second-largest economic superpower; it also demonstrated Washington's indifference to the distinction between a global leader and a global mercenary. A leader picks up the tab so that it can tell others what to do; a mercenary gets paid to be told what to do. In a multipolar world, America can no longer tell others what to do; but the world's only superpower does not need to become a superpower-for-hire, either. There is no better way for the United States to damage its position as a world leader than to begin defending freedom and peace for hard cash.

Finally, the United States must learn to share responsibility, rights, and influence in international, financial, and development institutions with its allies, notably Japan. American unilateralism in multilateral institutions was always a questionable way of exercising leadership, even when the United States had the monetary might to back it; now such practice has begun to affect the functioning of these organizations, as Washington cannot even put up the money to support the weight of its mouth. For example, as Japan—partly in response to U.S. pressure—assumes an increasing share of the financial burden in these organizations and expresses its eagerness to do even more, America only retards that process by blocking Japan from assuming a greater share of the power. The refusal of the U.S. government—in particular the Congress—to share power with Japan has been so pervasive and persistent since the early 1980s that one could write a whole book on this subject alone. For our purpose, however, it will suffice to illustrate this element of U.S. foreign policy with a few examples from three multilateral institutions: the World Bank, the International Monetary Fund (IMF), and the Asian Development Bank (ADB).

In all three institutions, a simple principle guides U.S. policy: maintain American political power and maximize Japanese financial burden. The United States insists on maintaining its initial status as the only member-country with a veto power in the Bank and the Fund. And it zealously protects its parity with Japan in voting power at ADB. Following the practice that the regional development banks are headed by a national from the region, combined with the fact that Japan is both an Asian giant and a global economic power, a Japanese heads ADB. But, the tradition that an American heads the Bank and a European heads the Fund persists without any legal support from the charters of these institutions.

The U.S. veto power—or, more generally, a member's voting right, based on its share in the Bank's total capital base—does not significantly influence much of the Bank's policy direction, lending decisions, or day-to-day operations. Yet it is undeniable that the U.S. insistence on maintaining its veto power and the presumption that the U.S. presidency of the Bank is an eternal American prerogative reflect a unilateralist attitude that those rights are too precious to share, as they allow the United States to use the Bank as a limited but leveraged instrument of U.S. foreign policy.

America's insistence on maintaining its veto right and European countries' resistance to allowing Japan to move ahead of them kept Japan until August 1984—the world's number-two aid donor at the time and soon-to-become the number-one creditor—as the fifth-ranking member in the Bank. Thereafter, Japan moved to the number-two position by inching ahead of West Germany, Britain, and France. Japan has since made progress in strengthening its number-two position; but even in 1989, its share was 9.5 percent of the Bank's capital (and its voting right commensurate with that figure), whereas the United States maintained its veto right by refusing to reduce its share below 16.5 percent of the total.

The irony is that Japan—often taken to task for shirking its global burden—had to fight tooth and nail to shoulder this burden, and had to bribe and appease America and Europe by picking up a disproportionately high share of the tab for many *special funds*. For example, Japan put up as much as the United States in the $15 billion ninth replenishment of the International Development Association (IDA), and made a special contribution of $300 million to break the deadlock in negotiations among the donors. Japan also made the biggest contribution to a World Bank special facility for Sub-Saharan Africa. While critics routinely chastise Japan for taking a free ride to economic supremacy, it seems that in multilateral institutions, America has been taking a free ride to political supremacy.

Japan's "burden-power gap" is even more serious at the IMF. Japan is the only member of the Fund that supplemented the Fund's resources with substantial contributions for financing the Brady Plan; it contributed the lion's share of the money needed to finance the Fund's several new facilities; and it is eager to do much more. Yet, with 4.5 percent of the total quota (capital), Japan remains the IMF's fifth-ranking member, while the United States retains its veto power with 20 percent of the capital. After more than two years of negotiation and horse-trading, in June 1990, the Fund's board of governors agreed to move both Japan and Germany to number-two positions within the context of a 50 percent increase in total quotas, but this change may not take effect until the end of 1991.

ADB is the only major multilateral organization where Japan's financial, intellectual, and political role is dominant, but the United States and its European allies have difficulty accepting Japanese leadership even in this Asian institution. While some of the tension reflects genuine differences in policy issues, exacerbated by the high-handed management style of the former head of the Bank, Masao Fujioka, the critical element remains the American kneejerk resistance to Japan's assumption of "an unfairly high share of global responsibility." Japan contributes almost 40 percent of the financing of the Asian Development Fund (ADB's private-sector lending arm) and 57 percent of the Technical Assistance Special Fund (a fund specially created for providing technical assistance to recipient countries); the U.S. contributions to these two funds have been 18 percent and 2 percent, respectively. Yet when Japan moved to increase its capital share of ADB in 1988, Washington followed suit to maintain parity with Japan's voting rights.

Another example of Washington's constant efforts to undermine Tokyo's leadership at ADB is its vehement opposition to President Fujioka's 1989 proposal to establish a private-sector lending agency—the Asian Finance and Investment Corporation—capitalized jointly by ADB and private banks and financial institutions. The irony is that the United States has been the most vocal critic of ADB for excessive focus on the public sector and neglecting the needs of the private sector, and Fujioka's proposal was a concrete response to the recommendation of a U.S.–initiated advisory panel that ADB establish a body to grant private-sector loans.

The principle of global partnership implies that America's unilateralist instinct in dominating the multilateral organizations must be contained; the tendency to hold on to political power while prodding Japan to shoulder the ever growing financial burden only erodes the credibility of American leadership and subverts the emergence of a new world order conducive to promoting global peace and prosperity.

Japan's Foreign Policy

While Japan has embraced the rhetoric of global partnership, it has yet to conduct its foreign policy on this basis. It must do so, however, to help free U.S. foreign policy from the relic of burden-sharing and move it toward the vision of global partnership. Global partnership is, by definition, a nonunilateralist concept: no nation can practice it alone. And Japan, because of its military-monetary deficit, has a comparative advantage in catalyzing the U.S. transition from a frustrated superpower resentful of the allies' unfair share of the burden to a confident senior partner of "The World Inc." To play this role, Japan needs a "Heisei Reformation": It has to undergo a revolutionary restructuring of its attitudes and behavior.[25] Two elements of this reformation are worth stressing.

First, while Japan is increasingly undertaking global initiatives on its own, fundamentally it remains a "reactive superpower." Even its "independent" initiatives seem to spring from the premise that "we should do this either because the foreigners, in particular the Americans, will like it, or because if we do not do it, 'they' will attack us." *Gaiatsu* (foreign pressure) is a risky basis for conducting domestic or foreign policy for any nation, let alone a superpower; it encourages foreigners to "bash

Japan," but it also creates a "victim mentality" at home, thus fueling mutual resentment and recriminations.

Japan's long history of isolationism, followed by the devastating defeat at its only attempt to become a regional hegemon, partly explains Japan's "global irresponsibility." An island nation prone to earthquakes with little arable and inhabitable land, dependent on foreigners for oil and other natural resources and at the mercy of the United States for military protection, Japan suffers from a small-island psychology and a sense of acute vulnerability that are totally at odds with its global position and influence. Also, largely because of its manufacturing sector's enormous competitive gains, Japan has become an economic superpower too quickly, with national mentality failing to adjust to the demands of global reality. Additionally, the postwar preoccupation with catching up with the West in economics, finance, and technology has kept Japan's standard of living low relative to other advanced nations, making Japan into a rich country with poor people—not a condition commensurate with exercising bold and visionary leadership.

Most critically, a vanquished nation that has achieved economic superpower status under conditions of dependency—economic, political, and psychological—on the victor (which happens to be a greater economic and military superpower), and that still remains dependent on the victor—for nuclear and military protection—is bound to have difficulty in becoming a proactive and confident global leader. In modern history, Japan's global position is unique: Japan is an economic superpower, but not a military and nuclear superpower; in fact, it depends on its greatest economic competitor for military and nuclear protection. This uneasy mix of monetary power and military dependence may indeed be unsustainable in the long run, and the Gulf crisis has already exposed one dimension of that unsustainability.

Meanwhile, however, Japan will remain a militarily dependent economic superpower, exerting its monetary weight around the globe and expected to make substantial financial contributions to the international community. To play this role in the manner of a confident world leader, Japan must learn to over-come its "vulnerable little island uninvolved in others' affairs" mentality, clearly define the guiding principles of its foreign policy, and stick to them. Japan should do things that it believes are the right things to do—not because it thinks others believe so, or because it wants to appease others or avoid criticisms. In multilateral organizations, Japan not only should fight for in-creasing voting power, but it should exercise intellectual and policy leadership. And it can turn its constrained military pos-ture into a comparative advantage: It can play the role of a "peace superpower," promoting arms control and mediating regional conflicts. The first step, however, is to conduct an open debate and national soul-searching on its role in World War II; only then can it gain the credibility and confidence to give up its passive pacifism for active pacifism.

Second, at the bilateral level, global partnership means Ja-pan must abandon its "appease America" policy. To be sure, Japan has a special relationship with the United States, but it should derive the principles guiding this relationship from its overall foreign policy framework. For example, *gaiatsu* is not a sensible basis for conducting global partnership; neither is it a rational way of managing—to borrow a phrase from Ambas-sador Mike Mansfield—"the world's most important bilateral relationship." In short, what this world needs is not a Japan that can say yes or no, nor a Japan that first says no and then says yes under pressure, but a Japan that can yes or no on its own.

Premise of Aid Cooperation

Within a reformed foreign policy framework, successful aid co-operation will require agreement on a number of points. Three of them are highlighted here.

First, both countries must clearly distinguish development aid from nondevelopment aid. The latter can be divided into three categories: humanitarian (including disaster relief), strate-gic (security, political, and "appeasement" aid), and transna-tional (the environment, drugs, and other global concerns). These distinctions are critical; for example, labeling political aid as development aid is bound to hamper effective aid cooperation and make a mockery of the goal of helping countries to help themselves. Furthermore, evaluations of the effectiveness of aid must take account of its goals: The effectiveness of development aid should be measured in terms of its success in promoting self-sustaining development, whereas the effectiveness of strategic or humanitarian aid should be measured by the degree of its success in achieving the strategic or humanitarian goal at hand.

Second, while the United States and Japan subscribe to similar—if not quite the same—theories of development and of the role of aid in promoting self-sufficiency, aid experts from both countries need to discuss these theories in depth and identify the areas of disagreement. Each government's complete understanding of the other's point of view is a critical prerequisite to successful cooperation in development aid.

Finally, Washington and Tokyo should cooperate on foreign aid at both bilateral and multilateral levels. For example, as Bloch and Hanabusa stress, joint training and exchange of views at a bilateral level can be very helpful. By contrast, as Hanabusa points out, in the area of environment, aid cooperation is likely to be more effective if carried out multilaterally involving not only other donors but recipient countries, as well. Bloch identifies another rationale for multilateral cooperation: A multilateral framework that also involves recipient countries can avoid the potential for tension and resentment that may result if developing countries see bilateral cooperation between Washington and Tokyo as the world's top two donors ganging up against them.

Aid Cooperation: Do's and Don'ts for America

Global partnership on foreign aid does not only require a common ground between the two donors, it also demands that each donor meet certain conditions. In the case of the United States, three items merit special attention.

First, as a number of authors in this volume have pointed out, any U.S. attempt to collaborate on development aid by complementing "American mind with Japanese money" will be a nonstarter. Thus, the suggestion that cash-short Washington can teach skills-short Tokyo how to give development aid is not the basis for fruitful collaboration. While a severe shortage of development professionals clearly constrains Japan's aid efforts, the fact remains that Japanese aid has been a great deal more effective than American aid in fostering development. Japan can certainly benefit from joint training and by hiring consultants from AID in areas where it lacks expertise, but a general presumption that America has clear superiority in development know-how is neither correct nor a helpful starting point for productive aid cooperation.

Second, cooperation is a two-way street; if the American attitude is that cooperation means Japan does what Washington tells it to do, we will return to the bilateral cycle of bashing and appeasing, driven by the confrontational concept of burden-sharing. This is especially true for strategic, or security, assistance. Global partnership means that Japan should decide where its aid ought to go for strategic reasons; then, if interests match, cooperation can take place. Twisting Tokyo's arm to give where Washington alone has security interests is not cooperation, but coercion.

Finally, the United States should practice what it preaches on development aid. The end of the superpower Cold War has ushered in an era not of global peace and tranquillity, but of regional hot wars, mostly in the Third World and Eastern Europe. This new reality makes it imperative that the United States undertake a comprehensive review of its aid policy—the 1989 report of the House Foreign Affairs Committee Task Force on Foreign Assistance is a commendable step in that direction—and reform its aid legislation. The United States should reorient its foreign aid program toward promoting development, away from fostering aid dependencies through its "security charity" and "U.S. farm and arms assistance" programs. While ethnic, religious, and other factors will continue to fuel regional conflicts in various parts of the world, self-sustaining and participatory development is the best way of promoting freedom, democracy, and peace. If Washington moves in the direction of helping countries that help themselves, then a whole new world will open up for aid cooperation between the two nations.

Aid Cooperation: Do's and Don'ts for Japan

Fruitful aid collaboration also requires that Japan change its manner of giving as it becomes the senior partner of global partnership on aid. Two of these changes merit mention. First, Japan should clearly articulate its aid philosophy—why it gives aid, why it gives in the way it does, and for what purpose—and not recycle a philosophy borrowed from abroad. Japan should clearly communicate this philosophy to her own citizens and the international community, build support for it, and adhere to it until the changing world demands a review and revision. A clearly articulated aid philosophy can become the guiding principle for cooperating with the United States. Without this anchor, aid can become another area of bilateral confrontation rather than cooperation.

Second, whereas the United States needs to move toward development aid, Japan is likely to move some distance away from it. As an economic superpower, Japan cannot avoid throwing its political weight around, and thus Japan's global responsibility in foreign aid can no longer be limited to development aid; Japan must offer humanitarian, strategic, and "transnationalist" aid. Japan has been providing strategic aid for some time; but it tends to publicly deny this. While the reason is the fear of domestic opposition, the root of the feared opposition is not the provision of such aid per se, but the fact that so far strategic aid has meant putting up money to support Washington's strategic interests. If Japan can openly articulate and communicate its own strategic interests, then local public opinion is unlikely to oppose strategic aid. And Japan can effectively collaborate with America where both nations' strategic interests coincide.

CONCLUSION

There is great wisdom in the adage that all politics is local. It may be fitting to end this chapter (and this volume) with two thoughts that spring from a variation of this adage: Globalism begins at home. First, a hegemonic superpower long accustomed to the privilege of unilateral exercise of power is bound to resist sharing it with others—especially those that prospered under its protective wing and transformed into powers challenging its supremacy—and the United States is no exception. But America's difficulty in making the transition is compounded by its loss of self-confidence as its international economic competitiveness and global edge in high technology erode. This erosion, in turn, has occurred not simply because Japan and others have caught up, but because weak domestic leadership has resulted in poor economic policy and inferior technological performance. Thus, as the United States adjusts to its status as the first among equals, it must restore credible leadership and renew the economy at home. Only an economically secure and technologically confident America can rise above the petty politics of burden-sharing, demonstrate global statesmanship, and share responsibility in areas of international importance, including foreign aid.

Secondly, in a similar vein, Japan needs to overhaul its domestic economy to reform its external behavior. It needs to eliminate its "rich country, poor people gap," which is one major source of its apparently selfish response to international problems. Japan must improve the living conditions of its people—in particular, housing and the urban infrastructure—for only when the Japanese people feel rich will they act as citizens of a rich and prosperous nation do. Also, Japan must open up, not only economically and socially, but psychologically: It needs to learn to communicate better within, and with the outside world. These elements of "Heisei Reformation" will make the Japanese more sensitive to the problems of the citizens of the world and prevent them from becoming "the ugly Japanese." Furthermore, these internal reforms will accomplish something else: Japan will transform from a whipping boy of burden-sharing (and a push-button cash dispenser) to a confident senior member of global partnership, sharing responsibilities with America and others in maintaining peace and promoting prosperity.

NOTES

1. This is now standard practice. For example, see House Armed Services Committee, *Report of the Defense Burden-Sharing Panel* (Washington, D.C.: 1988); and Pat Schroeder, "The Burden-Sharing Numbers Racket," *New York Times,* April 6, 1988, A23.

2. Malcolm MacIntosh, *Japan Re-armed* (New York: St. Martin's Press, 1987), 114; and Susan J. Pharr, statement before the Subcommittee on Asian and Pacific Affairs, Committee on Foreign Affairs, U.S. House of Representatives, September 28, 1988.

3. James D. Robinson III, chairman of American Express and chairman of the Council on Foreign Relations' study group that led to this volume, coined the term "Japanese Marshall Plan." See James D. Robinson III, "Defining the Time Bomb: A Proposal for the Tokyo Economic Summit," remarks delivered before Keidanren, Tokyo, February 18, 1986.

4. Uma Lele and Ijaz Nabi, eds., *Transitions in Development: The Role of Aid and Commercial Flows* (San Fransisco, Ca.: International Center for Economic Growth, 1990).

5. World Institute for Development Economics Research, *The Potential of the Japanese Surplus for World Economic Development* (Tokyo: 1986); and ———, *Mobilizing International Surpluses for World Development* (Tokyo: 1987).

6. Hobart Rowen, "Japanese Aid Plan Could Cost U.S. Dearly," *Washington Post,* October 12, 1986, H1.

7. Arjun Sengupta, "What Is To Be Done with the Japanese Surplus?" *Finance and Development,* September 1988. Dr. Sengupta reports an International Monetary Fund simulation that shows that "a $10 billion transfer from Japan to all developing countries for one year would increase U.S. exports by $2.26 billion, whereas an increase in Japanese fiscal expenditures of the same amount would result in increased U.S. exports of only $620 million" (26).

8. Pharr, statement before the Subcommittee on Asian and Pacific Affairs, 166.

9. AID, *Development and the National Interest: U.S. Economic Assistance into the 21st Century* (Washington, D.C.: 1989).

10. Quoted in "Cooperation Fosters Economic Development," *United States AID Highlights,* 6, no. 2 (1989).

11. Task Force on International Economic Development Policy and the Bretton Woods Committee, U.S. Chamber of Commerce, "How U.S. Firms Can Boost Exports Through Overseas Development Projects," Washington D.C., October 1986, 16.

12. U.S. General Accounting Office (GAO), *Economic Assistance: Integration of Japanese Aid and Trade Policies* (Washington, D.C.: 1990).

13. Ibid., 6.

14. Pharr, statement before the Subcommittee on Asian and Pacific Affairs, 161.

15. GAO, *Economic Assistance,* 19; and author's estimate.

16. Robert Orr, Jr., "Collaboration or Conflict? Foreign Aid and U.S.–Japan Relations," *Pacific Affairs* (Winter 1990): 476–489.

17. Economic Cooperation Bureau, Ministry of Foreign Affairs, Japan, personal communication, February 1990.

18. U.S. Department of Commerce, *Business America*, July 31, 1989, 10–11.

19. Eduardo Lachica, "Ex-Im Bank Says U.S. Exports Are Hurt By Other Countries' 'Tied' Aid Credits," *Wall Street Journal*, May 9, 1989, A4.

20. AID, *Development and the National Interest*, 111.

21. Ibid., 111.

22. House Committee on Foreign Affairs, *Report of the Task Force on Foreign Assistance* (Washington, D.C.: 1989).

23. Dennis T. Yasutomo, *The Manner of Giving: Strategic Aid and Japanese Foreign Policy* (Lexington, Mass: D.C. Heath and Co., 1986), 28.

24. Ibid., 28.

25. The phrase "Heisei Reformation" invokes a comparison with a watershed in Japanese history, Meiji Restoration—the collapse of Tokuguwa Shogunate in 1867–1868 and restoration of power to Emperor Meiji that led to the *modernization* of Japan. With the death of Emperor Hirohito in January 1989 and enthronement of his son Emperor Akihito, Japan is at another watershed in its history: it has ended the turbulent *Showa* (enlightened peace) period and entered the era of *Heisei* (achievement of universal peace) at a time when Japan and the world have been going through rapid changes. *Heisei* Reformation thus calls for a wholesale restructuring of the society that will lead to a genuine *internationalization* of Japan.

APPENDIX

The C. Peter McColough Study Group on
Japan's Role in Development Finance

James D. Robinson III, *Chairman*
Shafiqul Islam, *Group Director*

C. Michael Aho
Shinji Asanuma
Andrew Bartels
Richard E. Bissell
Julia Chang Bloch
Stephen W. Bosworth
Richard G. Darman
Gina Despres
Takashi Eguchi
Richard E. Feinberg
Tim W. Ferguson
Richard N. Gardner
Robert R. Gilpin, Jr.
William H. Gleysteen, Jr.
George J.W. Goodman
Martin Gruenberg
Masamichi Hanabusa
Yasuhi Hara
Ryokichi Hirono
Richard C. Holbrooke
Richard L. Huber
Takashi Inoguchi
Yoshihide Ishiyama
Yukio Iura
Lal Jayawardena
Helen S. Junz
Anatole Kaletsky
Makoto Kuroda
Pedro S. Malan

David W. MacEachron
Bruce K. MacLaury
Yoshiji Nogami
Shoji Ochi
Guy Pierre Pfeffermann
Ernest H. Preeg
Moeen A. Qureshi
Alan D. Romberg
Robert V. Roosa
Eugene Rotberg
Sir William Ryrie
Makoto Sakurai
Michael P. Schulhof
Arjun Sengupta
John Sewell
Lee Smith
Joan Spero
Ernest Stern
Bruce Stokes
Makoto Sunagawa
Peter Tarnoff
Donald Terry
Migel Urrutia
Rodney B. Wagner
William N. Walker
Koji Yamazaki
Toru Yanagihara
Nancy Young

GLOSSARY OF
ABBREVIATIONS AND ACRONYMS

ADB	Asian Development Bank
AFDB	African Development Bank
AID	U.S. Agency for International Development
ASEAN	Association of Southeast Asian Nations
DAC	Development Assistance Committee
ECA	U.S. Economic Cooperation Administration
ECAFE	UN Economic Commission for Asia and the Far East
ECLAC	UN Economic Commission for Latin America and the Caribbean
EPA	Economic Planning Agency
ESF	Economic Support Fund
Exim Bank	Export-Import Bank of Japan
FILP	Fiscal Investment and Loan Program
FY	fiscal year
GAO	U.S. General Accounting Office
GATT	General Agreement on Tariffs and Trade
GDP	gross domestic product
GNP	gross national product
IDA	International Development Association
IFC	International Finance Corporation
IMF	International Monetary Fund
JAIDO	Japan International Development Organization
JICA	Japan International Cooperation Agency
LDC	less-developed country
MDB	multilateral development bank
MIGA	Multilateral Investment Guarantee Agency
MITI	Ministry of International Trade and Industry
MOF	Ministry of Finance
MOFA	Ministry of Foreign Affairs

NATO	North Atlantic Treaty Organization
NEDA	National Economic and Development Authority
NGO	nongovernmental organization
NIC	newly industrialized country, also known as newly industrialized (industrializing) economy, or NIE
ODA	official development assistance
OECD	Organization for Economic Cooperation and Development
OECF	Overseas Economic Cooperation Fund
OPEC	Organization of Petroleum Exporting Countries
OTCA	Overseas Technical Cooperation Agency
PHILCUSA	Philippine Council for U.S. Aid
P.L.	Public Law
SDR	special drawing rights
UN	United Nations
UNCTAD	United Nations Conference on Trade and Development
UNDP	United Nations Development Programme
WIDER	World Institute for Development Economics Research

SELECTED BIBLIOGRAPHY

Development Assistance Committee (DAC). *Development Co-Operation: Efforts and Policies of the Members of the Development Assistant Committee, 1990 Report.* Paris: OECD, 1991. See also previous years.

Grimm, Margo. "Japan's Foreign Aid Policy: 1990 Update." *Japan Economic Institute Report.* no. 47a (December 14, 1990).

Lele, Uma and Ijaz Nabi, eds. *Transitions in Development: The Role of Aid and Commercial Flows.* San Francisco, Ca.: International Center for Economic Growth, 1990.

Japan Ministry of Foreign Affairs. *Japan's Official Development Assistance: 1990 Annual Report.* Tokyo: 1991. See also previous years.

Orr, Robert M., Jr. "Collaboration or Conflict? Foreign Aid and U.S.–Japan Relations." *Pacific Affairs* (Winter 1990): 476–489.

———. *The Emergence of Japan's Foreign Aid Power.* New York: Columbia University Press, 1990.

Rix, Alan. *Japan's Economic Aid.* New York: St. Martin's Press, 1980.

Stallings, Barbara. "An Increased Japanese Role in Third World Development." *Overseas Development Council Policy Focus.* No. 6 (1988).

U.S. Agency for International Development (AID). *Development and the National Interest: U.S. Economic Assistance into the 21st Century.* Washington, D.C.: 1989.

U.S. House of Representatives. House Committee on Foreign Affairs. *Report of the Task Force on Foreign Assistance.* Washington, D.C.: 1989.

World Bank. *World Development Report 1991.* New York: Oxford University Press, 1991.

Yasutomo, Dennis T. *The Manner of Giving: Strategic Aid and Japanese Foreign Policy.* Lexington, Mass.: D.C. Heath & Co., 1986.

This is by no means a comprehensive bibliography, but it does include the primary resources relevant to the themes of this book.

INDEX

ABOUT THE AUTHORS

Shinji Asanuma is a Director in the Asia Region of the World Bank. He was the representative of Lehman Brothers in Tokyo (1974–1984), and was also involved in international financial advisory activities with developing-country governments. He is the author of *International Development Assistance,* published in Japanese in 1974.

Julia Chang Bloch is the United States Ambassador to Nepal. She was the Assistant Administrator of the Bureau for Asia and Near East at the U.S. Agency for International Development (AID) from 1987 to 1988. Prior to that appointment, she was for nearly six years AID's Assistant Administrator of the Bureau for Food for Peace and Voluntary Assistance.

Anne Emig is a Ph.D. candidate in Political Science at Columbia University. She is currently a Fulbright Fellow in Tokyo doing doctoral dissertation research on Japan's response to the Third World debt crisis.

William H. Gleysteen, Jr., is President of the Japan Society. He served as Director of Studies at the Council on Foreign Relations from 1987 to 1989. A former Foreign Service Officer specializing and serving in East Asia, his various assignments included U.S. Ambassador to Korea and Deputy Assistant Secretary of State for East Asia and Pacific Affairs.

Masamichi Hanabusa is Consul-General of Japan in New York. He joined the Ministry of Foreign Affairs in 1958, and served as the Director-General of the Economic Cooperation Bureau before coming to New York in 1988.

Ryokichi Hirono is a Professor of Economics at Seikei University in Tokyo. He served as Assistant Administrator and Director of the Bureau for Programme Policy and Evaluation at the United Nations Development Programme (UNDP) from 1985 to 1989. He has published widely on aid and development issues, with a special focus on Asia and the Pacific region.

Hiroya Ichikawa is Director of the Industry and Telecommunications Department at Keidanren. Prior to this appointment, he was Deputy Director of the Economic Cooperation Department (1988–1989), and played a key role in establishing the Japan International Development Organization (JAIDO).

Takashi Inoguchi is a Professor of Political Science at Tokyo University. He has also had various visiting positions at the universities of Geneva, Australian National, Harvard, Johns Hopkins, and Delhi. Specializing in Japanese politics, political economy, and international relations, he is the author of numerous books and articles in Japanese and English.

Shafiqul Islam is Senior Fellow for International Finance at the Council on Foreign Relations. Before joining the Council, he was a Visiting Fellow at the Institute for International Economics (1986–1987) and Chief of the Industrial Economies Division at the Federal Reserve Bank of New York (1984–1986). He has published widely on international monetary and financial issues.

Shoji Ochi is Deputy President of the Japan Center for International Finance. He spent a long and distinguished career with the Bank of Japan (1951–1983), holding such positions as Auditor, Director of Bank Relations and Supervision, and Deputy Director of the Foreign Department.

Filologo Pante, Jr., is President of the Philippine Institute for Development Studies, a public policy research institute. Formerly, he was Deputy Director-General of the National Economic and Development Authority (NEDA)—the Philippine planning ministry—where his principal responsibilities included development planning, policy analysis, and aid coordination.

Ernest Preeg holds the William M. Scholl Chair in International Business at the Center for Strategic and International Studies in

Washington, D.C. A former Foreign Service Officer, he was Chief Economist and Deputy Assistant Administrator at the U.S. Agency for International Development (1986–1988) and U.S. Ambassador to Haiti (1981–1983). He is the author of numerous books and articles on trade and international economic relations.

Romeo A. Reyes is Director-General of the National Economic and Development Authority (NEDA), the Philippine planning ministry. His past experience includes Director of the External Assistance Staff at NEDA and Chief Economist at the Philippine Chamber of Industries. He is the author of many articles on Philippine development issues.

Barbara Stallings is Professor of Political Science at the University of Wisconsin-Madison. She has written extensively on international finance, including *Banker to the Third World: U.S. Portfolio Investment in Latin America, 1900–1986* (1987). Her most recent work has been on Japanese economic relations with Latin America.

Ernest Stern is Senior Vice-President for Finance at the World Bank. He also served as the Bank's Senior Vice-President of Operations (1980–1987). Before joining the World Bank in 1972, Stern was Assistant Administrator for Policy and Program Administration at the U.S. Agency for International Development (AID), where he had a distinguished career beginning in 1959.

Toru Yanagihara is Professor of Economics at Hosei University in Tokyo. A Research Officer at the Institute of Developing Economies from 1977 to 1989, he has served as a consultant and adviser to Japanese and international agencies, including the Ministry of Foreign Affairs, the Economic Planning Agency, and the World Bank. Yanagihara has published widely on debt, development, and adjustment issues.